A Short History of European Law

A Short History of European Law

THE LAST TWO AND A HALF MILLENNIA

Tamar Herzog

Harvard University Press

Cambridge, Massachusetts

London, England

First Harvard University Press paperback edition, 2019
Fifth printing

Library of Congress Cataloging-in-Publication Data

Names: Herzog, Tamar, author.
Title: A short history of European law : the last two and a half millennia /
Tamar Herzog.
Description: Cambridge, Massachusetts : Harvard University Press, 2018. |
Includes bibliographical references and index.
Identifiers: LCCN 2017019315 | ISBN 9780674980341 (cloth : alk. paper) |
ISBN 9780674237865 (pbk.)
Subjects: LCSH: Law—Europe—History. | Common law—History. | Civil law
systems—History. | Law—Europe—International unification—History.
Classification: LCC KJ147 .H47 2018 | DDC 349.409—dc23
LC record available at https://lccn.loc.gov/2017019315

Contents

Introduction

THE MAKING OF LAW IN EUROPE

A FEW YEARS AGO, an undergraduate student reported to me with excitement that she had just visited Washington, D.C., where she saw a copy of the great charter of liberties, the Magna Carta. Not wanting to dampen her enthusiasm, I asked myself how I could explain to this student that what she saw was a feudal document whose original intent had very little to do with what it came to symbolize, and whose importance was acquired over time because, centuries after it was enacted, it was given new meaning and a new role.

The question I first had to tackle was whether this mattered at all. Was it significant that an early thirteenth-century document such as the Magna Carta was misread by a twenty-first-century student? What would this student stand to gain had she understood what the Magna Carta really was and why and how it had come to acquire the status it now has? Was this history relevant to her present-day concerns? Was myth-breaking as important as myth-making? Is the past gone, or does it tell us something essential about the present and the future?

Understanding the thirteenth-century Magna Carta would entail remembering a feudal past in which powerful lords sought to protect their jurisdiction and property against an expanding monarchy. It would require imagining how society changed over time—mainly, how the privileges of a few barons became the rights of all Englishmen—and how, in the process, claims for rights limited what kings could do. Given its projection in the United States, this narrative would also include the story of how these ideas crossed the

1

Atlantic and mutated. Within a larger history of European law, the explanation would have to engage with the question of not only why the Magna Carta acquired this mythical status but also why similar feudal charters, abundant and frequent elsewhere in Europe, did not.

As a legal historian I know that what the Magna Carta currently stands for has nothing to do with the text itself and everything to do with how it was used and remembered. If my student knew this history, I reasoned, she might understand the past better, but she might also acquire a means to imagine differently her present and future. It could supply her with instruments to question narratives, understand the processes that led to their formation, and suggest where they could take us next.

The Magna Carta, of course, is not the only legal remnant that still determines our present or allows us to imagine our future. Plenty of other instruments, institutions, and texts inherited from the past fulfill the same role. As both relics of a time gone and important features of our everyday life, they give things certain meanings, they supply solutions, and they offer techniques through which to analyze and understand reality. Take, for example, "due process"—the obligation of courts to follow a particular procedure. Intuitively, many among us would consider it a relatively modern phenomenon linked to society's ambition to ensure the implementation of justice. Yet, due process, if not in name then at least in practice, was born long ago in medieval England. The story of its emergence is linked not so much to guaranteeing the right result (which it did not) but to the insistence that judges of common-law courts obey very strict procedural rules. Understanding why procedural rules became so important in English law and how, over the years and because of very odd transformations, they came to be seen also as instruments protecting litigants, would allow us to have a better grasp, for example, of why certain things were covered by due process while others were not, or why this set of rules developed in England rather than elsewhere.

Engagement with the past would also enable us to comprehend how European law came to refashion itself both as the epitome of reason and as a system with potentially universal applicability. The enormous influence European law has had around the globe could of course be explained by political and economic factors, but it also required an intellectual elaboration. Ancient Romans already linked community membership to law and both of these to the extension of political hegemony, but these links metamorphosed dramatically in the Middle Ages. The advent and propagation of Christianity allowed the projection of Roman law to new areas in Asia, Africa, and Europe. With colonialism, new explanations were adopted to justify the imposition of European law on non-European territories and peoples. The same happened during the eighteenth-century revolutions and nineteenth-century construction of nation-states. Tracing the evolving need to explain the relevance of European law elsewhere would illuminate, for example, some scholars' criticism of contemporary international law, which they trace back to Europe and which they consider a European rather than a truly global human heritage.

Having taught legal history for some twenty years in both law faculties and history departments in various countries and universities in Europe and the United States (at the University of Chicago, Stanford, and now Harvard), I often felt the need for a short, useful introduction to European legal history that could be used to discuss the evolution of law over time. Weary of big surveys that were heavy on details but light on explanation or on tracing development and change, and unhappy with those that endlessly repeated stereotypes and misconceptions or were provincial in their outlook, I intentionally wrote this book with both my history and law students and my colleagues in mind. What would they need to know to appreciate both how foreign and nonetheless familiar the past was? In a field so abundant with nationalistic affirmations, which myths needed to be put to rest and how could this be done? How could one integrate the history of law in Europe in a single narrative that would allow for local variations while also respecting the profound unity across Europe, including England? How could one communicate the preoccupations of Continental legal history with which I grew intellectually (and which seeks to establish overreaching principles) to an audience more familiar with other types of legal history that are traditionally focused on concrete examples? How can a short book reproduce what we know and what we don't, what we are sure of and what we hesitate to affirm, and yet give a narrative of how things have changed over time and (sometimes) why they did?

This book attempts to answer some of these questions in manageable and clear language. Its main goal is to give readers useful instruments with which to understand both the present and the past. Rather than supplying endless details, it engages with the most essential elements required to rethink our own standards by indicating when and how they emerged and developed.

Denaturalizing our present-day legal systems, it demonstrates that we reached these systems after a haphazard and complex progression whose trajectory into the future is far from evident. Today we might take it for granted that law is something that is created and can be changed, but as I demonstrate in this book, this vision is a relatively recent invention. For many centuries, law was said to exist because it simply did, because it was spontaneously created by the community, or because God had handed it down. Even if these perceptions were untrue, in the sense that law was always made by someone somewhere, the fact that people believed them was of great significance to how they viewed, interpreted, or obeyed the law, to whom they listened, and why. If today we take it for granted that each country has its own law, this too is a relatively recent phenomenon, law in the past being embedded in communities that shared things other than political allegiance. Knowing which factors justified legal obedience and why they mattered is essential for understanding how law functioned historically, as well as how it does today.

To describe the complexities of the past and demonstrate its relevance to the present, in this book, which surveys almost two and a half millennia, I ask how in different moments in time Europeans constructed their legal systems, where they thought norms came from, who they allowed to make, declare, or implement these norms, and what the results were. Rather than describing specific legal institutions or rules, I am interested in deciphering how norms were generated, in order to indicate how they should be read and understood given their particular historical context. I am also keen on demonstrating that their comprehension may tell us something important about whom we came to be.

Throughout the pages of this book, I constantly engage with two major narratives that have accompanied most research on legal history. The first portrayed law almost as a given. Sensitive to how particular solutions changed over time, for example, how contracts were drawn up or what proving a case in court required in different periods, on most accounts it implicitly assumed that law was law. It was as if society had changed, and so had its rules, but law as a field of action and a depository of knowledge and techniques remained the same. For most authors, law included norms that people obeyed, as if where these norms originated, how they were comprehended, which other types of norms existed, and who implemented them and in which way mattered very little. This narrative often seemed to imply that it was almost inconsequential whether law was attributed to communal creation (as in customary law), God (as in canon law), legislators, or judges. Neither did it matter whether law aimed to innovate or maintain the status quo, or whether lawyers and jurists presumed to interpret it literally or believed it represented a higher truth, which was not directly evident and which they sought to uncover.

As already indicated in my treatment of the Magna Carta, in this book I do the exact opposite. I describe the development of law in Europe as a phenomenon that involved not only choosing between rival solutions (as most scholars supposed) but also identifying basic assumptions regarding the rules themselves. Returning to the Magna Carta, to understand its meaning one has to comprehend, not only what it dictated, but also the normative system in which it operated. It is only by considering contemporary notions regarding the making, modifying, and imposition of rules that we can appreciate what the Magna Carta sought to institute. Its changing meaning over time was likewise linked to transformations not so much in the text itself (which remained surprisingly uniform despite constant copying and corrections) but in the legal contexts in which it was read. That it came to symbolize what it does today, in short, has everything to do with context (or, rather, contexts), which radically altered over time and which this book seeks to uncover and reconstruct.

The Magna Carta also teaches us that, in their quest to obtain certain goals, agents often played with continuity and change. They argued for continuity when they innovated, or they clamored for change when in reality they allowed for none. To understand the past, we need to know not only what happened but also how it was reconstructed, used, and comprehended both by contemporaries who lived through these events and by future interpreters who looked back to them in order to reform their present. Over the course of history, law was elaborated, re-elaborated, and reworked once again, as different individuals, communities, and institutions sought to identify, construct, reconstruct, manage, and re-manage different rules to regulate their activities.

If my first aim is to destabilize the idea that legal solutions changed but the legal framework (who imaged these solutions, who implemented them, which was their authority, and how they gained it) was inconsequential, the second narrative I wish to question is the presupposition that English common law and Continental law (also known as civil law) were utterly distinct. My own experience as a lawyer trained in a universe that used both of these legal systems and as a historian working in both Europe and the United States suggested that this separation could not be true. Instead of treating either one system or the other, as most legal histories do, or observing the specific instances and ways by which the two systems on occasions influenced one other, I adopt an analysis that observes English and Continental law at the same time by using a similar methodology.

To do so, in my description of developments from the late Middle Ages to the present, I deliberately alternate between Continental and English law, with the intention of placing them into dialogue with one another. My aim is to showcase both what these systems shared and how they differed. Above all, I wish to demonstrate the degree to which, even when they took different paths, they were largely propelled to do so in response to similar developments and pressures. I also suggest that the paths they took were inspired by a common tradition that supplied not only questions but also a horizon of possible solutions.

Thus, I examine the formative period of Continental *ius commune* alongside common law, I analyze how both systems responded to challenges and changed in the early modern period, I compare their eighteenth-century mutations, and I scrutinize them throughout the nineteenth century and into the formation of the European Union in the second half of the twentieth century. Rather than being foreign to each other, as many previous authors concluded, I argue that English common law and Continental civil law formed part of a single European tradition from which they both drew and were enriched. They were, in fact, substantially much more similar than meets the eye.

I begin my analysis with Roman law because of its continuing presence throughout European history. Among the endless ways in which Roman law's hegemony is still felt today is our constant dependence on presumptions, which were a Roman invention allowing one to assume the existence of things without having to prove them first. Not only was the employment of presumptions a Roman technique, some of the presumptions we currently use originated in Roman times. Take, for example, the legal presumption that children born to a married couple are the natural offspring of both spouses. This presumption allowed parents to register their children without having to prove their descent, a function it still fulfills today despite scientific advances allowing us to prove ancestry. Constantly present throughout history, this presumption, however, could come to satisfy new needs. Used under radically different social conditions, in present-day Spain, for example, it authorizes the registration of a child born to a legally married gay couple as the natural offspring of both spouses.

Roman law is an important point of departure for European legal history not only because of its ongoing legacy but also because this legacy was eventually shared by most (if not all) Europeans. Penetrating slowly, first with the expansion of the Roman Empire and then with the conversion to Christianity, it became the common stock in Europe most particularly after it was taken up by medieval scholars and reworked to fit contemporary needs. Forming the basis also for the initial development of English common law, its validity and influence were tested during the early modern period and were affirmed or denied with the coming of modernity. Over the course of this history, paradoxically, even those who rejected adherence to Roman law often argued their case by analogy to it.

The understanding of Roman law, of course, changed over the course of history, and so did its use. What it meant in the classical period had very little to do with how medieval jurists used it, or what English common-law lawyers and German nineteenth-century jurists made of it. Despite this huge variation in the way it was understood and incorporated, Roman law nevertheless maintained its prestige, and so did some of its basic methodologies and tenets. As usually happens, this interpretation and reinterpretation of the past enabled a creative engagement, not only with what had transpired in the past, but also with constructing the present and the future.

The constant invocation of Roman law also required as well as explained the permanent strain experienced in Europe between stability and universality, on the one hand, and dynamism and local responses, on the other. If Roman law supplied the backbone for a common European legal tradition, it could not solve the constant tensions between local and global, individual solutions and overreaching principles. These tensions were already present in Rome itself, where historians distinguished between law as practiced in the center and as followed in the provinces, but they continued throughout European history. It was precisely in order to overcome such tensions that in the eleventh, twelfth, and thirteenth centuries, efforts were made, in both Continental Europe and England, to create a unifying common law (Chapters 5 and 6). This *ius commune,* a term the English initially also used to designate their common law, was meant to cement and give coherence to a legal world that in reality comprised hundreds of thousands of local arrangements. Whether the search for commonalities succeeded, and to what degree, is part of the story I describe. Another is how the struggle for unification affected how communities were defined. Moving from personal associations (that encompassed people according to their relations with one another) to territorial jurisdictions (that imposed law on all those who inhabited a certain territory) and sometimes adopting midway solutions, communities expanded or contracted according to the perceived sameness of members. Sometimes family was the factor that justified the imposition of a common law, but often as important were a shared religion, a shared subjection to a lord, the sharing of fields, or the maintenance of trade relations, to mention just a few examples.

The struggle to unite people under the same law was also taken up by the Church, whose authorities were the first to designate the law that was common to all Christians as a *ius commune*. Yet, if the Church played a major role in propagating Roman law (Chapters 2–4), it also affected European normativity in other ways. After the Roman Empire converted to Christianity, the distinction between secular and religious lost much of its saliency. This was particularly true in late antiquity and the early Middle Ages, but it continued to be a fairly accurate description of European law even in later centuries because of the omnipresence of canon law and the commanding role of Christian morality. At a certain moment in time, some European actors began searching for a system that would no longer depend on external authorities or traditions but instead would be self-explanatory. The reign of self-evident truth, where rules could be justified not because they had an authoritative foundation but because they made sense to those who created them, propelled what we now identify as modernity. But this modernity was not necessarily secular. In the minds of many of its eighteenth- and nineteenth-century proponents, human reason and a natural law that was said to be imposed by nature on humans could perfectly cohabit with a belief in God.

Modernity brought about major transformations, but regardless of the interesting question of whether these were revolutionary or not, legally, at least, these changes were often more radical in intent than in practice. In the end, their most pressing legacy was the belief in human agency and the conviction that humans were capable of improving themselves as well as their societies. Thereafter, law would come to exemplify the general drive to move away from the art of conserving a status quo (as has been the case before) to the art of innovating in order to create a seemingly better world.

Having started this book with Roman law, I end it with the establishment and growth of the European Union, which for me is both a point of arrival and a point of departure. To what degree can Europe today have a common law, and who are the agents and interests propelling such a legal unification? Are these processes of unification particular to Europe or do they also operate on a global scale? How can the nation-state, invented in the late eighteenth century, cope with the challenges of both Europeanization and globalization?

To answer some of these questions and make some of these points, the individual chapters that follow each address a certain topic, as well as describe its evolution. In order to make the narrative clearer, I sometimes sacrifice chronology for the sake of illustrating better what I describe. I do so, for example, in Chapter 1, where I discuss provincial Roman law codes that were enacted after the empire converted to Christianity. Similarly, in Chapter 2, which describes the Christianization of Rome, I deal with some of the issues also covered in Chapter 3, which focuses on the early Middle Ages. In Chapter 6, where I study the foundational period of common law, I sometimes venture into the early modern period.

If chronology is complex, so is the geographical and political entity I identify as Europe. Evidently, over the course of the period I cover, Europe and the definition of what belonged to it were both invented and had greatly mutated. An idea rather than a continent, Europe changed forms and shapes and eventually ventured overseas to territories we now identify as colonial. The projection of European law was just as amorphous. During Roman times, parts of the Mediterranean and Asia were subjected to it, as were European overseas domains later on. By the eighteenth, nineteenth, and twentieth centuries, the legal tradition I describe as European reached its utmost expansion due to the growing hegemony of the Continent but also because elites around the globe chose to use and adapt European law to their own needs and desires. Because of this extension, some of the most important developments in European law happened outside the Continent, as when the law of nations was turned into natural law in the colonies, or as in the constitutional innovations introduced in North America. These not only were a consequence of European law, they also greatly modified it.

Precisely because I was looking to describe the most fundamental developments, rather than all developments, not all European countries feature equally. In my story, some parts appear as protagonists, whereas others are only mentioned in notes. The places and times I describe sometimes were chosen because of their importance, but more often they were selected because they illustrate some of the main arguments I wish to make.

PART ONE

Ancient Times

Roman Law

NOW YOU SEE IT, NOW YOU DON'T

THE CITY OF ROME was probably founded in the early part of the seventh century BCE. Initially ruled by monarchs, at around 509 BCE it had converted into a republic, in which a senate (an assembly of elders) appointed annually two public magistrates *(consuls)* to govern the community. This system of government lasted until 27 BCE, when the senate declared Augustus emperor. Having traded and fought extensively with its neighbors, Rome gradually expanded its control, first throughout the Italian peninsula and then throughout the Mediterranean and into parts of central and northern Europe. In 285 CE, the empire was divided into a western and an eastern part. This division, justified by the enormous size of the territories under Roman control, gradually gained political saliency. In 476 CE, Germanic troops invaded the city, forcing the abdication of the emperor, thereby bringing about what has come to be known as the "fall of the Roman Empire." Despite these developments, which terminated Roman political hegemony in the west, the Eastern empire, with its capital in Constantinople (present-day Istanbul), survived until its conquest by Ottoman tribes in 1453.

Rome left an enduring legacy in many areas and multiple ways. However, one of its clearest bequests was its influence over the development of law. There is a saying attributed to Goethe according to which Roman law was like a diving duck. It could be swimming on the surface or diving deep in the water, but whether you saw it or not, it was always there.[1] This belief in the persistence of Roman law throughout European history was not unique to Goethe or the nineteenth century in which he lived. It is currently shared by most historians, who usually begin the story of the development of law in Europe with Roman law. Of course, Romans were not the first people to have a normative system, and, like all other societies, they constantly borrowed from neighboring polities, most particularly from the Hellenistic world. It is also clear that Roman law evolved dramatically over time, continuously adapting to new circumstances and challenges.

Yet there is a general agreement among scholars that Roman law, most particularly as practiced in the six hundred years between the third century BCE and the third century CE, featured some of the most important elements we identify today with law as practiced throughout European history. Among them was the emergence of a secular law (even if applied by believers), the centrality of conflict resolution, and the emphasis on private law. Rome also experienced the emergence of specialists in law. As I will argue below, these specialists, identified as jurists, transformed the normative system into a professional field involving specifically designed procedures that had to be followed if the right answers were to be obtained. They coined terms and elaborated concepts that allowed them to translate everyday life into legal formulations. Roman law, in short, supplied new ways to think about normativity, which Europeans ever since have followed in different intensities according to time, place, and subject.

Ancient Courts and Divine Judgment

Experts of Roman law disagree about genealogy and dates, argue about the meaning of terms, and differ over why certain developments took place. However, most approve of a narrative that points to a gradual process that led to the secularization of the law, the creation of new remedies, their subsequent abstraction, and the rising importance of jurists and juridical training, which featured organized methods for understanding the law as well as generating and applying it. Most point out that, as far as we can tell, Roman law began as a system to adjudicate conflicts among individuals that, from archaic times (eighth to fourth century BCE), was centered on society's responsibility to guarantee order. This was done by providing mechanisms ensuring that, rather than engaging in violence, those who disagreed could find redress at the courts. Initially the use of courts was optional and required the consent of plaintiffs and defendants. Over time, however, courts acquired additional powers allowing them sometimes to compel litigants to appear before them as well as to impose their decisions.

This emerging system was identified as the *ius civile,* that is, the communal law (the law of the *civitas*). In the archaic period, questions of law as well as actual conflicts could be presented to a body (college) of patricians who were also priests (pontifices). Guardians of communal norms, as well as experts in ritual performance, these patricians ruled on whether certain behaviors conformed to social expectations, and they suggested what could be done in order to obtain remedy.

As far as we can tell, patricians who served as pontifices followed oral traditions that captured unwritten customs *(mos)* that were both religious and secular in orientation. Their responses to litigants, formulated as revelations of a secret truth, were considered by definition final and required no external proof. Supreme interpreters of the law, pontifices closely guarded their knowledge, passing it from one generation to the next.[2]

During this period, law was rigid and formal. Rather than a free narrative of what had transpired and what required remedy, there was a closed list of causes of action *(legis actiones)* that litigants could invoke. These acknowledged that the plaintiff was injured in ways that should be investigated and redressed. Different causes of action entailed different procedures, with some sending plaintiffs to a judge and others allowing him or her to obtain immediate reparation. The decision to adopt one cause of action or another was determinant. Not only did it define what the parties wished to achieve, but choosing an inadequate cause of action could lead to the termination of the proceedings.

Litigants invoked these causes of action before the pontifices. This invocation required the taking of a ceremonial oath, the utterance of certain words, and the performance of certain acts. Defendants responded in the same way, using preset responses. Religious in origins, this ritual had to be followed accurately, as pronouncing the wrong words or doing the wrong thing could lead to dismissal.[3] The pontiffs then determined whether the cause of action that was invoked was correct and whether the parties used the right rules and procedures.

The oldest written source we have from this period is a fifth-century BCE set of rules best known as the Twelve Tables. Although no complete copy of the Tables has been found to date, several reconstructions made by historians are available. These historians sought to recreate the Tables by arranging the quotations found in the writings of subsequent jurists. It is unclear, however, how much was lost and what the original design of the Tables was. Neither is it completely clear that all that was said to have originated in the Tables was indeed included in them.

Allegedly written down in order to diminish the monopoly of pontifices by making the law better known, the Twelve Tables list the obligation of litigants to appear in court, sanctioning them if they did not. The Tables also spell out procedural rules, regulate forms of legal transactions, and list other basic norms of communal life, enumerating elements of family law and the management of property (contracts, torts, inheritance, loans, real estate, theft, and so forth). Casuistic, partial, and incomplete, according to testimonies dating from later periods the Tables were nevertheless considered sufficiently fundamental to the proper functioning of Roman law that their contents were memorized and recited by children, and copies were inscribed on bronze, ivory, or wood panels that were displayed in public places.

The publication of the Twelve Tables was an important turning point in the history of Roman law not only because a secret law, collectively shared by the pontifices, was made public but also because it marked the appearance of *lex,* that is, of a law that was distinguishable from the religious order controlled by priests. This law would operate not between the community and its gods but among community members, and it would eventually designate a new secular and political sphere of action controlled by lawmakers who published the law rather than religious experts who guarded it.

It took some time, however, before the Twelve Tables fulfilled this potential of creating a sphere of legality that would be distinguishable from the religious order. Initially their interpretation and application was still in the hands of the pontifices, who were seen as those most capable of understanding and implementing their instructions. Around the end of the fourth and the beginning of the third century BCE, though, secular officers began taking their place. Also during this period, giving answers *(responsa)* as to what the law included became an aristocratic prerogative that was no longer based on religious expertise.

The Rise of Civil Litigation

From around 367 BCE, special officials called *praetors* (later identified as *praetor urbanus*) were nominated annually in order to oversee the resolution

of conflicts.[4] Initially praetors mostly followed existing procedures, ensuring that the right cause of action was employed and that it was employed correctly. However, soon after—the debate continues as to when exactly—significant modifications were introduced, instituting adjudication the way we think about it today.

The first and most important change for which historians have had difficulty establishing a time line—there is a debate whether it happened in the archaic period, in which pontifices ruled over the procedures, or afterward—was the division of adjudication into two distinct parts, the first dealing with questions of law and the second with questions of fact.[5] In the former, praetors decided on the admissibility of the case. In what today would be conceptualized as a preliminary hearing, they determined whether the courts would be willing to hear the case and which remedy should be given. This first part (*in iure,* that is, "within the law") was concerned with identifying the legal issues at stake and the appropriate remedy; in the second part (*apud iudicem,* "in the presence of a judge"), actual adjudication took place. In this part, the presiding judge (called *iudex*) had to ascertain the facts of the case, that is, what actually happened. The *iudex* heard the parties and considered their evidence. After he determined what had transpired, he proceeded to apply the solution that the praetor had identified in the previous stage.

The division of adjudication into two parts, the first concerned with establishing the legal question and the second with applying it to concrete circumstances, was essential to the development of law. This division registered the institutionalized awareness that it might be useful to isolate the normative order (the rule) from the chaos of everyday life (the particular circumstances of each case). Freed from the burden of the details specific to place, time, and parties, thereafter pontifices and / or praetors (depending on when this division took place) could begin formulating general rules that could be applied to all similar cases.

While the division of the process into two parts was important, the second innovation, which was as crucial and which most historians date to the third century BCE, was the introduction of new causes of action. No longer were praetors forced to follow the old causes of action and the religious rites that dominated the work of the priests. Instead, they were now at liberty to create new solutions embracing both the admissibility of cases as well as the types of remedies that the courts would supply.

This development was gradual. It probably began as a procedure specifically targeting the adjudication of conflicts involving foreigners, who were ineligible to use legal actions reserved for citizens.[6] However, sometime around the second or first century BCE (exact dating is still unsettled), it was also introduced into litigation among citizens after praetors were allowed to create new legal actions. These new actions—identified as "formulas"—usually consisted of short pronouncements that categorized the issue legally. Praetors drew these up after they heard litigants' claims and understood what they aimed to achieve. Offering ad hoc solutions to specific conflicts and often adopted after negotiation between the parties, most formulas included the identification of the person who should act as a *iudex,* a summary of the questions at stake, the facts required to support it, and an order stating how to proceed if the facts of the case were proved. For example, if there were a case of a conflict between individuals named Titus and Agrippa over the ownership of a horse, a formula would begin by stating who would be the judge (say, a citizen named Marcus). It would continue by declaring that it appeared that the horse in dispute belonged to Titus. If Agrippa, who held it, refused to return the horse to Titus as he was instructed by the judge, he should pay Titus its just price. If, on the other hand, it appeared that the horse was not Titus's, then Agrippa should be absolved. The formula could also specify the defenses (excuses) litigants could use; for example, it could allow Agrippa to argue that Titus had promised not to sue him.

After praetors clarified the legal issues at stake and prepared the formula, the parties would take their business to a *iudex,* whose role was to decide whether the facts of the matter justified the application of the rule set by the praetor. Unlike praetors, who were public officials nominated to a yearlong term, *iudex* were private individuals usually chosen by the praetor from a list of eligible men. A typical *iudex* would hear witnesses and consider other evidence. In the case mentioned above, he would verify whether the horse belonged to Titus and what its just price was. If Agrippa raised a defense, the *iudex* would decide on its veracity and would or would not free him from his obligation. Decisions of the *iudex* could not be appealed.

A Growing List of Formulas

It is possible that in the first few decades in which this system operated, formulas were mostly tailored to the parties and their specific concerns and reflected the evolution of Roman society and its needs. However, we know that relatively soon, praetors began drawing up standardized formulas that no longer included reference to the particular conditions of the case. Worded hypothetically, these formulas could specify, for example, that the praetor could rule against a seller who refused to hand to the buyer what was agreed upon, unless the seller showed no fault.

As formulas became more abstract, they could easily apply to more than a single case. Realizing this potential, some praetors began issuing lists of formulas that they would be willing to use in the future. Praetors working in Rome tended to post these lists in the Forum Romanum, the main square of the city, for all to read. The lists enumerated, seemingly in random fashion, the cases the praetor would agree to hear. For example, going back to Titus and Agrippa, the list could include the praetor's promise to rule in favor of a person whose property was taken away without compensation. Identified as edicts (edictum), eventually the lists of remedies were published annually by praetors before they assumed office. From the mid-first century BCE they were considered binding on the individual praetor who published them.

Initially each praetor published his own edict, with his particular list of remedies that would be valid only during the year in which he was in office. Yet gradually, first in the provinces and then in Rome, most praetors began copying earlier lists and referring to formulas already in existence. By the first century CE, repetition was so common and edicts were considered so prescriptive that praetors could no longer disregard what they had included by adding or subtracting from them. This became the rule in the second century CE when, under Hadrian (r. 117–138 CE), edicts were collected in an official compilation that was declared to be sufficient and final.

This development marked both the maturity and the end of an important period of Roman law. Before formulas were fossilized by the continuous repetition of the same edicts, praetors could create new formulas as well as deny the admissibility of old formulas. By granting or refusing to grant access to the courts, by indicating which circumstances deserved a remedy and which did not, and by allowing defendants to invoke certain defenses but not others, praetors intervened in the legal order by creating or denying what today we would identify as rights. Their intervention was so important and so massive that the norms they created by granting or refusing to grant remedies were identified as forming a new source of law, which paralleled the old *ius civile* and was later designated as *ius honorarium,* literally, the law that was made while they exercised their office *(honos).*

The importance of *ius honorarium* as a legal source allowed historians to characterize Roman law as a "law of remedies." Focused on how to redress the breach of peace and guarantee the return of the status quo, *ius honorarium* was mainly concerned with what individuals could do when they were wronged. It prescribed where they could go and which remedies they could receive. Much less interested in coining general principles or developing guidelines, this law was practical and casuistic. It collected the accumulated experience of Roman praetors but also authorized legitimate expectations as to what a wronged person could do. Alongside the existing law *(ius civile),* this magistrate-made law *(ius honorarium)* shaped Roman law as a synthesis between expert opinion based on customs, rituals, and systematic presentation *(ius civile),* on the one hand, and everyday conflicts and their resolution *(ius honorarium),* on the other.

The Emergence of New Procedures

Over time, new procedures emerged. Most important among them was the *cognitio* (literally, "investigation"), which reserved both the preliminary hearing of the case and the reception of proofs to an imperially nominated and salaried judge. Having begun during the reign of Augustus (27 BCE–14 CE) (or earlier, according to some historians) as a measure taken only in certain types of cases, *cognitio* eventually expanded to include most litigation. This marked the end of the division of the process into two distinct parts, one assigned to a praetor (and perhaps pontifices) and the other to a *iudex.*

With the gradual institution of *cognitio,* and most particularly starting in the third century CE, new officers were selected to serve as judges, and the emperor himself began hearing some cases, as did Roman governors in the provinces. The result was that conducting trials was no longer part of the public duty of prominent individuals (who could be appointed for one year as praetors or be nominated *iudex*) and litigation was no longer based on an agreement between parties who consented to the way their discord would be translated into a formula and agreed to subject themselves to the jurisdiction of the praetor and *iudex.* Instead, trials were now under the privy of officially appointed judges that both investigated the case and delivered the sentence.

The Contribution of Jurists

Sometime in the late third century, or during the second or first century BCE (the exact timing is still under debate), the work of praetors was accompanied by deliberations by a group of intellectuals we now identify as jurists (*iuris consultus* or *jurisprudentes*). Roman jurists were men who engaged with the normative order as part of their public duty. Many were members of the Senate, and some might have served as consuls. They had no particular training or official appointment, nor were their activities remunerated, yet they advised praetors on how to proceed by suggesting new formulas. They also answered questions from individuals who sought advice on which remedies could be requested or on how to manage their affairs or draw up documents in ways that would be legally useful and efficient. Jurists sometimes analyzed real cases, but they also gave their opinion on hypothetical cases meant to help interested parties plan their activities.

Although jurists were private individuals, many of whom held no official appointment, their influence on Roman law cannot be overestimated. Jurists guided the praetors and the parties, they creatively interpreted the formulas, and, above all, they profoundly transformed the law by molding its different tenets into a professional knowledge that only they shared. They elaborated a method to think about legal phenomena, invented a terminology, coined principles, identified organizing units, and referenced a series of ideas that would guide European law ever since.

The way jurists set about to create this new knowledge was both simple and ingenious. Beginning with a set of individual cases and a long list of casuistic solutions, jurists compared real cases against one another as well as against hypothetical cases. They asked what were the similarities and the differences. They distinguished between elements that, although mentioned in the rule or formula, were not normative and those that, on the contrary, were normative, by identifying the legal problem *(quaestio iuris)* that the case, norm, or formula was meant to resolve. Going back to Titus and Agrippa, rather than simply ruling that Agrippa had to give Titus the just price for the horse, by comparing his case to others, jurists came up with the concept of "good faith" *(bona fides)*. According to that, agreements must be settled on without simulation or dissimulation. If Titus retained the horse because Agrippa agreed not to sue, Titus could be accused of committing fraud.

Employing these procedures, Roman jurists elaborated many essential concepts that are still with us. They typified an enormous range of activities and social relations into a list of preset categories, including such things as "obligations," "contracts," "guardianship," "partnership," "inheritance," and "sale," to mention just a few examples. This enabled them to distinguish between different forms of sale, or a variety of ways to obtain ownership. It also allowed coining rules that would be valid for all sales or all ownerships, and others that would not. According to some historians, this process resulted in a true metamorphosis that conceptually transformed "acts of will" (the actions of individuals) to "acts of knowledge" (which translated what had happened into an intellectual abstraction).

The result was a new model for thinking about social relations. This new model, which we now identify as legal, consisted of a method to comprehend how people dealt with one another and what the consequences of their actions should be. This method was said to operate abstractly and adopt procedures that were completely indifferent to and independent of attachment to particular people, places, or times. In other words, regardless of its specific stipulations, where and when it was agreed to, or by whom, according to Roman jurists a sales contract was a sales contract. As such, it could include elements that were individual to this particular contract, but it was also subject to common rules that applied to all sales contracts of that type.

Roman jurists also invented quintessential juridical instruments, such as legal presumptions *(praesumptio iuris)*. Legal presumptions allowed jurists to assume that certain things were true without having to prove their existence. Reversing the burden of proof by placing it, not on the person who wished to demonstrate the presumptions, as is usually the case, but on the person who wanted to refute them, presumptions allowed jurists to infer, from what they knew, what was not known or could not be proved. A typical presumption from this period involved the conclusion that all property possessed by a married woman was given to her by her husband. A commonsense observation in that particular society and time, it could be used in legal proceedings and be adopted as a truism unless there was proof to demonstrate the contrary. Other presumptions included the idea that cancellation of a deed testified to the extinction of the debt, or for resolving questions of inheritance, that various individuals who died in a shipwreck all died at exactly the same time.

Although much of this scholarly production was oral, by the second century BCE some jurists began collecting their responses *(responsa)*, summarizing important cases, and recording court decisions. Others produced commentaries or treatises on certain topics or wrote general essays on Roman law. As this literature proliferated, new genres appeared. In the second century CE, a jurist named Gaius proposed a practical manual to introduce the uninitiated both to the law and to legal thinking. The manual, titled *Institutes,* divided Roman law into three parts: the law of persons (personal status), the law of things (including obligations), and the law of actions (what kinds of actions were available to litigants who wanted to achieve certain things). Although not particularly important when it was written, this manual became a model to follow. By the fifth century, it was also subject to interpretation and commentary.

Jurists and the Law

Although jurists were not formally appointed and their advice had no binding force, their answers could be normative. This was the result not of an official appointment (which they lacked) but of the reputation and prestige of the jurists themselves and the belief that their analyses embodied reason. Because the degree to which their advice was followed depended on how renowned the person who gave it was, not all opinions by all jurists were considered equally prescriptive.

The fact that private individuals could express opinions about the law and that these opinions were abided by was not always agreeable to the Roman authorities. Several emperors attempted to control these processes by instituting, for example, a system of licenses to give advice, or by drawing up lists that prescribed which jurists were to be followed and in which order of preference. Best known among these efforts was Augustus's listing of jurists having the right to give responses, Constantine's (r. 306–337 CE) fourth-century-CE instructions that only certain works by certain classical authors could be cited in Roman courts, and the fifth-century (426 CE) Law of Citations that allowed only the use of the opinions of five selected jurists. The Law of Citations also instructed that if these jurists disagreed, the majority opinion would prevail and that, if there was no majority because the various jurists pointed at various (rather than only two) solutions, the opinion of Papinian (140–212 CE) should be followed.[7]

Despite their persistence, these imperial efforts at controlling juridical creation were mostly in vain. Juridical literature continued to develop, and its usage continued to depend mainly on the reputation of jurists, not on imperial decision making. In the long run, imperial control over this legal source was achieved more efficiently by co-opting jurists, not by attempting to manage the normative reception of their opinions. To this end, several emperors employed prestigious jurists in their court or arranged for them to give responses on their behalf. Some jurists even became members of the council that advised emperors on the most important matters of state.

This cooperation between jurists and the emperor led to important changes. By the third century CE, most juridical activity was centered on jurists giving responses as members of the imperial bureaucracy. In their capacity as imperial officials, their determinations were now binding not because of their inherent goodness but because they were considered orders of the emperor.

Juridical Training

Initially jurists had no special preparation other than living in the community and being involved in its affairs. As members of the Roman elite, most were trained in rhetoric, the art of persuasion, but they had no legal training per se. With the growing importance and number of jurists, however, something akin to a professional preparation began appearing. Instruction mostly took place orally, with a group of apprentices following a master as he gave advice or delivered speeches. As this practice became popular, individual preparation was replaced by communities, or groups of people, who came to listen to jurists publically expound their opinions on points of the law. Although teaching continued to be informal and voluntary, those habitually listening were sometimes identified as "students" who formed "societies" and paid some remuneration to their "teachers."

By the first century CE, the following of masters became so institutionalized that two rival schools of thought made their appearance. Identified as the Proculians and the Sabinians, these schools were named after the jurists who founded them. Historians disagree as to the difference between the two schools. Most believe that they were probably distinct in their approach to legal analysis, one adhering more closely to the letter of the law and the other caring more about material justice.

The congregation of students around masters was particularly noticeable in the second century CE, when several locations were identified as places where law teaching habitually took place. In these locations, teachers gave courses on a variety of subjects, including juridical thought and imperial legislation. At the end of their studies, students received a certificate. By the fourth century CE these schools came under the control of emperors, who appointed the teachers and gave them the status of civil servants. In 425 CE, Theodosius II (r. 408–450 CE) declared illegal the teaching of law outside these state-sanctioned institutions.

Legislation

Another means to create legal norms was legislation. Assemblies (meetings of all male, adult, Roman citizens) could pass statutes *(leges)* as well as *plebiscita* (laws made in assemblies of plebeians). According to some historians, the Senate, where leading men of the republic met to discuss the affairs of the day, was a legislative body that not only recommended but also prescribed certain solutions *(senatus consulta),* most particularly under the Republic (ca. 509–27 BCE). In the late Principate (ca. 27 BCE–284 CE), a new form of legislation, the *oratio principis,* appeared, allowing emperors to deliver speeches telling the Senate which norms it should adopt.

These various legal sources fared differently in diverse periods. Laws and statutes passed by assemblies were an important source of law until the first century BCE. Senate decrees were important in the first and part of the second century CE. The accumulation of imperial legislation led to the appearance of collections of imperial constitutions such as the third-century CE *Codex Gregorianus,* which included legislation from Hadrian to Emperor Diocletian (r. 284–305 CE), or the more famous early fifth-century *Codex Theodosianus,* formally promulgated by Theodosius II and including sixteen books divided into titles and covering legislation dating from 306 to 437 CE. But even at the height of their prominence, these sources were of little weight when compared to the production of praetors and jurists. Among other things, legislation tended to add to and explain, rather than change, the legal situation. Furthermore, its most frequent field of action was public, not private, law. Legislation also covered such issues as criminal law, testamentary succession, and family law.

The relatively secondary role of legislation in the making of Roman law was paradoxically confirmed with the advent of the empire. Roman emperors, who sought to influence the legal order, legislated massively.

However, to justify their growing legislative powers they often disguised themselves as judges and jurists. They published edicts (as the praetors once did), rendered judgments *(decreta)*, or gave answers to questions of law presented to them either by the interested parties or by praetors *(rescripta)*. These answers were often written not by the emperors themselves but by jurists working for them and in their name. Contemporary jurists consented to these practices, yet they continued to uphold the centrality of juridical thought and insisted on their role as custodians of a legal methodology. The emperor, they argued, was free to legislate, but examining the legitimacy of his enactments rested with jurists. After all, jurisprudence, not imperial pronouncements, embodied knowledge of matters divine and human and distinguished what was just from what was not.[8]

Ius Gentium

Owing to the conviction that polities depended on agreement among members to live together under the same normative order, Roman law was applied exclusively to the citizens of Rome. Because each community had its own laws, which were the laws of its *civitas* (its community of citizens), in theory foreigners *(peregrini)* had no right to Roman law even when they were present in Rome. Foreigners of the same group were to use their own *ius civile,* that is, their own communal law. But what would happen when individuals of distinct communities came into contact? Which laws would apply?

To take care of such situations, a different system had to be devised. Born sometime in the fourth or third century BCE—the dates are not very clear— this system was eventually identified as *ius gentium* (literally, the Law of Nations, Peoples, Gentiles, or Tribes). Managing it would be a new figure, a special praetor for foreigners *(praetor peregrinus),* a post created in 242 BCE.[9]

The emergence of *ius gentium* rested on the assumption that while some norms were particular to a specific community, others were common to all. *Ius civile* represented the former; *ius gentium* represented the latter. From its birth, therefore, *ius gentium* was imagined as a universal system that could fit any person of any community or legal tradition. To discover what it included, in theory the *praetor peregrinus* (or provincial governor) was to identify the legal principles shared by all humans. Because what this meant in practice was not always clear, those dealing with *ius gentium* had a much greater liberty to add, subtract, or change the law than did other officials who were charged with applying Roman law. Thus, although much is unknown about how the *praetor peregrinus* proceeded to identify the contents of *ius gentium* and whether his understanding of it truly differed from his understanding of Roman *ius civile,* it is nevertheless clear he enjoyed a relative liberty that allowed him to, for example, abandon the old causes of action and, as we saw earlier, and introduce new formulas. The quest to identify a *ius gentium* also allowed the *praetor peregrinus* the pioneering adoption of important principles, such as the obligation to have good faith *(bona fides)* in contracts. The formulas the *praetor peregrinus* created, the remedies he supplied, and the edicts he published established important new practices and doctrines soon imitated by other praetors and since used by jurists.

Imagined as a law that was not based on the specific historical experience of a particular community but instead was anchored in human experience, eventually *ius gentium* was said to represent human reason and the nature of things. As a result of this understanding, on occasions Romans considered it also as embodying a natural law *(ius naturale).* They suggested that it was so reasonable and compelling that nature, rather than human convention, was responsible for its creation.

The Extension of Roman Law throughout the Empire

Conceived as the law of a particular community, Roman law was thus tied to citizenship, which was an inherited status exclusive to the inhabitants of the city and their descendants. However, in a long process extending from the fourth to the first century BCE, Roman citizenship was extended to most individuals living in the Italian peninsula and Gaul (present-day France). In 212 CE, Emperor Caracalla granted it to all free residents of the empire. As a result of this extension, Roman law was no longer the exclusive system of the citizens of the city, but instead the common stock of all imperial subjects.

The way this legal extension took place was particularly interesting. Rather than reimagining Roman law as a territorial law that ruled first over a city, then over a region, then over an empire, as eventually many powers would do, what Romans did in order to broaden the validity of their legal system was to grant Roman citizenship. In other words, rather than making the territory Roman, they transformed foreigners into citizens, and rather than arguing that Roman law should be universally applied, they redefined the extension of the Roman community by including in it all the inhabitants of the empire. Roman law theoretically remained the same; what changed was the definition of who Romans were.

The expansion of citizenship and, with it, of Roman law, throughout the empire led to important developments. One that has drawn the attention of many scholars was the emergence of a series of peripheral or provincial Roman legal systems. These included local expressions of Roman law, which were radically different from place to place and vastly diverse over time. Once portrayed as "vulgar" because of their distance from the centers of creation and from juridical debates, their more salient feature was that they were greatly influenced by local conditions and customs, most particularly in the Hellenistic East, where Romanization was harder to achieve than elsewhere.

Although the emergence of local variations of Roman law probably predated the extension of Roman citizenship to all the inhabitants of the empire, it is generally believed that this extension accelerated the fragmentation of Roman law. By ordering that Roman law would immediately replace all previous legal traditions, the Antonine Constitution, which sanctioned the extension of citizenship in 212 CE, unilaterally imposed the trappings of Roman law onto preexisting native systems. In theory mandating a complete legal overhaul, in practice, however, this goal was unattainable. The result was an extremely complex structure that allowed the development of multiple and parallel legal systems that, although formally identified as Roman and sharing some characteristics, were nevertheless radically different from one another.

This extreme pluralism was not formally acknowledged. Roman jurists, of course, knew that differences, sometimes substantial ones, existed among the laws operating across the empire, but they did their best to conceal this. They did so by redefining the scope of customary law. They argued that, after the imposition of Roman citizenship, all persisting differences between the (original) Roman law and the (local) Roman law were but exceptions anchored in local customs. Reimagining all legal differences as part of a local customary law allowed jurists to sanction and legitimize the survival of a vast body of native law despite the fact that, in theory, the empire tolerated only the existence of one common (Roman) law.

Whether they predated the imposition of Roman law or emerged after it was imposed, paradoxically, the reclassification of legal differences as customs greatly transformed Roman law. By recognizing as legitimate (Roman) customs what were in reality foreign norms, and by giving them normative value within Roman law, Roman jurists opened the door for the massive penetration into their legal system of non-Roman concepts and legal arrangements. One example is that Hellenistic forms of contract or foreign understanding of possession could thereafter give rise to a *ius civile* litigation even in Rome itself.

The complexities that resulted could be demonstrated by observing developments in the Iberian Peninsula. Rome intermittently controlled Iberia from the end of the third century BCE, and its final conquest is said to have been completed in the year 19 BCE. Roman domination persisted until the end of the fourth century, when Iberia was conquered by the Visigoths. This convoluted history was reflected in the way local law developed. Initially several systems coincided in the territory. There was Roman law for Roman citizens, indigenous law for the natives, and complex rules, based on different principles, for assigning cases involving Romans and non-Romans. None of these systems, however, existed in isolation. They interacted to such a degree that indigenous law gradually became Romanized to the point that, rather than ensuring separation, its imposition led to acculturation. Its employment allowed indigenous people to familiarize themselves with Roman law and accept some of its basic tenets under the guise of their being local. Provincial edicts and pronouncements added to this growing body of local law, as did Senate decisions that specifically targeted Hispania.

Over time the number of local inhabitants recognized as Romans grew substantially through individual concessions of citizenship to "worthy" natives. Several indigenous cities received the status of Latin municipalities, and their inhabitants acquired Roman citizenship. After all free residents of the empire were made Roman citizens, then, at least in theory, only Roman law persisted in Hispania. Yet this transition was neither immediate nor complete. Customary indigenous law persisted because it was considered known or good, because there was an insufficient number of experts in Roman law, and because it was gradually merged with Roman law.

This amalgamation of Roman and non-Roman was further enhanced after the Western Roman Empire fragmented. This became particularly evident in the early sixth century, when the Visigoths (who conquered Hispania at the end of the fourth century) proceeded to recompile the local Roman law. The *Lex Romana Visigothorum* (also known as the Breviary of Alaric), which they elaborated, was in the Middle Ages considered a trustworthy source for late Roman law. However, although the Lex Romana reproduced some essential Roman texts, such as abstracts from the second-century *Institutes* of Gaius or the fifth-century Theodosian Code, compilers of this law selected which parts to include and how to interpret them. They incorporated and reproduced in their collection a simplified and abbreviated version of Roman law based on very few sources that were repeatedly used and cited. It is also possible that by the time the Lex Romana was enacted, Roman law was already under the influence of not only local Iberian customs but also the laws and customs that the Visigoths brought with them to Iberia. If this was true, then not only did the Lex Romana capture only some parts of Roman law, but it is possible that it contained a not particularly faithful representation of how Roman law fared in Iberia before, during, or after the Visigoth conquest.

If the extension of citizenship was one challenge, another was Emperor Diocletian's (r. 284–305) decision in 285 CE, in the midst of a prolonged crisis, to divide the empire into two parts. Diocletian apparently wished to facilitate the administration of this vast polity by naming two rulers and building two capitals. Yet what began as a mere administrative and political tool ended up forming a true divide. In the post-Diocletian period, Constantine (r. 306–337) materialized the division of the empire by erecting in the east a New Rome, which he called Constantinople, where he transferred his residence.

The growing distinction between East and West was also noticeable legally with the gradual emergence of an Eastern and a Western Roman law. It became particularly prominent after the Western empire fragmented in the fifth century and was overrun by a great variety of tribes we now identify as Germanic (see Chapter 3). Thereafter, Western Roman law became heavily influenced by Germanic legal traditions. Meanwhile in the East, Roman law came under the renewed yet intense influence of Hellenistic culture.

Most historians tend to categorize the survival of Roman law in the East as marking the emergence of a separate and distinct legal tradition, which they identify as Byzantine. Yet, paradoxically, this so-called Byzantine law eventually gave rise to the most important compilation of Roman law that survives to date, the *Corpus Iuris Civilis*.

The *Corpus Iuris Civilis*

The *Corpus Iuris Civilis,* as it came to be known in the sixteenth century, was a collection of various pieces of Roman law.[10] Sanctioned by Justinian

(r. 527–565), emperor of the Eastern empire in the sixth century CE (that is, after the fragmentation of the Western empire), in reality the *Corpus* included several independent compilations that were enacted successively. Common to all of them was that they were prepared by a committee of experts with the aim of guarding, even restoring, the glory of Roman law as well as supplying a practical code for the Eastern empire and a teaching tool for students.

First among these compilations was the *Code (Codex)*, which in a first edition of 529 and a second edition of 534 outlined various texts of imperial legislation, some ancient, some less so, some general and some pertaining specifically to the Eastern empire. The *Codex* mostly sought to fuse selectively three preexisting compilations (the *Codex Gregorianus*, the *Codex Hermogenianus*, and the *Codex Theodosianus*), adding to them the most recent imperial legislation and omitting what was considered obsolete or contradictory. The second edition of the *Codex* also included decisions by Justinian as to how to solve certain conflicts and promote reform. The *Code*, which was meant to replace earlier collections, was arranged according to subject matter, and inside each subject the laws were arranged chronologically.

The second compilation carried out under the auspices of Justinian was the *Digest* (or *Pandects*). Finalized in 533 CE, it reproduced extracts from the writings of some of the most influential Roman jurists who had worked between the first century BCE and the fourth century CE. Arranged by topic, the *Digest* dealt with important areas of private law, mostly family law, property law, contract law, and inheritance.[11] It was divided into fifty books that followed the arrangement of the Code.

The third compilation, titled *Institutes*, was promulgated in 533. Mainly based on the manual for students authored by Gaius in the second century CE as well as containing elements from other students' manuals, Justinian's *Institutes* described the principles of Roman law and divided them by the law of persons, things, and actions.

Although meant to collect and reproduce the law, the *Corpus Iuris Civilis* nevertheless innovated a great deal. The quantity of material considered for inclusion was enormous, forcing the editing committee to choose what should be incorporated and what not. Historians have estimated that, to prepare the *Digest,* which compiled jurists' opinions, some thirty-eight authors and two thousand books were consulted but that only about 5 percent of this material made it into the last version. Committee members were also told to settle conflicts and produce a unitary body of law and were mandated to adapt this law to the conditions and legislation of their time.

If the process of elaboration implied change, so too did the inclusion of this material in legislation sanctioned by the emperor as the law of the realm. The juridical opinions that were reproduced in the *Digest* now acquired the status of law. The same happened with the *Institutes,* a manual for students that thereafter was authorized as the formal vehicle with which to understand Roman law. Justinian was so adamant about giving his collections the power of law that he prohibited references to the original material or to previous recompilations. He also forbade the elaboration of commentaries and glosses, forcing jurists to center their attention on his compilations and on them alone. Often unsuccessful, these measures nevertheless exemplified the degree by which Justinian desired to ensure the beginning of a new age.

The Afterlife of the *Corpus Iuris Civilis*

Despite the fragmentation of the Western Roman Empire in the fourth and fifth centuries CE, what we now identify as the Byzantine Empire (the Roman empire of the East) survived until the conquest of Constantinople by the Ottomans in 1453. From the sixth century (when the *Corpus* was elaborated) to the fifteenth century, therefore, in theory at least, Roman law as compiled in the *Corpus* continued operating in the East.

Formal continuity, however, could not mask what were in reality substantial mutations. Most remarkable among these was the gradual adoption of Greek rather than Latin. Used since the mid-sixth century—Justinian himself began legislating in that language—ultimately Greek became the legal language of the East, forcing jurists and practitioners to translate, summarize, and interpret some of the major Latin texts.

The adoption of Greek, the continuing reference to the Justinian codification whose presence in the West was at best patchy, and the need to apply Roman law to constantly evolving new circumstances, gave rise to the creation of a distinct Roman legal system that was particular to the East. The eleventh-century schism that enshrined a distinction between a Latin and an Orthodox Christian Church, the former observed in the West and the latter observed in the territories of the Byzantine Empire, also contributed to a widening gap between Western and Eastern traditions of Roman law.

Despite this growing divergence, practitioners in the East constantly asserted their ongoing association with and reliance on Roman law. Subsequent Byzantine emperors presented their legislation as amendments (rather than derogation) of the *Corpus,* and the *Institutes,* the manual for law students included in the Justinian compilation, also maintained its place in legal education. It is therefore paradoxical that the division between East and West, which was not particularly clear in the early Middle Ages, would eventually become clearer and to some degree definitive only after the Eastern Justinian *Corpus* would reemerge in the West, where it would fuel the "revival" of Roman law in the eleventh and twelfth centuries.[12]

2

The Creation of Latin Christendom

IN THE FIRST CENTURY CE an important agent appeared on the horizon of what was to become European law. Its initial impact was timid and partial, but by the fifth century it became a major player. This transforming agent was a new religion, Christianity, and it was about to turn the ancient world upside down.

Christianity was born as a Jewish sect sometime in the early part of the first century CE. With relatively humble beginnings, it expanded rapidly, first in the Eastern Mediterranean and then along its western shores. Roman officials initially rejected the new religion and, thinking it subversive in both method and creed, persecuted its followers. But by the fourth century CE, the tide had turned. In 312 Constantine recognized Christianity as one of the permissible religions, and in 383 Theodosius I declared Christianity the official religion of the empire.

The combining of Christianity with the Roman Empire produced an earthquake. It shook some of the basic foundations of Roman law, and once the seismic activity was over, what emerged was a new system. This system no longer linked law with citizenship. Nor did law become territorial. Instead, normativity was now tied to a shared creed. In theory, it united all Christians, regardless of their origin or location. This new system was also propagated by new actors, the believers. It was through the missionary activities of these individuals and following their path that, in the early medieval period, both Christianity and Roman law were introduced across Europe. Gradually forming part of the legal and cultural stock even in territories that never formed part of the empire, this introduction created a space we now identify as Latin Christendom.[1] What it meant for European legal development is the subject of this chapter.

The New Religion

Historically, the new religion was an offspring of Judaism. Although eventually moving away from it, Christianity shared the Jewish vision of God as a lawmaker. According to this tradition, at the basis of the relationship between the believers and the divine was an agreement (a covenant) that ensured that if the believers obeyed God's law, they would be rewarded. Their observance of that law would guarantee that God would favor and protect them.

This understanding of the relationship between God and believers, which Judaism introduced and Christianity then followed, portrayed God not as a capricious being that reproduced human faults and passions but instead as a virtuous power that acted through legislation. God's rules were, in theory, clear, and those who entered into the covenant knew what they included.

This conceptualization of lawgiving was new with respect to Roman law. Whereby Roman law focused on conflict resolution, Christianity featured a law that was based on a contract, an agreement between parties. Rather than being anchored in customs and elaborated by praetors and jurists as in Rome, the Christian law was divine in origin. And rather than being open to all citizens of an imperial polity, this law was offered by God only to the Israelites.[2] Roman and Christian law were also distinct because the norms they adopted were radically different, as were their identification of right and just behavior and their conceptualization of what the community consisted of and what it was destined to achieve.

The Christianization of Roman Law?

Given these vast differences between Roman and Christian law, many historians rushed to assume that the advent of Christianity greatly and immediately affected Roman law. They expected to conclude that the rise of Christianity in Rome brought about major changes and that these would be easily traceable in the historical record. They also anticipated that after

Rome Christianized, Roman law and the behavior of Romans would have substantially mutated.

But many historians now disagree about how important or pervasive the influence of Christianity on Roman law was or, most particularly, how immediate. They also question whether legal changes (even when they occurred) affected practices, or whether they remained a dead letter, more revealing of the intentions of a small elite than of what happened in society at large.

Those holding the view that little changed after the Christianization of the empire argue that the new conceptualization of law as divinely mandated did not immediately influence Roman law. As long as the empire lasted, Roman officials continued to operate as before, inventing, reinterpreting, and applying the existent law. Criminal law also continued to uphold Roman traditions and was not greatly affected by the new, radically distinct, Christian morality. Families continued to function as they did in the past, with children maintaining their role as guardians of familial memory despite the new Christian promise of afterlife and Christian criticism of Roman earthly commemorations. Social stratification and status were essentially preserved despite the new ethos that Christians were to live in brotherly and nonhierarchical communities.

While many historians sought to answer the question whether the conversion of the empire affected Roman law by comparing the norms before and after it took place, others suggested that not all contemporary legal changes were necessarily tied to the adoption of the new religion. Mutations, they argue, could easily be motivated by an evolution common to both Christians and non-Christians. After all, Roman law had constantly changed even when the religious belief of Romans did not. Was it possible, for example, that some innovations, such as demands for female chastity, reflected notions coming from the provinces and from non-aristocratic circles that adhered to customary practices rather than to the new Christian beliefs?

Some historians reached the conclusion that Christianity introduced no substantial or immediate changes. Others affirmed that even if the authorities, modalities, and language remained the same, the contents of Roman law shifted in what was to become a long and slow process of integrating Christianity with Roman law. These scholars point to legal adjustments adopted after the conversion of the empire, mainly through imperial legislation. For example, beginning in the fourth century CE, sins were added to the existing lists of crimes, and new regulations were made regarding pious bequests. Also innovative was the distinction between appropriate and inappropriate public entertainment, the idea of indissoluble marriage, the legitimization of natural children, and the duty to pay alimony to wife and offspring. Beyond imperial legislation, it is possible that Christianity might have influenced the way Romans conceptualized and sought to control sexual conduct. It might have led to new practices regarding charity and welfare. In short, Christian elements and a Christian agenda may have gradually penetrated Roman law, and Christianized Romans behaved (at least to some degree) differently than pagans.

Historians of late Roman law also debated why Roman emperors introduced Christian ideas into their legislation (when they did). Some argued that the emperors were motivated by true religious belief; others said that they were politicians seeking to maximize their power and capitalize on new societal trends that were beneficial to them. For example, was Constantine's legislative work motivated by Christian zeal or by traditional Roman concerns? By referencing customary legal practices, was it possible that Constantine nevertheless created new norms that introduced Christian ideas, fusing them with Roman precedents and values? Taking into account his legislation regarding the emancipation of slaves, was his support for the idea of freedom a result of his wish to free individuals who were enslaved because of their Christian belief (as some have argued), or was it part of a more general move against his opponents, allowing him to portray these opponents as tyrants and himself as a liberator? How did introducing new methods for emancipation, mainly by allowing Christian masters to free their slaves in church, affect Roman laws on slavery? How did it help the propagation and consolidation of Christianity?

The Romanization of the Church

If historians disagree on whether the introduction of Christianity led Romans to reconsider their legal traditions and adapt them accordingly, and to what degree, there is nevertheless a general consensus that the empire's espousal of the new religion radically affected Christianity. The first and clearest sign of that was the Romanization of the Church. Born in the Eastern Mediterranean and prospering in Asia Minor and the Near East, early Christianity was deeply influenced by Hellenistic culture. It was predominantly Greek-speaking and took on many Hellenistic traits. Yet once it reached

Rome and became the official religion of the empire, Rome gradually emerged as an important Christian center, and in many areas Latin replaced Greek as the main vehicle of communication.

Other important changes also took place. Early Christianity was very local in character and contained many different communities who agreed on hardly anything. These communities were self-regulated and often confronted one another. After Christianity became the religion of the empire, this extremely nucleated structure gradually came under attack. Now that Christianity was endowed with a state (the Roman state), an additional system of law (to Church law was now added Roman law), and a series of authorities (Roman authorities), these began regulating Christian life. What followed was a slow process of centralization that eventually led to the formation of the Church as we think of it today—a structure of authority with a more or less fixed canon of beliefs and a set of authorized texts.

The institutionalization of Church authorities and the definition of a common creed was a mission that late Roman emperors undertook with great expediency. This imperial positioning vis-à-vis the Church had Roman precedents. Pagan Roman emperors were considered representatives of the gods, with whom they were believed to have direct communication. Because the gods favored them, the emperors were under the obligation to ensure that the gods would be worshipped. Applying this understanding to Christianity, late Roman emperors presented themselves as defenders of the correct faith and as leaders responsible for its propagation. As benefactors of the Church, they adjudicated conflicts among Church members and among different Christian communities and decided who was right and who was wrong in matters of faith.

Following these beliefs, from as early as the fourth century CE emperors also called meetings to declare the basic tenets of Christianity. The Council of Nicaea (325 CE), organized by Constantine, settled the issue of who Jesus was and what his relationship to God was. It adopted the so-called Nicene Creed, later expanded at the Council of Constantinople (381 CE), which affirmed the divinity of Jesus and the existence of a trinity (the father, the son, and the Holy Spirit). The Council of Carthage (397 CE) identified the official canon of the Church and selected the texts that would be included in the authorized scripture.[3] Early councils also provided procedures to ordain the clergy and to call for meetings of bishops (synods) and adopted some of the principal liturgical practices.

Over time, imperial intervention grew exponentially. Subsequent emperors interfered with Church matters not only by dictating solutions but also by forcing them on opponents by persecuting and punishing them. By the end of this process, Christianity and its dogma became a matter of imperial law. Imperial law determined, as the fifth-century Theodosian Code did, what true Christianity was and which religious practices were to be followed.

Defining Heresy

The gradual definition of what Christianity was and what believers should follow also led to the identification of what it was not. This process of delegitimizing certain positions began long before the conversion of the empire, but it greatly accelerated thereafter. It was so quick and powerful that, disregarding past divisions, by the fifth century CE Christian authors could argue that Christianity included "all which has been believed everywhere, always, by anyone."[4] Recognizing some debates among the faithful as legitimate (these were identified as *schisma*) and others as not (heresy), the result was the division of Christians into orthodox (those who believed correctly) and heterodox individuals (those who did not).

As these opinions propagated, Roman emperors began legislating against heretics. Because of the identification between empire and Church, they defined heretics as criminal offenders. Their disobedience, it was argued, constituted contempt for the emperor and his imperial law and endangered the community. It therefore could, and indeed was, equated with treason and was punishable by death. Thereafter, St. Augustine (354–430 CE) could advocate persecution of heretics, believing that they were dangerous dissenters whose opinions could pollute the community and bring about its downfall.

Promoting Conversion

If the union of empire and Christianity generated mechanisms leading to a single dogma imposed on all believers and punishment of those who refused to adhere to its tenets, it also provided opportunities to promote conversion. Wishing to achieve this goal, different emperors legislated in this direction, granting converts special privileges. They also inflicted on pagans legal and economic limitations, such as prohibiting their rites, ending state subsidies to support their religion, and removing the immunities of their priests. On occasion, emperors confiscated treasures found in pagan temples or consented to the destruction of these temples. In the 340s and 350s, laws were enacted prohibiting pagan worship under penalty of death. Many regulations favored Christians in public office or prohibited the employment of pagans. Particular pressure was place on elites, who were to be rewarded or punished because of their creed in ways that were much more severe and meaningful than the treatment meted out to simple folk.

As a result of such measures, by the early fifth century St. Augustine, one of the fathers of the Church, could openly advocate the use of coercion and violence to promote conversion, arguing that Roman emperors had the unquestionable right to employ all means at their disposal to prohibit paganism. External pressure, he argued, could provoke a genuine change of heart and could lead to true faith. His views were accepted by emperors such as Justinian, who in the sixth century legalized the forced conversion of pagans. Thereafter, Roman law became an instrument for advancing, even imposing, conversion, a move presented as a necessary means to ensure the well-being of all humankind.

The Church as a Roman Institution

From the perspective of European legal history, however, the most meaningful development during this period was the growing identification between the Church and the law and structures of Rome, which the Church continued to uphold even after the Western Empire fragmented. Bishops, for example, were fashioned after Roman consuls or praetors. They received similar judicial, administrative, and legislative powers in both the religious and the secular realms, they were to follow procedures that originated in Roman law, and they were expected to take into consideration what Roman law instructed. Like Roman officials, bishops also met in assemblies to coordinate their activities as well as to legislate, and they were exempt from public service, controlled extensive properties, and enjoyed great prestige. In the absence of local government, most particularly after the Western empire fragmented, bishops often undertook responsibilities as state officials, such as overseeing inheritance and succession, supervising public works, settling private disputes, and operating schools.

The Church's adoption of Roman structures and laws was also clear in other ways. Dioceses were conceptualized as Roman units, and the Church itself was legally constructed as a corporation *(universitas),* a status that in Roman law was held by the state and other public bodies, allowing them to own property, receive gifts, and make contracts. Church buildings were called *basilicas* after the old Roman spaces where assemblies met and where praetors rendered judgments on elevated platforms. Church canons (rules) used the imperial style and were read, interpreted, and obeyed as if they were imperial decrees. Roman jurisprudence became a vehicle through which to discuss theological questions, and bishops responded to petitioners by using the forms and formulas of Roman jurists. One result of this merger was various books, such as a fourth-century discussion of why paganism was false and Christianity was true that was titled "Divine Institutes" after Gaius's manual for law students. This allusion was purposeful, according to the author, because just as Roman jurists used Gaius's *Institutes* to settle juridical disputes, his book would do the same with regard to religious creed.

Historians thus conclude that early ecclesiastical law grew out of the constant interaction between Roman legal practices and the requirements and needs of the Church. The Church, of course, also preserved the Roman language (Latin) as well as Roman forms of oratory, expression, literature, architecture, and art. By the time of Pope Gregory I (590–604) some authors portrayed their world as one "in which most Romans had been Christened, the empire itself sometimes was called a *res publica christiana* and the Church long since granted peace *(tranquilitas).*"[5] Criticizing this situation a thousand years later in 1651, Thomas Hobbes remarked that "the papacy is no other than the ghost of the deceased Roman empire, sitting crowned upon the grave thereof."[6] As for historians, they have long asked if the empire was swallowed up by the Church, or the Church by the empire. Most agree, however, that Christianity transformed Rome and that Roman society transformed Christianity, and that, in the process, law acquired a new character.

Christianization and Romanization after Rome

In the centuries following the fragmentation of the Western Roman Empire (during a period we now identify at the early Middle Ages), Christianity spread throughout Europe and so did Roman culture and law. This process of diffusion was long and complicated. Initially, conversion efforts were fairly feeble. As long as the Church consisted of a multiplicity of bishops, each working in his diocese, there were insufficient means or coordination with which to bring about the conversion of large populations. However, with the foundation of the monastic orders (which produced dedicated missionaries, most particularly from the sixth century onward) and the gradual affirmation of the papacy (during approximately the same period) the Church moved into an expansionist mode.

From the sixth to the twelfth century, Christianity gradually established itself in most of central, northern, and eastern Europe. Expanding westward from the Italian peninsula to present-day France and Germany, it reached the British Isles, and to the east it spread into Moravia, Slovakia, Serbia, Bulgaria, Poland, Hungary, and the Baltic states. Next came northern Europe, with the Netherlands, Denmark, Sweden, Norway, and Iceland. At times incremental, at others advancing and retreating, by the end of the twelfth century this process of conversion produced an important homogenizing effect that, among other things, introduced Roman law and Roman structures all over Europe.

As a result of these processes, the new Christianized understanding of Roman law, which initially was limited to the territories of the empire, won primacy throughout much of European territory. Missionaries and Church officials responsible for this dissemination might have cared about the conversion of the so-called pagans, but while they spread the word of the gospel, they also propagated the language, rhetoric, art, ceremonies, culture, and law of Rome. They introduced Roman administrative structures, formulas, and procedures and imposed Roman ways of thinking, arguing, and resolving conflicts.

Particularly transformative in this regard were the processes taking place in territories that had not been part of the Roman Empire. There, the accumulated effect of Christianization and Romanization was especially noteworthy, eventually replacing earlier traditions. According to some historians, the diffusion of Romanized Christianity throughout much of the Continent resulted in the "making of Europe." That is, it brought about the gradual buildup of the cultural, administrative, legal, and political characteristics that enabled Europe to cohere.[7] By the tenth century if not earlier, Europeans of very distinct regions with vastly diverse pasts and cultures could feel themselves identified with Christianity and present themselves as heirs to Rome.

While this was happening in much of southern, western, central, and northern Europe, in the East a different strand of Romanization made inroads. There as elsewhere, converts to Christianity were introduced not only to a new religion, but also to Roman trappings. Yet these trappings were distinct. They were mostly Hellenistic in orientation and conducted in Greek and disseminated an Eastern, rather than a Western, Roman tradition.[8] Their effect, however, was as important and as enduring. After the conquest of Constantinople, the capital of the Byzantine Empire, by the Ottomans in 1453, Eastern Roman law survived in the institutions and laws of the Orthodox Church. Applied to the Greek population living under Ottoman occupation, it was administered by the patriarch of Constantinople and other Church officials who, by implementing Orthodox canon law, also preserved a Roman legacy.

PART TWO

The Early Middle Ages

3

An Age with No Jurists?

THE APPROXIMATELY FIVE HUNDRED YEARS between the demise of
the Western Roman Empire in the fifth century and the year 1000 are usually
characterized by historians as highly chaotic.[1] The religious unification of
Europe under a gradually expanding Christianity led to the emergence and
imposition of canon law across the Continent. Yet initially this canon law had
highly disjointed structures of authority and a great variety of contradictory
norms and sources. Meanwhile, the conversion of Europe was accompanied
by extreme political fragmentation with the emergence of a multiplicity of
small polities, each independent of the other. The Continent also experienced
the massive movement of human groups from the north to the center, south,
and east. Many such groups, often identified as "Germanic," had initially
allied themselves with the Roman Empire, with which they traded, to
which they supplied soldiers, and where they wished to immigrate. However,
by the end of the fourth century some of these groups began seizing sufficient
power to bring about fall of the Western empire (according to some historians) or its radical modification (according to others). As they took over
formerly Roman territories, the growing political and economic hegemony
of several of these groups, which established kingdoms in areas now belonging to Germany, France, Spain, Italy, Switzerland, and North Africa,
led to the introduction and dissemination of new legal cultures across the
Continent. These mixed with existing native and expanding Roman and
canon law in diverse ways, creating complex amalgamations that were different from place to place and period to period.

47

In approximately the year 800, a combination of local, Germanic, Roman, and canon law crystallized. Although it had different expressions in distinct locations, it nevertheless featured some common notions regarding what law was and where it came from. According to some scholars, this emerging consensus allows us to view this period—which many historians consider to have witnessed the emergence of Europe as a cultural, religious, and economic space—as exhibiting the first genuinely common law. How this vision emerged and what it consisted of is the subject of this chapter.

Early Canon Law

Church leaders had always legislated, and they continued to do so after the Roman Empire converted to Christianity. Yet in the aftermath of the fragmentation and dissolution of the Western empire in the fifth century, the character of Christian law was greatly modified. No longer sanctioned by emperors or supported by state institutions, this law was now wholly dependent on Church authorities and on their claim to have the duty as well as the power to regulate the lives of all believers independently of where they resided.

The normative system that resulted was identified as canon law (*canon* being the Greek word for "rule" or "guide"). Building on what was decided by Church assemblies and emperors and continually referencing and borrowing from Roman law, early canon law was nevertheless distinct from its Roman precedent. No longer the product of a political authority that could impose its will on those who resided in the territory, as was the case under Rome, instead it was theoretically based on a spiritual authority that was to be levied only on Christians. Spread over many territories and polities, Christians were said to share a common legal order because, by virtue of baptism rather than citizenship, they were members of a community whose laws could be enforced on them even against their will.

The emergence of the Church as a nonterritorial entity based not on political power but on a shared belief, bishops' growing responsibility for producing and applying norms, and the lack of competing powers, allowed the Church to expand its legal activities and substantially increase the volume of its law. Church officials often provided solutions for quotidian matters such as adjudicating commercial contracts or overseeing inheritance. Mostly local in focus, orientation, and application, early medieval canon law could differ substantially from one place to the next, and, lacking an efficient central authority, different Christian communities could disagree about almost everything.

In the quest to reinstitute a central authority for the Church, beginning in the sixth century and more clearly in the following centuries, successive bishops of Rome began claiming a special role for themselves. Arguing that after the demise of Rome the Church was the only structure that could claim universality and the only administration left with an imperial vocation, these bishops identified themselves as *Pontifex Maximus* (the high priest in ancient Rome) as well as popes (from the Greek term *pappas,* meaning "father"). As such, they insisted they were to lead the Church and be superior to all other bishops.

Although it took several centuries to complete, the institution and consolidation of the papacy led to the desired centralization. So did the calling of periodic assemblies of bishops. Having begun in the fourth century under the auspices of Roman emperors, by the early Middle Ages these assemblies became important agents in regulating the relations among the different Church authorities and communities, as well as in defining the content of Christian dogma.

The massive accumulation of norms that resulted led to the need for compilation. From the sixth century onward, different individuals and organisms sought to collect canon law and ensure that copies of its main tenets would be available at least to those in leadership positions. Well known among these efforts were the collections made during the reign of Charlemagne, the late eighth- and early ninth-century Frankish ruler. Charlemagne's aim was to create authorized versions of important texts and ensure their distribution throughout his realm. Despite these and other efforts, however, no single authoritative compilation of Church law came into existence before the twelfth century.[2]

The plurality of sources and the absence of a general and authoritative compilation led to the emergence of a great assortment of canon laws that were radically distinct. Local churches formed their own collections, which they followed, often disregarding instructions from Rome. There was so much uncertainty as to what the common tenets of Christianity were, that even as late as the ninth century savvy authors could introduce into the Christian dogma what today we know were forgeries. One famous example is the production and dissemination of false papal decrees, including

declarations on points of law. Mixing authentic material with newly invented ideas, with cut-and-pasted sentences that did not belong together,
some of these false decretals reconstructed the contents of letters that had
existed but were lost, while others modified the meaning of what had been
determined. They were inserted into a collection said to have been authored
by Isidore Mercator, probably a pseudonym. The collection included sixty
letters and decrees attributed to early popes, of which it is now believed that
fifty-eight were forgeries. It also contained a treatise on the early Church
and the authentic canons of fifty-four early councils. It ended with an enumeration of papal decrees by popes from the fourth to the eighth century,
most of which were pure invention.

The forged decretals limited secular rulers' control over bishops and Church
property and made important changes in the way ecclesiastical trials were to
be handled. Defending the jurisdiction of bishops against intervention by
archbishops and provincial synods, they also included instructions regarding
liturgy, the sacraments, and marital law. Inserted alongside genuine material, these forgeries, spreading throughout Europe, were considered reliable
and were widely followed. They were instrumental to the affirmation of
Church authority until the fifteenth century, when scholars began expressing
serious doubts about their validity.

Particularly important in this regard was a document identified as "the
donation of Constantine." This document, completely fabricated and included in the false decretals, affirmed that Constantine had transferred imperial powers onto Pope Sylvester I (314–335) and his successors. According
to what was stated, Constantine not only recognized the pope as the successor
of the apostles Peter and Paul, and Rome as the main Christian center, he
also allowed the pope to appoint secular rulers. Unsurprisingly, this document became essential in the eleventh and twelfth centuries during debates
between popes and kings regarding the breadth of their powers.[3]

On occasions inserting anachronistic information about real events or
using a style that was inappropriate to the period, the false decretals were
nevertheless sufficiently well executed to have fooled even the highest authorities of the Church and the most important compilers of Church law.
Other less famous falsifications also existed, most probably written by canon
law experts who, while falsifying some decrees, also collected unadulterated
material. It is now believed that most of the fake documents were created by
collectivities rather than a single individual in a single location, and that

those involved in their elaboration must have had access to rich enough libraries and sufficient knowledge to obtain such trustworthy results.

The Continuing Presence of Rome

The predominance of canon law in early medieval Europe ensured the continuing presence of Roman law, as Church legislation continued to resort to Roman forms and formula and theologians continued to produce exegeses by drawing on Roman terminology and analysis. To allow for this to happen, Roman law was taught in many abbeys and cathedral schools and was considered such an authoritative source that it could be used in cases where canon law was silent. Early Christian texts, such as the sixth-century Rule of St. Benedict (for monks living in communities) or the *Etymologiae* of Isidore of Seville (which sought to systematize all knowledge in an encyclopedia-type publication), also made references to Roman law. They appealed to Roman law categories as well as to terms and normative solutions. This continuing relationship between Roman and canon law was captured by the contemporary saying *Ecclesia vivit lege romana* (The Church lives by Roman law).

Yet Roman law also persisted in Europe in ways other than its conservation by the Church. In territories under the control of the Eastern Roman Empire, such as parts of present-day Italy in the sixth and seventh centuries, the *Corpus Iuris Civilis* (the sixth-century compilation of Roman law made under Justinian) was known and used, and legal transactions recovered by scholars demonstrate frequent references to Roman law. Mostly in Latin, these transactions also followed Roman forms or implicitly reproduced Roman discussions. This was particularly clear in areas of law covering land or contracts.

The enduring presence of Roman law was also registered elsewhere. In the Frankish empire, sixth- and seventh-century clerks imitated Roman notarial practices in order to draw up donations, testaments, sales, and marriage contracts. The same thing happened in Gaul (present-day France), where there were ninth-century compilations of Roman notarial formulas that had been in use from as early as the sixth century in both secular and ecclesiastical administration. Many royal officials, who often served as judges, had knowledge of both Roman and canon law. As many as twenty famous experts in Roman law may have been active in Gaul between the fifth and the eighth century, and Roman citations and formulas were prevalent in a great diversity of transactions. In cities of Roman origin, Roman law also persisted in commercial dealings and urban administration continued to emulate Roman practices.

Persistence was also clear in Iberia. In the kingdom of León (present-day Spain), tenth-century judges continued to apply the legal procedures of Visigothic Spain, which were Romanic in origin. In Galicia (northwest Spain), copies of the *Forum Iudicum* (a collection of laws promulgated in the seventh century by the Roman Visigoths, also known as *Lex Visigothorum* on which, see below) circulated and were used by judges who held the Roman title of *Iudex*. Roman-Visigothic law also survived on the Iberian Peninsula in territories under Muslim occupation, where it was considered the "personal law" of all Christians.

The Germanic Element

Historians of the early Middle Ages have long disagreed whether the many distinct groups that immigrated from northern to central, eastern, and southern Europe that we now identify as "Germanic" shared a common legal tradition. Some historians have pointed out that the movement of these groups was haphazard, carried out in small units, and placed their members in such intense contact with other cultures that it is difficult to assert what their original mores had been. It is also possible that, because documentation regarding the seventh and eighth centuries is more abundant than records from earlier periods, our understanding of these groups and their practices is both profoundly anachronistic and incorrect. Historians who express such doubts conclude that if these groups shared anything at all, it was an Indo-European rather than a specifically Germanic tradition. This Indo-European tradition featured a "primitive" attitude to law that relied on orality and supported no central institutions, no clear procedures, and no set structures.

Other historians nevertheless suggest that even if there was no single Germanic law, the groups that immigrated from the north to the south, east, and west did introduce to the European mainland certain elements that could be identified as distinct, most particularly when compared to Roman traditions. Rather than being Indo-European (and thus also shared with Rome), they were Germanic. Most important among these elements was a different organization of public life. Whereas Roman law sustained the existence of a *res publica,* or a state, the Germanic family of laws did not. Germanic society was divided into large kin groups led by elders, who were responsible for rendering judgment on disputes among members as well as making most other decisions regarding the management of communal life. In their deliberations, the elders appealed to an unwritten and flexible order that could be constantly negotiated. Although we have very limited information regarding how this transpired, the assumption is that, rather than being abstract, these legal systems were concrete, relational, and strongly influenced by rituals and formulas. The decisions reached by the assemblies of elders reflected a constantly mutating normative horizon that was meant to fit the circumstances of place, time, case, and parties rather than to pursue an abstract justice or obey an abstract principle.

Regardless of the important question of whether the northern immigrants did in their origin share a common legal Germanic tradition, it is clear that by the third and fourth centuries CE their members (who gradually came to dominate Europe) were already greatly affected by both Roman law and Christianity. Under Roman influence, the newcomers' legal attitude changed and their political structures underwent centralization and aristocratization. There is some evidence, for example, that by the sixth and seventh centuries, participation in assemblies was mostly restricted to the elites, and military leaders began claiming the status of hereditary kings. Other areas of the law might also have undergone dramatic transformations. Gradually the popular, oral, and flexible elements of legal creation disappeared and, under Roman influence, leaders of the so-called Germanic tribes began promulgating statutes. In the sixth, seventh, and eighth centuries, law books that sought to record and reproduce the erstwhile oral normative system also made their appearance. Mainly written in Latin rather than German, these books sometimes were used as instruments to ensure the survival of what was defined as "the good old order," but more often than not they confirmed the degree to which this order had already been altered. The written law that they included tended to be more systematic and abstract than what we believe the original law might have been, and it established kings as the main instruments for authorizing (if not outright creating) the legal order.

These important mutations were already evident in the sixth-century Salic laws (*Pactus Legis Salicae,* also known as *lex salica*) that both collected older norms and sought to replace vengeance by *compositio,* that is, a monetary arrangement. Best known today as the legal basis by which European monarchs excluded from succession those who descended of female line, the Salic laws enumerated a long list of remedies available to injured parties instead of violence. Written in Latin and organized to some degree as a Roman edict, the laws were nevertheless interwoven with German terms and also sought to reproduce Germanic traditions.

Another striking example of the fusion between Roman, canon, and Germanic law was the mid-seventh century *Liber iudiciorum* (also known in the Middle Ages as *Lex Gothica* or *Forum Iudicum*), which collected laws of both Germanic and Roman origin and also included royal legislation enacted by the Visigoth kings. The *Liber,* which was greatly influenced by the writing of theologians and was approved by local bishops in the eighth Council of Toledo (653), was applied by the Visigoths to their Iberian subjects of both Roman and Germanic origin. Written in Latin and demonstrating familiarity with Roman concepts, it covered such diverse aspects as legislation, the administration of justice, family law, obligations, penal law, and sanctions against Jews and heretics. Designating a territorial rather than a personal law, its success was so spectacular that it survived the conquest of Iberia by Muslims in 711 CE. Thereafter it regulated the life of Christians living under Islamic rule.

Changes in administrative practices were also noticeable. There is ample evidence, for example, that orality, usually associated with Germanic traditions, by the eighth century was no longer as central to the medieval legal order as it had been. By that time, codices appeared across Europe enumerating legal arrangements. Some were conceived as collections of laws, whereas others sought to reproduce different types of legally useful documents. Most popular among the latter were books containing formularies that scribes could copy, amend, abridge, or reorganize. During this period, recording offices (chanceries) were also founded, and seals became instruments demonstrating the authenticity of their production. Thereafter, written law and written records circulated in a legal world that was still profoundly oral but that was gradually undergoing important transformations.

As a result of all these processes, by the tenth century it becomes extremely difficult to distinguish Germanic from Roman law, or Germanic from canon law. Of course, some legal institutions clearly originated in one system or the other, but in practice, Latin expressions and Latin and Christian ways of thinking, interpreting, and organizing the material dominated to such an extent that a Germanic law was no longer easily recognizable.

Divine Intervention

Until the thirteenth century, God's direct participation in communal assemblies was considered both possible and desirable. This mostly happened in difficult cases, in which it was hard to establish what had happened. In such cases, contemporaries believed that God would intervene by indicating who told the truth and who lied, who was guilty and who innocent. His ruling would take the form of a miracle that would save the person who was worthy of being defended from suffering unnecessary injury. To solicit this intervention, assemblies would subject the parties to an ordeal, that is, to a test. There were several ways in which this could be done. The defendant could put his or her hand in boiling water, walk on fire, or eat too much bread too fast. These activities, it was reasoned, would normally result in an injury. If this did not happen, it was because God wanted to help the defendant. This was his way of indicating that the person was innocent or was telling the truth. Thus, those who were not harmed during an ordeal were held to have proved their case.

The Church initially encouraged these tests because they gave concrete proof of the immediateness and mercy of God and helped solve difficult questions, but by the turn of the millennium it began disapproving them, and in the thirteenth century (in the Fourth Lateran Council of 1215) it withdrew its support for them altogether by prohibiting the participation of the clergy. During this period, ordeals were gradually reclassified as both irrational and pagan. Historians have long debated why these changes took place. Some have suggested the aim was to cleanse the Christian community from its pagan past or to ensure that only practices that found backing in the scriptures would be authorized. It is also possible that the authorities of the Church were unhappy with "demanding" that God perform a miracle (to prevent an innocent person from suffering) or with involving clerics, who were present in all ordeals, in decisions regarding the shedding of blood. Also essential to the gradual abandonment and then prohibition of ordeals might have been the fact that by the early thirteenth century *ius commune* (see Chapter 5) provided society with new professionals, identified as jurists, who were experts on how to manage (and solve) conflicts. To the difficult problems ordeals sought to solve these professionals offered new solutions based on the collection, examination, and evaluation of both written and oral proof. Attempts to centralize criminal justice in the hands of both secular and ecclesiastical authorities enhanced these tendencies, by demanding a move from a judgment of God to a judgment of men.

Although historians contest the reasons for the gradual abandonment and eventual deauthorization of ordeals by the Church, most agree that these processes produced major legal changes. As ordeals lost their legitimacy, Europeans searched for (or were already in the process of developing) new mechanisms for solving difficult questions, such as determining criminal responsibility in cases with no direct witnesses to the crime. On the Continent this led to the adoption of a new legal procedure (the Romano-canonical procedure also known as *ordo iudiciarius* or the inquisitorial process) that had judges investigate the alleged crime and decide on a verdict according to their analysis of the proof. This process was introduced in the twelfth century before ordeals were abolished, but it was greatly enhanced, and its practice expanded from ecclesiastical to civil courts, after 1215. Charging judges with both finding out the truth and ruling on it, this process—which could be initiated by a magistrate who suspected a crime had been committed but had not received a formal complaint or accusation—specified which proofs would be deemed sufficient, what to do in cases where evidence was lacking, how to interrogate, and which punishments could be inflicted in the cases in which there were indications but not a certainty regarding guilt. Searching to ascertain empirically what actually happened and not only guilt or innocence, by the late thirteenth century this procedure also involved, on occasion, the use of torture against suspects and witnesses as a means to achieve certitude in difficult cases.

According to historians of common law, in England these same developments—the gradual delegitimization of ordeals and their eventual abandonment—encouraged a different response, namely, the increasing powers of lay juries in criminal cases. Lay juries existed in Europe (and England) before 1215, when they mainly operated (as grand juries would today) to bring accusations against people suspected of having committed crimes (presentment juries) or to dismiss private accusations of crime on the basis of prior hate or spite *(de odio et atia)*. Although the use of juries expanded over time to encompass new duties and new offenses, it was only after 1215, in direct response to the Church's deauthorization of ordeals, that the English monarchs assigned juries with the task of issuing final verdicts.[4] From that point in time, juries, rather than God, determined the veracity of the accusations. The qualifications of jurors were not based on professional preparation or logical deliberation. Instead, they depended on the fact that jurors were locals who knew the defendants and were familiar with the case. Because such was the assumption, contrary to Continental judges, juries did not have to hear and evaluate evidence, neither were they outside, detached observers. Instead, what they ruled was largely based on what they experienced personally, and on what they already knew.

The Result: A Fragmented Yet Unified World

Regardless of the question where norms came from, during the early Middle Ages most individuals lived in a world in which the geographical extension of political entities as well as their laws was extremely confined and in which norms could be radically distinct from one place to the next. Made of fragments of Roman, Germanic, local, or canon law, the legal universe that contemporaries inhabited was highly segmented, multivalent, and compound and reflected a great variety of norms that originated in multiple orders. This universe also conflated morality and law, and suggested that human order was but a (poor) imitation of a superior, divine order.

Although we do not know much regarding how this complex universe actually functioned, because documentation is scarce and often deficient, the general assumption is that during this period the most difficult task was to identify how disputes could be settled. To help establish that, authorities and parties occasionally requested the intervention of local experts identified as *iuratores* (jurors). As people under oath (which was what *iuratores* meant), these local individuals met to discuss how a specific conflict brought to their attention should be resolved.

Conflicts that were not brought before jurors were adjudicated by village or town assemblies, which could include up to a few hundred people. Contrary to the activities of jurors, village and town assemblies were open to all. Conducted as rituals as well as festivities and having a clearly sacred character, these assemblies were both a confirmation of the role of justice in communal life and occasions to implement it. As happened in archaic Rome, the rituals followed in these assemblies mandated the use of particular formulas and the taking of specific actions. Often a mixture of Roman, canon, local, and Germanic law, these formulas and actions were fairly repetitive and followed a precise script that was thought to be fundamental for the attainment of justice. In most cases they required that the plaintiff or defendant formally repeat their version of what had transpired, usually by taking an oath. Other ritual acts could consist of grasping a symbolic rod to express consent or invoking divine intervention in the form of ordeal.

How such ceremonies varied across time and space, we are not sure. However, because of their local character, they must have varied by location and must have changed dramatically over time. Historians have traditionally suggested that whatever their origins might have been, whatever formulas were invoked, rituals followed, and votes taken, all of them reproduced a customary law that was particular to that community. In recent years, though, other scholars have insisted that, rather than being customary as they were once described, these practices were constantly negotiated. They allowed for the dominance of some individuals over others and often showcased profound divisions within the community. If they were to represent an "old" way of doing things, or a custom, their antiquity was usually limited in time. Appeals to tradition were usually strategic, and the tradition that was invoked was normally tied to perhaps only one generation's memory. It is thus possible that by calling things "traditional," contemporaries referred to their inherent virtue, not necessarily their longevity. In other words, that a thing was old indicated a heuristic quality, not a genealogy.

Appeals to norms, which were often tied to the need to resolve conflicts, could also take place ceremoniously as part of a routine adopted by community members to bolster their relationship with one another as well as to recognize their subjection to the local authorities. In such cases, norms were recited orally in public meetings that were both theatrical and celebratory. Educational in orientation, the recitation of norms was meant to fix them in people's memory, but it was mostly directed at socializing members, teaching them what was good and what was desirable. Here too, although norms were presented as old and permanent, historians have remarked that they were far from stable. Under the guise of continuity, modification was persistent, memory serving as both an instrument for conservation and as a means to introduce change.

The Fusion of Sources

Local, Germanic, canon, and Roman law thus coexisted in early medieval Europe. Emblematic of such mixtures were the activities of Charlemagne.

King of a Frankish empire that covered large parts of present-day France and Germany, expanded north to the Netherlands and east to the Baltic region, and that was also in control of Northern Italy and the northern fringes of what is now Spain, Charlemagne was a secular ruler of Germanic origin who also oversaw spiritual matters. Ruling over a loose association of territories, some more Latinized than others, in the year 800, he was anointed by the pope as "emperor of the Romans." For the pope, this move guaranteed Charlemagne's mostly military support and was also a step in freeing the Western Church from control by the Eastern Roman Empire. For Charlemagne, this coronation suggested that he was both king and emperor and that he, in this later capacity, could also intervene in ecclesiastical affairs as Roman emperors once did.

Although Charlemagne is remembered as a formidable legislator, what he instructed and what he enacted was not legislation in the sense we give it today. Like all leaders at that time, Charlemagne had no pretension to create a new order that would depend only on his will. Instead he sought to arrange and systematize existing solutions and ensure obedience to them. A guarantor of justice rather than the maker of norms, and in charge of peace-making rather than imposing his personal rule, theoretically his role was to declare the law by making it manifest and to ensure obedience.

Charlemagne intervened in both religious and secular affairs and instructed both religious and civil authorities on how they should proceed. Fashioning himself as the protector of the Church as well as of the physical and spiritual well-being of his subjects and all Christians everywhere, he reformed ecclesiastical institutions and sought to restore clerical discipline, recover Church properties, and encourage the use of authorized collections of canon law. Charlemagne also ordered the writing down of local laws and the Romanization of norms of Germanic origin. Pursuing some measure of unity in his kingdoms, he promulgated edicts that were designed to introduce centralization, not necessarily standardization. His quest was to establish the authority of his court, not to secure uniformity, and his empire indeed remained a fragmented structure with a great diversity of regimes, norms, and legal sources.

The actual management of this chaotic amalgamation of local, Roman, Germanic, and canon law was not always easy. Canon law, for example, which theoretically was relevant to all Christians, affected not only religious duties but also such diverse activities as contract making or debt collection.

Local law, which only covered members of concrete communities, coexisted alongside princely norms. Though some topics were typical of local arrangements and others more appropriate for princely dictates, the distinction between local and princely was often problematic, and both could govern alongside canon law in questions of contracts and debt. The orientation and instructions of these parallel normative systems could of course harmonize, but they could also bitterly conflict.

Yet despite their potentially contradictory nature, as far as contemporaries were concerned this amalgamated system never lacked coherence. Contemporaries did not ask (as subsequent generations did) whether certain norms were Germanic, canonic, or Romanic. Neither did they perceive of the possibility that their religious duties would vary from their duties to family, community, or prince. Instead they assumed that, together, these various legal sources represented how things were and ought to be because such were the ways of the world and because this was what God desired.

Were There No Jurists?

Historians thus usually conclude that early medieval law mostly embodied the personal duty to behave correctly. This duty was anchored in family and communal obligations as well as in religious duties. Norms were mostly oral and were supposed to be learned, or negotiated, through living in the community. There was no single authority or body with a monopoly on legal production, nor was there any need for formally sanctioned rules. Enacted by human interaction and sometimes guided by the clergy, this normative universe could envision the direct participation of God through ordeals and, in the absence of ordeals, sought to find other procedures to mediate between the parties or to discover the truth.

Although such a system required no jurists in the sense of individuals trained in law or who earned their living by giving legal advice, experts were not lacking. Among them were the elders who agreed on how to adjudicate conflicts and the theologians who indicated to believers how they should behave. Also abundant were canon lawyers and moral theologians who defined the structures of authority inside the Church and debated the extension of ecclesiastical jurisdiction, the meaning of certain sins, or which price was just and which abusive. Emperors and kings also continued to employ legal advisors who helped them collect, systematize, and write down local and canon law. Without the existence of such experts, the ninth-century legal forgeries of canon law would not have succeeded. After all, the individuals who fabricated them must have been sufficiently familiar with both Roman and canon law to create these successful imitations.

Expertise was also part of the day-to-day practice of the law. In the ninth century, glosses and commentaries on different parts of Roman and local law began appearing in Europe. In Pavia (present-day Italy), the study of law was so intense that scholars were divided among the *antiqui,* who mostly centered their attention on Roman law, and the *moderni,* who also dealt with Germanic law. Roman and canon law also sustained the work of scribes and notaries, two professions that came into prominence in Europe during this period alongside the growing use of written documentation. Scribes and notaries were responsible for producing legally efficient documents. They drew up and recorded a great variety of transactions, often by resorting to old formulas they found in textbooks. The early Middle Ages, in short, was perhaps a world with no jurists, but it was certainly a universe in which many professionals gave advice, suggested to kings and their subjects how to proceed, indicated to their community what was right and what was wrong, and pondered on how God's laws could be discovered and implemented.

4

Lords, Emperors, and Popes
around the Year 1000

THE YEAR 1000 CARRIES an enormous weight in the European imagination. It stands for the maturity of an early medieval society that soon after would disappear or at least would mutate sufficiently to be considered as new. This story of change begins with chaos. After the demise of the Western Roman Empire, no other polity emerged to replace it. This so-called power vacuum led to extreme fragmentation. Beginning in the sixth century, the inhabitants of Europe experienced processes of conversion and Romanization, but despite growing homogeneity in some respects, around the year 800 Europe could be imagined as an archipelago, with villages controlling their hinterland but no common authority to unite them or dictate common rules. Attempts at unification, such as under Charlemagne, were relatively brief or failed in the long run. Experiencing constant migratory waves that led to settlement, conquests, and reconquests by various Germanic, Slavic, and Viking groups, instability from within was accompanied by invasions from outside by Muslims approaching from the southern Mediterranean and Magyar tribes arriving from Asia.

The precarious situation that resulted led to important economic changes, mostly the decline of commerce and the move to a subsistence economy. It also led to the rise, sometime between the ninth and the tenth century, of a series of social, economic, and political institutions traditionally identified as "feudal." What feudalism was, when and where it originated, how it was practiced in different parts, and whether it was a historical reality or a narrative created by scholars a posteriori to explain what had transpired, have all been contested issues for many years. Yet most historians agree that whatever forms existed in Europe around the year 1000, by the eleventh and twelfth centuries they had come under attack. With new authorities who identified themselves as kings, the eleventh and twelfth centuries also witnessed the consolidation of the Church. The struggle for both secular and religious centralization and the growing competition within kingdoms between kings and lords and within the Church between the pope and other bishops was further complicated by the tense relations between secular and religious authorities fighting over who was superior to whom. In what follows, I survey these developments, ask questions about them, and explain how and why they were important to European legal history.

The Conventional Portrait of Feudalism

There are many theories about what feudalism was and how and why it had emerged. Clearly, though affecting many areas in Europe, it was not practiced identically everywhere and may not have constituted a "system" in the way historians once described it. Furthermore, much of what we know about feudalism comes from descriptions written in the twelfth and thirteenth centuries, when it was already undergoing decline and change and when those describing it had their own motives to present it in particular ways. Regardless of whether they identify it as "feudalism" or not, whether they agree on what precisely it included, or if it comprised of a system or only encompassed a range of disparate practices, most historians concur that in the ninth, tenth, and eleventh centuries many parts of Europe shared several fundamental characteristics that were lacking in the earlier times.

According to the conventional portrait, most important among these characteristics were relations of personal dependency between powerful individuals (lords) and subject populations (vassals). These relations featured unequal exchanges whereby the lord protected and cared for vassals and they, in return, had to be loyal and obedient and give their lord aid, service, and advice. Highly regulated practices indicated how the bond between lords and vassals was to be created and how it was to end. In its classic formulation, feudalism appeared as a deeply ritualized affair with feudal relations being established in an elaborate ceremony identified in the literature as "homage." Varying according to place and time, homage usually required that the vassal put his hands between the lord's and declare his wish to become part of the lord's household as well as take a solemn oath of fidelity, usually on the holy Scriptures or a relic. The lord then hugged and kissed the vassal and recognized him as "his" man.

Feudal relations initially mostly covered mutual protection, which was understood as military defense. By the tenth century, if not earlier, in many areas these also began involving property relations. It is hard to establish why this happened. Perhaps protection was now not only military but also economic, including the duty to provide subsistence. Perhaps because of extreme instability, landholding individuals and communities were willing to relinquish their control over their properties, which were transferred to a lord in exchange for protection. Although we are not sure of the nature of these processes or their precise chronology, their results were fairly clear. In large parts of Europe, powerful lords appeared who were now considered the proprietors of large domains. In most places these lords allowed vassals to have usufruct or tenure rights over the land in exchange for some sort of compensation, either tribute, military service, or labor. Part of the payment vassals made was also symbolic and included recognition of subjection and an oath of allegiance.

As economic concerns became central to this system, lords began ensuring that their vassals had the financial resources they deserved according to who they were. This was typically done by giving them use of the land, but it could also be achieved by granting them an office or another type of income. Eventually the duties of lords also extended to judicial protection, and lords began holding sessions in which they acted as judges, applying what was said to be the customary law of the land. This allowed lords to acquire many of the functions we identify today with government. They policed their territories, adjudicated conflicts, and dispensed punishment. They collected taxes and applied, if not outright created, the norms that governed the community. In many places these developments marked the end of the kind of communal justice that was practiced by local assemblies and juries in the early Middle Ages. In other places communal justice persisted, though radically modified because now controlled by the lord and his men.

Although according to the classical formulation feudalism was based on an agreement between parties to constitute a personal relationship, it was nevertheless clear that even if originally some choice was allowed, most vassals did not enter into this relationship by exercising free will. By the tenth century, furthermore, feudalism had lost most of its initial purpose as a defensive mechanism and evolved mainly into an economic system of exploitation. Rights and obligations became hereditary for both lords and vassals, and the degree of exchange between them substantially diminished. This system of personal dependency came to dominate the European landscape. It expanded throughout Europe, reaching present-day France, Italy, England, Scotland, Ireland, Wales, the Slavic territories, and parts of the Iberian Peninsula.[1]

A Feudal Society?

As a result of these developments, according to the traditional portrait, by the year 1000 most Europeans lived on rural estates where they were tied as vassals to a lord who exercised jurisdiction over them. In most places, the lord accumulated what today would be classified as legislative, executive, and judiciary powers. He made the rules, he applied them, and he adjudicated conflicts. In his decision making, he might have been guided by the existing local law—that was usually the pretension—and he was certainly supposed to care about canon law, but it was his word and his interpretation that carried the day.

Feudalism, however, was not a simple two-tier system. Instead, it was imagined as a multilayered one in which (minor) lords could be vassals of (greater) lords. The hierarchical structure that resulted allowed a megalord—for example, the German emperor—to be the master of several lords who, in turn, had vassals of their own. Because the lords' vassals were not the emperor's vassals, the emperor could not directly request their collaboration. Instead he had to address them through their immediate lords. This pyramid of command guaranteed the loyalty of important lords and the submission of their vassals, but it also imposed restrictions on the emperor. Not being able to directly command the vassals of his vassals implied that when the emperor wanted them to do or refrain from doing something, he had to depend on the mediation of the lords, who could ask for concessions in return.

This situation, which was necessary in the ninth century when feudalism probably emerged, became unsustainable after some lords—now identified as monarchs—began to expand their jurisdiction. Beginning in the eleventh and twelfth centuries, they sought to diminish the power of their peers or control them by summoning them to the courts and converting them into their servants. Through these mechanisms, lords not only became members of royal households, they also lost their power base in the countryside where their vassals resided, from which they were mostly absent.

To further facilitate the submission of all those inhabiting their kingdoms, kings also encouraged the growth of cities. Recognizing these cities as "free" because not under obedience to a feudal lord, kings placed them and their inhabitants under the king's direct authority. Although this policy was successful, and cities grew in number and size all over Europe, in the long run the most efficient tactic kings used to consolidate their powers was to institute themselves as supreme adjudicators. They claimed a role as arbiters between lords and established royal courts throughout the realm. This method, which most monarchs attempted to implement, first succeeded in England and resulted in what we now identify as the English common law (see Chapter 6).

Questioning Feudalism

For many years, the above description was the standard textbook narrative regarding the nature and history of feudalism. Beginning in the 1990s, however, some historians began asking whether there was one type of feudalism or several, and whether feudalism as classically defined had existed at all. They questioned the term used to describe these developments ("feudalism") but they also disagreed over whether an institution that fit this description ever materialized in real life. They suggested that it was only a model that rarely (if ever) was put into place. Or they maintained that the large variety of situations and practices they uncovered in the archives could never be reduced to a system with clear principles. In short, they saw "feudalism" as a theoretical abstraction that obscured rather than enhanced our understanding of the past.

Scholars also insisted that despite the pervasive presence of lords and vassals in many parts of Europe, not all contemporaries lived under a feudal regime. Some territories were more "feudalized" than others, and even where classic feudalism might have been the dominant form of economic, social, political, and legal order, there also existed free peasants and urban dwellers, their numbers varying by region and period. Feudalism, these scholars sustained, had captured our imagination far more than it ever deserved.

It is nevertheless clear that something of importance happened in ninth- and tenth-century Europe. Whether we call it feudalism or not, whether we believe it to be a single phenomenon or various, a coherent system or disparate practices that were packaged together by scholars who disregarded their heterogeneity, and regardless of the question of whether it affected all of Europe or only parts thereof, it is evident that during this period the structures of European polities vastly changed. Many autonomous villages became dependent, demand for protection became pervasive, and power structures became pyramidal with the gradual appearance of lords and overlords who monopolized many functions of government and justice. Interactions among those inhabiting the same village or town might have been only slightly modified, but relations between communities and between them and local authorities suffered important mutations that eventually led the way to the formation of monarchies and states.

Lords, Emperors, and Church Authorities

To solidify their position, German emperors sought support from the Church. The alliance between powerful individuals and the Church was, of course, much older than the ninth and tenth centuries, yet it is commonly assumed that this mutual dependency reached new heights during this period. The place where this took place was the Carolingian Empire.

The Carolingian Empire was a loose association of polities that covered parts of present-day Germany, France, Switzerland, Austria, Italy, Belgium, Luxembourg, and the Netherlands. It was headed by Charlemagne, who in the year 800 was anointed by Pope Leo III as "emperor of the Romans."[2] Charlemagne's empire fragmented after his death, but in the tenth century a new dynasty emerged that was able to extend control once again over large territories. Leading it was Otto I (912–973), whom Pope John XII in 962 crowned emperor of the "Holy Roman Empire," which was the name the German territories pretending to be imperial now received.

Although on both these occasions, popes supported the German imperial claim, eventually the relations between these emperors and the Church would become extremely fraught. In the late eleventh century, tensions escalated into open conflict that scandalized many Europeans. The occasion was a disagreement over whether emperors could appoint bishops. As the action of handing over the staff (scepter) to the chosen bishop in acknowledgment of his spiritual authority was called "investiture," we usually refer to that conflict as the "Investiture Conflict."

From the perspective of European legal history, this episode brought to light the difficult question of what were the correct relations between the pope and the secular powers of Europe. Who was superior to whom? Could popes intervene in secular matters? Could emperors do so in religious affairs? Could the secular and the spiritual be distinguished at all, or was there only one community in Europe, a single Christian *ecumene*?

Roman traditions, which both secular rulers and the Church espoused, did not facilitate the distinction between a secular and a spiritual realm. Before their conversion to Christianity, Roman emperors were high priests *(pontifices maximi)* who were central to the Roman religious cult. After their conversion, Roman emperors kept this view, legislating on religious matters and actively intervening in religious affairs—for example, by calling for and participating in meetings of bishops where the Christian canon was fixed. After the Western Roman Empire was overrun by Germanic tribes, Popes Leo I (440–461) and Gregory I (590–604) actively fashioned themselves not only as leaders of an expanding Christendom but also as secular powers with near-universal reach.

Yet because they required the help of secular leaders, not only to subsidize and protect the work of missionaries and Church officials, but also, on occasions, to secure their control of Rome, from as early as the sixth century successive popes habitually appealed to Germanic monarchs to assist them. These monarchs—for example, Charlemagne—could thereafter portray themselves as protectors of the Church. They legislated on religious matters and constantly limited Rome's control and autonomy in their territories.

With the rise of powerful lords, the autonomy of the Church was further compromised by local lords' growing control. During this period, it became customary for lords to appoint bishops in their territories. It also became common for these lords to elevate the bishops they selected by recognizing them as feudal lords (tenants-in-chief) and by granting them jurisdiction over both territory and people. Nomination as lords guaranteed bishops the administrative and financial powers to control their flock (now also vassals), but it also aided the overlords who nominated them to secure their loyalty.

Because ecclesiastical lordships were tied to a particular diocese and were granted to whomever was nominated bishop, if the overlords controlled nomination, they could also control who would lead these lordships. They would thus ensure that important feudal domains would remain under the overlords' direct control and would be granted periodically to whomever they saw fit rather than becoming the perpetual property of a single family as would happen in other cases.

The linking of feudal powers with the holding of ecclesiastical office meant that, as far as the overlord was concerned, it was vital to guarantee that these ecclesiastical yet seigneurial domains not fall into the wrong hands. Hence, it was necessary for these overlords to control the nomination of bishops. But the popes also wanted to control the nomination of powerful bishops who were feudal lords, and equally considered the provision of offices to allies an important means to secure their loyalty.

Clearly expressing this preference, in the late eleventh century Pope Gregory VII (1073–1085) began a wide-reaching reform with the aim of obtaining control over these coveted offices. He or one of his close collaborators authored a decree (now known as *Dictatus Papae*) that listed twenty-seven important papal resolutions.[3] Among other things, it denied German emperors the right to nominate and depose bishops and invest them with their pastoral rod. The decree also stated that the Church was founded by God and that it was the only truly universal body. If emperors disobeyed papal orders, the pope could depose them and free their vassals of their oath of obedience.

While establishing the preeminence of Church over empire and popes over emperors, the *Dictatus Papae* also sought to secure the primacy of the pope within the Church. It determined that only the pope could establish new laws, form new congregations, transform the status of existing institutions, and control Church officials. Only he could move bishops between dioceses, call general synods, and identify the chapters and books that were sacred. The *Dictatus* further stated that the pope could be judged by no one and that his decisions could not be appealed. The pope had these exceptional powers, the decree said, because he was no ordinary bishop. A direct successor of Peter, the pope was the only living figure who could use the imperial insignia, whose feet should be kissed by all princes, and who should be the object of veneration by having his name, now considered "unique," recited in churches. Through the merits of Peter, he was holy. The *Dictatus Papae* also asserted that one could not be a believer without being in harmony with the Church.

The Investiture Conflict

The question of investiture was tested in 1076, when Emperor Henry IV (1050–1106) ignored the papal nominee for the archdiocese of Milan (a rich feudal territory) and instead appointed one of his own men. After Pope Gregory threatened Henry with excommunication, Henry called for a meeting of the German bishops. Under his inspiration and guidance, in a synod in the city of Worms in 1076, the bishops renounced obedience to Gregory, declared him deposed, and requested the election of a new pope. Though they censured Gregory, claiming that he had obtained the papacy by usurpation and deceit, the main accusation against him was innovation. According to the bishops, he had invaded their customary and legitimate powers to the point that he was creating confusion that was destroying the Church.

Pope Gregory responded to these challenges by excommunicating the emperor and freeing the German nobility from their duty to obey him. Isolated from his lords, who threatened to elect another emperor to succeed him, in 1077 Henry made an act of public capitulation to the pope. The story, however, did not end there. The nobles followed up on their threat and nominated another emperor (Rudolf, duke of Swabia); the pope supported this new candidate and excommunicated Henry a second time. Henry again declared the pope deposed and elected a new pontifex (known as Antipope Clement III) in his place. With Henry's armies at the gates of Rome, Gregory fled the city and died shortly thereafter.

In 1122 the successors of Henry and Gregory (Emperor Henry V and Pope Calixtus II) reached a compromise formally resolving the Investiture Conflict. At the Concordat of Worms, they recognized the elections of bishops as a papal privilege but allowed the emperor to preside over them and intervene in cases of dispute. According to the compromise, the emperor could no longer invest bishops with the staff, but he could require them to give him homage. Though an understanding was seemingly reached, both sides maintained their basic positions as to who they were and how they were to relate to one another. Neither was the conflict within the Church completely resolved. Subsequent popes continued to argue for a superior, perhaps absolute, power, and many bishops and theologians contested these claims.

And European Legal History?

Law in eighth- to eleventh-century Europe was still based on a combination of Roman, Germanic, canon, and local law, but it was also increasingly determined by locally powerful lords who controlled vassals. In some places where free cities or free peasants existed, local autonomy persisted, but it, too, was gradually limited by the emergence of superlords who fashioned themselves as emperors and kings.

Although many of these changes could be explained by the particular circumstances of place and time, what was perhaps most surprising about these developments was the constant reference to a covenant between unequal partners. Of course, unlike the covenant between Christians and their God, the covenant between lords and their vassals was not religious, but it was not altogether secular either, as lords were theoretically endowed with a Christian mission and their vassals obeyed them because, among other things, they had taken an oath. Furthermore, during this period lords often refashioned themselves not only as Christians but also as religious leaders who were responsible to both the secular and the spiritual well-being of their subjects.

The idea that lords had acquired their powers because of some sort of covenant or exchange between them and their vassals was extremely important. Even if partially (or wholly) fictive, even if abusive, even if not truly free, this foundational myth of consent, agreement, and exchange as the basis for political power would eventually become central to European history. It would appear in endless reiterations and forms throughout the centuries and would become the justification upon which monarchies and eventually states would be established as well as destroyed. The contractual vision of polities would come to supply both a justification for government as well as a means by which to criticize the authorities and demand that they behave in certain ways.

While relations between lords and vassals restructured the ways Europeans conceived of power and interacted with the normative system, now growingly at the hands of lords, the Investiture Conflict can be identified as a pivotal moment in the development of a new vision of European law. A first attempt at reestablishing a clear distinction between a secular and a religious sphere, it also featured what some conceptualized as a true revolution—allowing the Church to free itself of feudal control and institute an independent legal system. This system, which would come to regulate both the Church's internal affairs as well as the life of all Christians, would become the first legal system in Europe to rely mostly on legislated solutions created by a single authoritative voice, the pope. The Investiture Conflict was also instrumental in propelling the next great mutation in European law: the rebirth of Roman law in Italian universities in the twelfth and thirteenth centuries.

PART THREE

The Later Middle Ages

5

The Birth of a European *Ius Commune*

THE TWELFTH CENTURY is considered a pivotal moment in European history. The demise of feudalism (where it existed) and the rising power of monarchies were accompanied by economic prosperity and a demographic boom. With the growth of production and the emergence of new commercial routes and centers, the urban network was greatly enlarged and immigration intensified. New towns were established and depopulated centers were revitalized. As monarchical powers expanded, so did royal entourages, and as towns grew in size and importance, so did their administration.

Historians have long considered this period a true "Renaissance." They suggest that it was accompanied by a spectacular expansion in artistic, scientific, and intellectual production that also profoundly affected European law. The point of departure was a highly fragmented system that varied according to place, group, and subject matter. The point of arrival was the birth of a new constellation that was potentially common to all Romanized Christians and would thereafter be identified as their *ius commune,* literally, their common law.[1]

As we have seen, around the year 1000, law was fragmented, geographically confined, and dependent on local, Roman, Germanic, and canon law, as well as feudal legislation. These various normative regimes mutually influenced one another, but rules could differ dramatically from one village to the next.

The new circumstances of the twelfth century led to the search for a novel normative order. In contrast to law based on local regulation, differing from place to place, newly emerging communities that had no previous legal traditions, the intensification of relations between communities and with non-European trading partners, and the growth of immigration required a different type of law that would bridge such differences. The need for reform was also felt in other spheres, such as public law, which was insufficiently developed to support the needs of emerging municipal bodies and royal administration. Here, too, a new legal order had to be imagined. With economic prosperity and intensified support to learning, a larger segment of society could (and found it useful to) dedicate itself to intellectual pursuits.

Propelled by the political, social, cultural, and economic conditions and backed by municipal and royal authorities as well as by the Church, all seeking to solidify and augment their powers, a novel method to approach normativity began appearing in Europe, gradually yet dramatically changing its legal landscape. This innovative method was introduced in northern Italy, yet it quickly spread to other parts, where it remained in force until the nineteenth century, perhaps beyond. How and why this happened and how European law changed as a result is the subject of this chapter.

The Study of Law in Europe

The legal revolution that took place in Europe in the twelfth and thirteenth centuries was shaped by three interlocking elements: the discovery and reconstitution of ancient Roman texts (mainly the *Corpus Iuris Civilis*), the adoption of a new method to analyze them (Scholasticism), and the invention of a new environment in which to do so (learning centers, which grew into universities). Historians have long debated which preceded what. Did the new method lead to the formation of new intellectual environments, or did the new environments encourage the formation of new methods? Was everything initiated by the discovery of ancient texts, or were texts sought after because they now mattered in new ways?

Whatever the exact genealogy and causality might have been, scholars agree that the combination of new sources, new methodology, and new intellectual environment produced a profound transformation. This transformation was not only intellectual but also social and political. It was driven by the growing prominence of kings who sought to justify their extending powers, by new municipal corporations and agents who wished to do the same, by papal desires for primacy; and by the intensification of commerce and learning. With new economic resources to support individuals dedicated to scholarship, the new European normative order not only assisted the pretensions of kings, popes, municipal officials, and urbanites, it also produced new professionals, the intellectuals, who made a living by teaching, advising, and writing books.

Reconstructing Ancient Texts

Scholars in Europe knew for centuries about the existence of the sixth-century compilations of Roman law ordered by Emperor Justinian.[2] Fragments of these compilations circulated in different parts of the Continent, but none of the available copies was considered trustworthy or complete. An abbreviated version of the Code (imperial legislation) was available, and so were parts of the *Institutes* (the manual for students), but the *Digest* (the volumes containing juridical opinions) was not.

Toward the end of the eleventh century, a copy of the *Digest* reached Bologna, in northern Italy. There are many accounts about how and why it miraculously materialized and who was responsible. It is currently agreed, however, that whoever the person was, the so-called discovery of the *Digest* was probably tied to the Investiture Conflict—the struggle between the German Emperor Henry IV and Pope Gregory VII regarding emperors' powers to elect bishops (see Chapter 4). Because during this conflict both sides, wishing to justify their positions, appealed to Roman law, both actively searched for new fragments of that law that would back their claims. It is thus possible that the "rediscovery" of the *Digest* during this period of conflict involved no true unearthing but instead could be explained as a strategic move by those who had known about its existence but now sought to capitalize on it in new ways.

Following the rediscovery of the *Digest,* several individuals began reconstructing the legal compilations undertaken by Justinian.[3] This effort included collecting different segments that were known as well as seeking new ones. Once sufficient material had been accumulated, the different parts were put together in what was believed to have been the original design. This done, scholars trusted that for the first time in centuries they had access to a correct and full copy of the Justinian corpus, which they believed accurately represented Roman law.

The Method

Satisfied with the text they had reconstructed, scholars began studying it. The methodology they employed was innovative. Identified as Scholasticism, it was based on the assumption (taken as a certainty) that Roman texts were imbued with a hidden harmony. The obligation of readers was to prove that such was the case by offering an interpretation that synchronized the different parts and enabled the reconstruction of a coherent message.

Most scholars following the Scholastic method began with a philological analysis of the texts, their terminology, order, and phrasing. Shaping their observations as a dialogue, they asked questions and debated the answers. This dialectical thinking and exposition was mainly geared toward comparing passages to one another. Working under the assumption that the various parts were not contradictory, scholars employed logical arguments in order to demonstrate that such was the case. One of their favorite techniques was the *distinctio*. Analyzing two fragments that seemed similar yet pointed to different solutions, these scholars proceeded to demonstrate that although the fragments appeared identical, they were in fact profoundly distinct. Because they were different, the solutions offered could be diverse without there being a contradiction. Hence, what appeared at first glance as a contradiction was instead part of a coherent system in which all the different pieces pointed to the same rationale.

By following this method, scholars hoped to reveal the criteria that guided Roman jurists and the techniques that organized their reasoning. Their aim was not to uncover the particular solutions Roman jurists adopted but instead to extract the rule *(regula)* that explained their consistency. By putting together what they learned from individual examples and cases, these scholars hoped to understand what they considered to be the inner core, the basic essence, of Roman law.

The adoption of the Scholastic method converted the *Digest,* which was unknown and hardly used in Europe up to this point, into a particularly attractive source of Roman law. Reproducing the opinions of different jurists, the *Digest* included an exceptional number of disagreements and contradictions. It therefore was an excellent source allowing scholars to make distinctions and elaborate terminology, concepts, and criteria.

Because Scholastic analysis used textual exegesis that paid close attention to the specific terms Roman texts employed, their order, and their meaning, it was essential for scholars to ascertain that the documents they examined were accurate. If they were not, then their discussion of them would be based on false evidence and would not lead to the ultimate truth. Thus, as the discovery and reconstruction of ancient texts led to their study, their study led to additional effort to ensure the accuracy of the texts. Textual reconstruction and textual exegesis, in short, mutually supported one another.

From the twelfth to the sixteenth century (considered the formative period of this new European legal science), scholars (now identified as jurists) debated the principles, terminology, and structures of Roman law. Though they were trying to explain ancient texts, their endeavor did not revive the ancient law of Rome, but instead reinvented it. Medieval jurists came up with new ways to assess, analyze, and relate to legal questions. Their interpretations were perhaps anchored in a prestigious Roman past, but, in reality, and as would be forcefully argued in the fifteenth and sixteenth centuries (see Chapter 7), they were entirely new.

The Environment

The individuals engaged in these debates mainly taught or studied in the various study centers and universities that appeared in Europe in the late medieval period. Whether universities formed part of a longer tradition or were a completely new phenomenon is a matter of debate. In late antiquity, there were schools in which instruction was given to students, usually in order to prepare them for a particular professional task. These schools taught grammar, dialectics (the art of reasoning), rhetoric (the art of exposition), arithmetic (the study of numbers), geometry (the study of figures), astronomy, and music. From as early as the first century CE if not earlier, Rome also featured schools where students of law congregated. These began as informal gatherings, but by the early fifth century they were sufficiently institutionalized that emperors could limit the study of law exclusively to them.

In the sixth century, monastic schools began appearing all over Europe. First emerging spontaneously and then encouraged by popes and emperors, these schools taught poetry, astronomy, and mathematics but were mostly focused on understanding the Scriptures. In some places, rhetoric and Roman law might have been studied, too. By the late eighth and ninth centuries, monastic schools were joined by episcopal or cathedral schools, which covered similar subjects but were mostly located in the large urban centers that began appearing throughout Europe.

Twelfth- and thirteenth-century study centers and universities were therefore both old and new. Appearing in several European cities where demographic growth, economic prosperity, and urban revival were particularly strong, they drew crowds that came to listen to masters lecture. The congregation of a large number of masters in certain locations, as well as urban regulations favoring it, brought several of these new learning sites into prominence. Paris, Bologna, Toulouse, and Oxford became famous among students and teachers because of the excellence of teaching but also because of the scope of what was being taught. Designated as *studium generale*—places where it was possible to study (almost) everything, including theology, medicine, and law—these centers were transformed into "universities" after they were legally recognized as corporations.

One of the most important characteristics of the new learning centers was that they were truly pan-European. Teachers and students came from all over Europe and they circulated from one university to the next. The teaching language was Latin, and most of the universities employed a similar curriculum and method. Popes and emperors, who fashioned themselves as global figures, typically encouraged the founding of these centers, although their enthusiasm sometimes met with opposition from local authorities, who resented the arrival of many foreign teachers and students who were habitually poor, unfamiliar, and—in the eyes of many—not particularly productive. The new learning centers were also criticized occasionally by local bishops who previously had controlled all education in their dioceses and gave licenses to teach. Despite this (often fierce) opposition, universities prospered. By the mid-fifteenth century, some sixty cities in present-day Italy, France, Spain, Portugal, England, Scotland, the Czech Republic, Austria, Germany, Belgium, Croatia, Hungary, and Poland had a university.

Universities were greenhouses for the creation of a group of scholars who shared not only a way of life and a profession but also ideas and ways of thinking. They produced the "intellectual," a new sociological figure whose main occupation was to study or teach. With the birth of states and with growing municipal powers, many intellectuals would come to occupy important public offices. Thereafter, studying at the university would open new career opportunities to individuals who could afford to invest time and money in their intellectual preparation. Studying would also become a mechanism allowing the advancement of the middle classes (to use an anachronism). It would enable the emergence of a new type of nobility whose prestige was no longer linked to soldiering or bloodline but instead was based on intellectual achievements.[4]

Among these new intellectuals, some would come to be identified as jurists, individuals dedicated to the study of law. Recognized as experts in this particular domain, by the twelfth, thirteenth, and fourteenth centuries jurists who studied in universities became particularly coveted councilors. They were acknowledged as professionals who could advise on juridical matters, plead for the parties, and help the expanding administration of cities and monarchies. Depending on time and location, their mediation would eventually become a prerequisite in all legal interactions.

How the New System Operated

The combination of new sources, methodology, and environment created a novel system of law. Until the mid-thirteenth century, discussions in universities mainly focused on the reading and comprehension of ancient texts. Though these discussions were mostly oral, we do have written fragments of how this was done. These fragments mainly contain *glossa*. A gloss was a brief annotation between the lines or on the margin of a text that explained its terminology, content, principles, and main points, asked questions, and compared this segment to a word, sentence, or paragraph that appeared elsewhere. Faithful to the Scholastic method, the authors of glosses (known as glossators) tried to harmonize the different fragments by demonstrating that what seemed to be a contradiction or lack of coherence was not. The gloss explained the text, but it was also used as an index to facilitate cross-references. Most importantly, it allowed medieval jurists to develop a specialized terminology, invent new categories, and suggest new ways of thinking about the law.

A short gloss attributed to Rogerius, a scholar who taught in Bologna in the twelfth century, exemplified this method.[5] Analyzing the *Institutes* (the sixth-century manual for law students), Rogerius observed that it defined "justice" as the "the constant and perpetual desire to give to each man his due right." Asking why the *Institutes* mentioned "desire" rather than requiring an actual implementation, Rogerius concluded that this was not an oversight but instead a purposeful choice. It was meant to explain to law students that even if the goal of dispensing justice was not reached, the intention to do so was sufficient to qualify the action as just. By adopting this explanation, Rogerius established the importance of "intent" in legal interactions. He suggested that what you did and what resulted from your action was important, but no less essential was the state of mind (intention) that accompanied your act.

Next Rogerius observed that, according to the *Institutes,* justice contained three central mandates: to live justly, not to injure others, and to render to each his own (ensure that each person received the treatment he or she deserved). Asking why there were three rather than one single mandate and how each differed, Rogerius concluded that the first precept ("to live justly") referred to crimes against oneself (sins). The second and third precepts ("not to injure another" and "render to each his own") dealt, on the contrary, with crimes against other people. He explained that because crimes against other individuals were more frequent and more severe, they were prohibited twice. Yet their doubling did not diminish the fact that in reality there were two ways in which one could hurt other people. "Not to injure another" (the first of the two precepts) pointed to "commission" whereby to "render each one his due" (the second of the two precepts) pointed to "omission."

By studying only a few sentences of the *Institutes* and by observing repetitions as well as the choice of words, Rogerius thus justified some of the most basic categories we still employ today. He demonstrated the importance of intent, and he clarified the distinction between performing a wrongful act and failing to do the right thing (commission and omission). None of these observations was truly necessary in order to understand the Roman text, yet the analysis of this text gave Rogerius an opportunity to imagine a new way to categorize legal phenomena.

Starting in the late twelfth century, some scholars began collecting legal questions and publishing them. These documents, reflecting intellectual engagement with actual practice rather than with theory, usually centered on real or hypothetical cases that jurists had to solve and presented points for consideration and discussion. Also common were collections of glosses in large bodies known as *apparatus,* some of which contained as many as 100,000 fragments. Other types of publications were the *summae,* which discussed the contents of an entire book such as the *Institutes* (the student manual) and the *commentum* or *lectura,* which reproduced lectures given by a law professor.

From the fourteenth century on, scholars began demonstrating a greater degree of freedom, focusing their attention less on the texts themselves than on the doctrine they sought to develop. Their main goal was the practical applicability of the legal principles that could be drawn from Roman texts, and they were less concerned than previous jurists with being faithful to the original source. Typically, fourteenth-century scholars often based their analyses not on the Roman texts themselves but on the glosses of preceding jurists.

During this period scholars also began giving *consilia.* Somewhat similar to ancient Roman juridical activity, *consilia* were written opinions on matters of the law. They were authored by jurists at the request of interested parties who had sought their advice on how to plan their activities or how to solve certain situations. Demonstrating the originality of medieval jurists, these answers creatively applied theoretical debates developed in universities to everyday situations. Dealing with juridical questions either hypothetically or post factum, jurists often acted as hired guns whose role it was to find the solution that best fit their clients. Nonetheless, their responses became an important source of law. Well argued and well expressed, many of these juridical opinions were followed as if they were authoritative statements of what the law dictated.

A particularly remarkable figure during this period was Bartolus of Saxoferrato (1313–1357). An extremely prolific jurist, teacher, and judge, Bartolus published treatises on a great variety of topics, wrote commentaries, and engaged in giving counsel. He wrote on some of the most important issues of his time, such as the power of German emperors over parts of Italy, conflicts between different jurisdictions, citizenship, and dowries. Typical of his work were his treatises on the legal consequences of changes in the course of rivers upon property rights and jurisdiction. Although rivers were useful dividers, Bartolus argued, natural changes in their course were constant. It was therefore essential that jurists reflect on how these changes affected rights. He concluded that rivers could add or remove land and that this had consequences for riverbank owners, whose property rights could be enlarged or diminished as a result. Bartolus also determined that if these alterations in the course of rivers were sufficiently slow to produce new customs and new ways of relating to the modified landscape, the territorial jurisdiction of riverine communities could also increase or be reduced.

This was a revolutionary conclusion because, contrary to property rights, which most jurists agreed could constantly mutate, before Bartolus's time territorial jurisdiction was thought to be permanent and unalterable. In his answer, Bartolus not only invented a new rule (jurisdiction can change), he also created a new vision of what territorial jurisdiction was. This vision, which comprehended territorial jurisdiction not as naturally given but instead as dependent on how individuals and communities related to space, allowed him to give an efficient response to the challenges that his contemporaries faced, among them the growth of cities and states and the constant redefinition of their boundaries. The idea proposed by Bartolus that both property rights and territorial jurisdiction were created and could be modified by human activity was so powerful and so convenient that it soon became recognized as the established norm.

Canon Law

Scholars have long debated whether discussions in universities began by studying Roman texts or canon law texts or whether both things coincided. Questions of chronology aside, it is clear that the same methodology (Scholasticism) and the same concerns expressed with regard to Roman law were also applied to the study of canon law. Here too, the first task scholars faced was the reconstruction of the corpus of that law, which was dispersed in a variety of sources and collections, some more global and authoritative than others (see Chapter 3).

In the twelfth century, a successful compilation was proposed by Gratian. Gratian (who may have also used the work of previous scholars) collected, examined, selected, and systematized the different sources of canon law (the Bible, legislation and decisions of Church councils, papal decisions, and the writings of the Church fathers and early saints).[6] Arranging this material logically in three parts, he enumerated the sources, described Church hierarchy, and listed the rules regulating the hierarchy's activities. Also included were instructions regarding judicial procedure, Church property, the religious orders, marriage, sins, repentance, and penance. Matters of doctrine and matters of law were intermingled throughout the work, but the latter predominated.

This compilation (*Concordia Discordantium Canonum*, literally the harmony of discordant canons, later known as the *Decretum*) was unofficial.

Yet it was considered so reliable that it ended up being followed as if it had been formally endorsed. Other compilations of canon law followed, most important among them the thirteenth-century *Decretales* (also identified as *Liber Extra* because it included what was left out of the five books of the *Decretum*) and *Liber Sextus* and the fourteenth-century *Clementinae*. By the early sixteenth century, these compilations together received the name *Corpus Iuris Canonici* in order to distinguish them, yet make them parallel to, the Justinian *Corpus Iuris Civilis*.[7]

As with the study of Roman law, after scholars were convinced they had recovered a genuine body of Church law, they began centuries of analysis, exegesis, and study. Gratian was the first to do so, adding to his compilation brief annotations *(dicta)* that addressed and explained apparent contradictions with the aim of harmonizing the whole. Other scholars soon followed. Applying the Scholastic method and constantly conversing with their colleagues studying Roman law, canon-law jurists ended up glossing, commenting, and writing treatises on canon law. They developed vocabularies, extracted principles, and systematized the juridical thinking of the Church. As a result of these similarities in method and places of creation, over time canon and Roman law tended to fuse to such a degree that it was sometimes hard to distinguish between them.

Typical of this amalgamation was the development of Romano-canonical court procedures *(ordo iudiciarius)* in the twelfth and thirteenth centuries.[8] A means to replace the ordeal after it was deauthorized by the Church, this procedure, inspired in Roman *cognitio,* was first adopted by popes and ecclesiastical courts and then taken up by secular jurisdictions, including royal, feudal, and municipal courts. Developed due to ecclesiastical impetus, it was propelled by Romanist and canonist jurists who taught at the various European universities. Heavily inspired by the Justinian *Corpus Iuris Civilis,* it was also greatly affected by canon law, mainly through its continuing regulation and elaboration by papal decretals.

Feudal Law

Alongside Roman and canon law, scholars also turned their attention to feudal institutions. Starting in the twelfth century they suggested that a "feudal law" had existed in Europe as early as the eighth century. This law governed relations between lords and their vassals as well as between the various lords. It identified lords and their duties and defined how individuals became vassals and what they owed to their masters. Feudal law also dealt with the jurisdiction of lords over their vassals, feudal courts, and conflicting claims of various lords over the same individuals or lands. It focused on issues typical to feudalism such as access to and use of land, as well as inheritance.

The genealogy of how this field of inquiry came into being is quite similar to what we know of Roman and canon law, and it is probable that it emerged contemporaneously. Already in the eleventh century, some scholars had begun discussing feudal law, yet juridical interest in that law began in earnest only with the publication in the mid-twelfth century of an authoritative text, the *Libri Feudorum*. This text, compiled in present-day Italy, collected decisions from so-called feudal courts, as well as feudal customs, legislation, and juridical writing. By the thirteenth century the literature on feudalism had expanded so dramatically that there were now experts *(feudists)* dedicated to writing commentaries on these laws.

The erudite literature on feudalism introduced the study of feudal law to universities. The result was the gradual Romanization of feudal law, which was discussed, analyzed, and understood by using Roman terminology, categories, and ways of reasoning. The fusion between the two fields was so complete that, in practice, they merged. One indication of this was that by the thirteenth century, for example, several scholars appended parts of the *Libri Feudorum* to their copies of the *Corpus Iuris Civilis* and glossed them together. Another was the influence of Roman law on discussions regarding feudal law—for example, allowing feudal jurists to apply the Roman idea of *dominum* to explain the relations between lords and vassals. They suggested that lords had *dominium directum* of the land (allowing them to direct what would happen on it, collect dues, and exercise authority) and vassals had *dominium utile* (giving them the right to use the land).

Why twelfth-century scholars cared about feudalism sufficiently to turn their attention to it is one of the least studied questions. As described in Chapter 4, by the time scholars began thinking about feudalism, it was already declining everywhere. Remnants of what it had been persisted in different parts of Europe in various intensities, but the powers of lords, as well as the number of unfree individuals, gradually diminished as monarchies, the economy, and cities grew. Historians who argue that our vision of feudalism is distorted would suggest that the reason twelfth-century scholars cared about it was relatively simple: they reimagined the feudal past for their own purposes, which was why we should not trust their interpretations. Looking back to feudalism allowed twelfth-century jurists to develop doctrines dealing with relations between lords, kings, and their subjects, the meaning and extension of jurisdiction, and land rights, all of which were very important at that time precisely because feudalism was dying. It also enabled jurists to conceptualize public authority as the outcome of a pact between rulers and ruled that included mutual obligations. According to this theory, subjects could legitimately rebel against monarchs who, by not respecting the pact, became tyrants. In feudalism, in short, these scholars identified elements that could serve not only to explain the past but also to structure and control their own twelfth- and thirteenth-century societies.

Ius Commune

The study of Roman, canon, and feudal law in medieval study centers and universities by scholars who reconstructed texts and then applied the new Scholastic method to them revolutionized European normativity. It created innovative ways to think about, analyze, and discuss the legal order. Scholars of course continued to disagree with one another, but they did so using common terminologies, concepts, arguments, and techniques.

The complex system of knowledge, organization, and interpretation that resulted included solutions to particular legal problems, such as who had the right to use land or who was a citizen of which community. But above all it proposed a new vision according to which, despite wide variations in the concrete answers proposed in different parts of Europe, juridical thought was not particular to a place, a society, or a time. Instead, it was based on reason. This implied that the new juridical method could have a universal vocation and embody, as it came to be known, a *ius commune*—a law potentially common to all. Thereafter, following the guidance of *ius commune* became identified as *rectum* or *directum;* that is, the right way of doing things.[9]

Comprising centuries of juridical opinions, this new legal constellation, now referred to as *ius commune,* was clearly different from classical Roman law, that is, from the law that regulated life in ancient (both republican and imperial) Rome. Said to be inspired by that ancient law, it was nevertheless entirely new in scope, method, intention, and solutions. It did share with Rome, however, the idea that jurists were at the forefront of juridical creation and that jurisprudence, the science of law, was the most important normative source.

Spreading *Ius Commune*

Replicated in universities across Europe and propelled by the constant movement of intellectuals from one city to the next and their employment by municipal, royal, and imperial governments as well as by Church authorities, and eventually by the relative abundance and wide circulation of printed material, the new juridical science expanded throughout Europe. Some European territories were affected earlier than others, some were affected more intensely, but by the sixteenth century at the latest, some version of *ius commune* was present almost everywhere.[10]

This process of dissemination was initially backed by secular rulers and municipal authorities who believed that the new science would solidify their powers and justify their growing demands for superiority. Following this strategy, in the thirteenth century King Alfonso X of Castile officially incorporated the new juridical method into Castilian law. He ordered his advisors to recompile its doctrines alongside canon and local law, producing a collection now known as the *Siete Partidas* because it has seven parts. Considered radical when it was enacted because of its dependence on juridical scholarly discussions, it was not until the fifteenth century (after *ius commune* penetrated into Castile through other channels, mainly the founding of universities and the circulation of jurists) that the *Partidas* became central to the Castilian legal system. By that stage, however, Castilian kings were already wary of *ius commune* and were no longer as enthusiastic about its penetration, which they could not control. As ancient Roman emperors had attempted to do with their own jurists, successive Castilian monarchs endeavored to limit the effects of *ius commune.* They established a hierarchy of legal sources, according to which royal laws would be at the top, followed by customs *(fueros),* and only then the *Siete Partidas.*[11] They also decided that new *ius commune* doctrines could not be adopted without their consent. These efforts, however, were largely unsuccessful. By that stage, the legal method proposed by *ius commune* was considered the most logical way to handle juridical questions. Whether permissible or not, recognized by kings or not, by that time it had become a repository of solutions that no jurist or lawyer could afford to ignore.

The New Juridical Science and Preexisting Law

Until fairly recently historians tended to think about *ius commune* as a substantive law that mainly included concrete solutions to particular problems. As a result, many suggested that it stood in opposition to preexisting local, municipal, royal, or canon law, which it sought to replace. According to this narrative, after *ius commune* expanded throughout Europe, authorities, jurists, and locals had to choose between following *ius commune* or remaining faithful to their legal traditions, as obeying both was impossible. This interpretation, which dominated the field for many years, has been largely discarded. Instead it is now proposed that the new method developed in universities did not necessarily replace the previous legal system but it came on top of it, suggesting new ways to organize, explain, and systematize the preexisting normative order.

According to this interpretation, preexisting laws and *ius commune* peacefully coexisted. This could happen because indigenous local law, legislation (where it existed), and native variants of canon and feudal law were all identified by *ius commune* jurists as including a *ius proprium* (a law proper to a specific community or place). The task that jurists who were trained in *ius commune* undertook was not to remove the *ius proprium* but instead to synchronize local arrangements (which continued to vary dramatically from one place to the next) by reinterpreting them in ways that would not be contradictory to the new *ius commune*. Jurists achieved this by arguing that *ius proprium* gave concrete solutions to specific problems, but both the problems and the solutions should be analyzed, interpreted, and decided according to the methods developed by *ius commune*. Furthermore, in cases in which local law gave no answer, in its capacity as a "general law" *(lex omnium generalis) ius commune* could intervene, suggesting solutions. *Ius commune,* in short, would supply the terms, concepts, procedures, and techniques of analysis that jurists would employ whether they debated local, Germanic, canon, municipal, feudal, or royal law. Meanwhile, *ius proprium* would be understood as the local expression of a *ius commune,* the particular, local, manifestation of an ultimate and shared technique.

Because European kings and municipal authorities called upon jurists to help them regulate their kingdoms and cities, over time the influence of *ius commune* became so pervasive that it greatly modified the *ius proprium.* Jurists not only offered advice and proposed legislation, they also compiled, collected, and arranged the existing law. As they documented institutions, processes, and regulations, they refashioned them according to their criteria and understanding. They incorporated, synchronized, and systematized the normative order to such a degree that by the end of this process it was no longer recognizable. By that time, rather than explaining ancient texts, what *ius commune* jurists mostly did was to intervene in the legal order. Answering questions, counseling, and surveying as well as chronicling certain practices, they radically transformed the preexisting law.

An example of how jurists proceeded to do the above can be found in juridical discussions of naturalization. The local laws of various Italian communes allowed for naturalization under certain conditions. Roman law also had instructions regarding the transformation of foreigners into citizens. By studying both, *ius commune* jurists invented a theory that explained what naturalization was and what it required. This theory held that individuals' adhesion to communities was normally tied to birth and descent. It was therefore by nature that certain people belonged to a polity. For naturalization to transpire, foreigners needed to change their nature. This change in nature could occur if sufficient time had elapsed since the foreigner arrived at the locality and if he could demonstrate that this prolonged residence had influenced him. Starting from these premises, jurists listed the conditions for naturalization and the type of proofs that were required, as well as how these could be substituted by legal presumptions. They also concluded that the different practices followed by the various Italian communities were but local manifestations of this common rule.

Observing how they operated, some historians concluded that by referencing Roman categories and texts, what these jurists mostly did was codify, systematize, and abstract principles from what they observed unfolding around them. To return to our example, the ways each Italian commune treated naturalization were different. Some communes wanted foreigners to marry locally, others demanded that they pay a minimum amount of taxation, or forced them to acquire real estate, but these differences, jurists sustained, were inconsequential because all conditions were directed to the same end. They all sought to establish the same thing, namely, that the person requiring naturalization had changed his nature and was no longer a genuine foreigner.

Historians have thus concluded that, rather than understanding ancient Roman law, what medieval jurists did was to develop methods with which to synchronize and integrate the various legal regimes that coexisted in Europe and the many sources from which they had emerged. Their main task was not to interpret ancient documents but to make Roman, Germanic, local, feudal, and canon law as they were practiced in different parts of the Continent cohere together into a common system, a *ius commune*.

The Results

The new techniques created by jurists did not remain an abstraction, nor did they penetrate only the highest echelons of society. Instead they percolated into and affected everyday life even in remote villages. In the late Middle Ages, ordinary peasants in tiny hamlets along the Spanish-Portuguese border often fought over their right to use the land. Although their description of why the land was theirs did not employ the correct terminology (possession), it nevertheless faithfully reproduced juridical doctrine regarding land rights. It suggested, for example, that entitlement depended on having utilized the territory for an extended period of time without encountering opposition. It also pointed out that the silence of rivals could be understood as consent. This conclusion, which referenced a juridical presumption (under ordinary circumstances, silence equaled consent) was also accompanied by the understanding that a violent response against invading neighbors did the contrary, that is, it manifested disagreement.

The illiterate peasants who engaged in these debates had not studied law, nor were their vindications prepared by lawyers. However, what they said and did was surprisingly identical to what *ius commune* jurists argued. It was based on abstractions offered by these jurists after they studied a great variety of customs and ways of doing.

How peasants came into this knowledge is hard to ascertain. They themselves gave no clear answer. When asked why they believed certain rules applied, they clarified that the norms they invoked were natural, that they were universal and that, as a result, they needed no proof or explanation.

Apparently, by that stage, the conclusions of *ius commune* were indeed seen as so logical and reasonable and were so widely accepted that contemporaries assumed that they were common to all humanity, they were immutable, and they were true.

The study of law that began in the twelfth century thus revolutionized European normativity. Having no formal means to impose itself, it spread across borders and through institutions with or without authorities' approval. Carried from place to place by jurists who were convinced of its superiority, it allowed them to rethink the existing normative order, refashioning it anew. By the end of this process, there was no place that *ius commune* did not touch, no field it did not affect.

6

The Birth of an English Common Law

ENGLAND FORMED part of the Roman Empire until the fifth century, and Roman and Romanized citizens as well as indigenous Celts and converts to Christianity formed part of its community. Roman law was introduced to the island and affected in diverse intensities both Roman citizens and Romanized natives. What happened next is a matter of debate. According to most scholars, with the withdrawal of Roman troops, Roman law as well as Christianity virtually ceased to exist in England. According to others, pockets of both persisted, most particularly among native Celts and in the western regions.

But regardless of what happened in the fifth century, most historians agree that in the late sixth century Roman and canon law were reintroduced to the island by Christian missionaries. Equally present was some version of Germanic law, carried to England by successive Germanic groups that invaded its territory. As a result of these developments, from the seventh to the eleventh century the legal situation in England was not dramatically different from that in other parts of Europe where native, Germanic (including Danish), canon, and Roman law all coexisted to some degree or the other.

Evidence from this period illustrates this complexity. In the seventh century, for example, Roman law was taught at a school in Canterbury. During the same period, Anglo-Saxon remedies for various offenses were written down.[1] The aim was to replace blood feuds with monetary payment, a move indicating, according to some scholars, the growing influence of Christianity and perhaps Roman law (the debate still lingers). In the sixth, seventh, and eighth centuries, Anglo-Saxon donations and testaments often cited *jus ecclesiasticum* (ecclesiastical law) as their guide and inspiration, and so did records of slave manumission as early as the seventh century. By the ninth century, Christian influence on legal remedies was particularly clear, many making direct references to the Bible.[2] Also during this period, some royal decisions used terms originating in Roman law and so did agreements that included oath. Seventh- and eighth-century Anglo-Saxon charters dealing with land imitated formulas used by papal administration, copied the practice followed in Italy, or bore signs of Frankish and Celtic influence. By the ninth century the number of charters written in vernacular (Old English) grew spectacularly, as did the use of legal formulas of Roman origin.

If canon and Roman law gradually penetrated the island, so did feudal institutions. Anglo-Saxon laws written down after the Norman Conquest (1066), allegedly in order to reproduce the legal situation predating the invasion, captured many of these trends. The *Quadripartitus* (ca.1108–1118), a collection of such norms that only survives in fragments, contained a Latin translation of Anglo-Saxon laws, a few Latin documents, and two treatises on status, pleading, and theft that followed the structure of Roman law and were influenced by Christian morality.

Despite striking similarities between developments in England and in Continental Europe, most historians suggest that beginning in the eleventh and twelfth centuries England took a different path. This path would allow the development of a distinct legal system that, according to most, was very different from the *ius commune* that came to dominate the rest of Europe. How and why this happened is the subject of this chapter, in which I trace the development of English common law and ask whether it was different from *ius commune* and, if so, how.

Law under the Early Normans

After the Norman invasion (1066), nothing indicated that England would take a different path.[3] Although early Norman kings established themselves as colonial rulers, taking over the properties of natives, this political, social, and economic upheaval was nevertheless accompanied by a legal continuity. Initially Norman monarchs appeared adamant that such would be the case and proceeded to record the laws that predated their arrival with the alleged aim of arresting any possible encroachment on the existing normative order.[4]

In line with what was happening elsewhere, Norman monarchs such as William the Conqueror (r. 1066–1087) and Edward I (r. 1272–1307) employed men of letters as aids and councilors. Among such experts was Lanfranc (1005–1089), archbishop of Canterbury. Lanfranc was an Italian-born teacher and canonist who, as a member of the King's Council, advised William the Conqueror also on secular matters and contributed to the compilation of existing laws and customs.

There is also evidence that the teaching of Roman and canon law was introduced into England in the middle of the twelfth century by a jurist from Bologna. This jurist, Vacarius, taught law at Oxford, a new learning center having no clear date of foundation that nonetheless was considered to have begun attracting students in around 1096. To help his students, Vacarius composed a manual *(Liber pauperum)* that included extracts from the *Digest* (the sixth-century Roman recompilation of juridical opinions) and the *Codex* (the book including imperial legislation) alongside gloss. Copies of the Roman *Corpus Iuris Civilis* soon became available on the Island, and in the late twelfth and early thirteenth centuries the study of Roman law expanded from Oxford to several additional centers. During this period, training in canon law was introduced into local universities and cathedral schools, and many Englishmen studied in Continental Europe, while others avidly purchased Roman and canon law books for their libraries.

It is also currently believed that canon law was practiced in the ecclesiastical courts instituted by the Normans in the 1070s. According to this new understanding, it was only after the sixteenth-century Protestant Reformation that a new doctrine emerged in England requiring canon law, now perceived as a foreign law, to be received or approved by kings before it could be applied in the kingdom.[5]

Thus, it is fair to conclude that England initially followed approximately the same path as many other European countries, where Roman and canon law were studied and practiced yet local legal arrangements also persisted. If this was the case, when, how, and why did England take a different path?

The Superimposition of Royal Jurisdiction

Historians usually begin the account of English particularism by explaining that Norman kings depended on the feudal lords who accompanied them to the island and ensured its control. Like most other contemporary monarchs,

however, they wished to limit the powers of these lords, obtain direct access
to their vassals, and acquire full mastery of the land. To achieve this goal,
they devised ways allowing them to relinquish gradually the mediation of
lords. The method they chose was to extend their jurisdiction throughout
the realm. Beginning with Henry I (r. 1100–1135) and substantially intensifying with his grandson Henry II (r. 1154–1189), Norman monarchs began
instituting a system of royal courts, which were to be superimposed on all
previously existing jurisdictions.

How they accomplished this task was beautifully described at the very
end of the nineteenth century. Although many historians now contest this
narrative, believing it a legend, it is nevertheless a story that deserves telling.
According to it, initially Norman kings demanded the right to intervene in
disputes and guarantee their peaceful resolution only when they were physically next to the litigating parties. This usually meant that their jurisdiction was limited to individuals who were in attendance at their court. In a
subsequent stage Norman kings began appropriating the power to ensure
peace on special days such as their coronation or the weeks of Christmas,
Easter, and Pentecost. Eventually they moved from protecting dates to
protecting territories. They first defined the jurisdiction of their court in a
comprehensive way that covered a perimeter of up to three miles from
where they were physically located and then applied special protections to
the main roads and waterways of the kingdom under the excuse that they
led to the court. Gradually the network of roads and waterways under royal
jurisdiction was broadened to include almost all roads and waterways. By
the close of the thirteenth century, lawyers at the service of the monarchs
developed a legal fiction according to which the king was present everywhere in the kingdom. Thereafter, the protection of the monarch, which
was once limited to his household, included the entire realm and "the
king's peace had fully grown from an occasional privilege into a common
right."[6]

The imposition of royal jurisdiction throughout the realm, which was first
temporal (protecting certain dates) and then geographic (protecting certain
places), was also carried out by assigning certain matters to royal hands. Here,
too, the process was gradual. Norman kings justified their growing intervention by indicating that certain issues were of particular interest to them
and were thus worthy of their attention. Among such issues were disputes
over the exercise of royal franchise or the protection of particular persons.

Despite this extension, local, municipal, feudal, and ecclesiastical courts persisted—except that now superimposed on them was a web of royal jurisdiction. This web was extremely thin: it is estimated that until the late eighteenth century, rarely were there more than fifteen judges in all royal courts. Furthermore, although placed on top, royal judges had no supervisory functions: their jurisdiction was entirely separate from that of ecclesiastical, local, and feudal courts. Adding royal courts on top of the existing system of adjudication, therefore, did not create a hierarchical pyramid. What it did was to allow litigants the choice whether to take their conflicts to local, municipal, ecclesiastic, or feudal courts, or to request royal involvement. Choice, however, was given only to freemen. Those who were unfree had no right to plead before the king and no ability to solicit his protection.[7]

The growing web of royal jurisdiction led to occasional tensions, but by the thirteenth and fourteenth centuries almost any free man owing allegiance to the monarch could request his intervention in a multiplicity of affairs. This extension was justified by invoking the crown's responsibility to guarantee peace, which involved primarily the ability to adjudicate conflicts.

A Growing System of Writs

The growth of royal jurisdiction required the development of new legal mechanisms. If, initially, kings could hear plaintiffs in person, they soon had to delegate this faculty to some of their men. As the number of individuals involved in hearing cases for the king grew, several royal courts were instituted.[8] As officials and institutions proliferated, additional instruments were created to regulate their activities. Together these developments, particularly noticeable in the mid to late twelfth century but continuing thereafter, led to the emergence of what we now identify as the English common law.

This development was gradual. Early royal intervention was administrative rather than judicial. When the king or his officials received reports of wrongdoing or a breach of the peace, they sent to trustworthy individuals an order to redress the situation. This order, written in Latin on a small parchment and bearing the king's seal, was known as a "writ."[9] Written in the royal chancery by royal officials, it reproduced the version of the offended party and gave instructions as to how to remedy the situation. For example, a lord might decide that because his tenant did not pay him feudal dues, he should be evicted. If the tenant disagreed and believed he could find no remedy at his lord's court, he could take the issue to the king. If the king (or his officers) thought the matter deserved their attention, they could issue a writ that instructed the addressee, a man of royal confidence, to make sure that the lord would not proceed to oust the tenant. Writs could instruct lords how to handle the conflict or they could order them to listen to the parties and adjudicate their claims.

Writs included an executive peremptory instruction meant to guarantee peace. They were considered an efficient tool allowing the king, who was charged with overseeing the welfare of the kingdom, to intervene in selected cases. Yet although they supplied an efficient and immediate solution to problems that needed redress, they were easily abused. Issued ex parte at the request of the interested party, their grant assumed that the petition was justified. Nonetheless, because those requesting royal intervention some-times misrepresented what had transpired, in the twelfth century a further development took place. Writs began allowing alleged wrongdoers to choose between complying with the order or appearing before a royal delegate in order to explain why he or she should not.

This development, which allowed wrongdoers to defend themselves, was revolutionary. It transformed writs from administrative documents into orders to initiate litigation. Writs now sent the parties to royal officials who heard their cases and decided whether the remedy included in the writ should be granted or not. The need to appear before royal officials, justifying why the writ should be applied or denying that it should, gave rise in the thir-teenth century to a procedure known as "pleading." Armed with a writ, a plaintiff would present himself or herself before a royal official in order to narrate the facts that justified the concession of a remedy. The defendant would respond by denying some or all the facts, by admitting the facts but giving them another interpretation, by denying the relevance of the writ, or by introducing additional factors (excuses) that explained why, notwith-standing, a remedy should not be given. The plaintiff would then respond by invoking a similar set of preestablished answers.

This exchange between the parties was extremely formal. Rather than de-scribing the facts of the case, it consisted of a set of pre-ascribed positions and responses that the plaintiff and the defendant could invoke. The ex-change continued until it became clear what was agreed between the par-ties, and what was contested. It was only after this clarity was achieved that the case went to "trial." Contrary to pleading (that concentrated on claim making), during the "trial" the parties had to prove the facts upon which their claims were based. Proof could be established in a variety of ways depending on time, issue, and place. The parties could take an oath, be subjected to an ordeal, or a jury could be called upon. After the facts of the matter were proven (or not), the adjudicating official (now properly functioning as a judge) determined whether the remedy included in the writ should be granted (or not).

How Writs Functioned

In the centuries following this transformation, writs became instruments allowing litigants to begin a lawsuit before royal officials. Issued by the royal chancery, they reproduced the decision (1) that the case was within royal jurisdiction and (2) that it justified the king's intervention. The writ instructed royal officials, now identified as "justices," to hear the case. If writs were a means to commence litigation, their denial marked the impossibility of addressing the royal courts. In cases in which the chancery decided that there was no reason or cause for the king to intervene, it refused to issue a writ. The immediate consequence was that royal courts had no jurisdiction over the affair. Litigants who failed to secure a writ were thus barred from pleading before royal courts, but they could still find redress in local, feudal, or ecclesiastical courts.

Initially writs were issued individually to the person requesting royal assistance and they covered the specific circumstances of his or her case. They were ad hoc and particular, were delivered sealed, and theoretically could be used only once. Obtaining a writ required a substantial investment in time, energy, and funds. Litigants had to convince the chancery that their case merited royal attention, which during this early period was always presented as an exceptional grant rather than a routine right.

Because writs depended on the willingness of the king to intervene, they were mostly granted to individuals whom the kings wanted to protect and they covered issues that the king was most keen to control (mainly those that could potentially curb the powers of lords) or that carried a greater risk for a serious breach of peace. They were the product of piecemeal decisions that reflected the monarch's conditions and interests. But if writs depended on the king's willingness to intervene, they also were conditioned by the existence of a party interested in obtaining them. Pragmatic and practical rather than abstract and theoretical, writs existed because there was a conflict that required resolution, a party who chose to bring it to a royal court, and a chancery that, representing the king, decided to intervene. Writs thus proliferated in areas in which individuals sought royal protection and the king was willing to give it. This meant that the creation of writs was driven by private interests rather than by considerations of public good, and it was shaped by the economic, political, and social circumstances of the time.

The Institutionalization of Writs

Although writs began as ad hoc, individual solutions to particular problems, over time some writs became institutionalized. By the mid-twelfth century, and more clearly in the thirteenth century, the chancery began keeping a record of which writs had been issued in the past, and it routinely expressed willingness to continue doing the same. As a result of these developments, writs were no longer ad hoc solutions given to particular plaintiffs on a case-by-case basis. Instead they became a fixed formula that litigants could obtain if they knew what to ask for. To facilitate the identification of existing writs, many received names, such as *praecipe quod reddat* ("command that he render"), which instructed local authorities to give plaintiffs the land they claimed as their own, or the *novel disseisin* ("recent dispossession"), which did the same with regard to possession. Contemporaneously, a public list of obtainable writs also made its appearance.

The growth of writs was spectacular. In around 1189 there were some forty writs; by the end of the thirteenth century their number was ten times larger. As writs became popular, royal jurisdiction extended, and as royal jurisdiction extended, new writs were produced. In the process, royal intervention, which was originally viewed as exceptional, became routine. By that stage it was possible to imagine that royal jurisdiction would become limitless, eventually supplying a remedy for almost every wrong.

The success of writs was tied to monarchs' ability to attract litigants to royal courts, which litigants preferred over feudal, local, or ecclesiastical courts. There were very few explicit statements of why this was the case, but most historians believe that if litigants preferred royal jurisdiction, it was because they thought it more equitable or more efficient than local or lordly decision making. One of the advantages of royal courts was the ability to compel defendants and jurors to appear in court when summoned. Also important was the fact that judgment rendered by these courts was recorded in rolls, which were safely stored in the Tower of London and could, in theory, be found when needed. It is also possible that royal courts were regarded as instances in which, contrary to what transpired in other courts, an impersonal, rule-bound process of dispute resolution took place.

The system of conflict resolution that emerged as a result of all these developments was gradually identified as "common law." This system was "common" because it was superimposed onto local, municipal, and feudal jurisdictions, it potentially encompassed the entire realm, and it was open to all those under allegiance to the king.[10] The commonness that it referenced was political. This stood in clear opposition to *ius commune,* which, combining Roman, canon, and feudal law, was identified as "common" because it was theoretically shared by all the inhabitants of Latin Christendom. These inhabitants were perhaps divided into a multiplicity of diverse, even rival, polities, yet they adhered, so it was alleged, to a single culture, a single religion, and a single (common) law.

Writs, Remedies, and the Growth of Common Law

In theory, by granting writs the king (and his officials) supplied the forum (the court) and the procedure (which cases would be heard and by whom) but not the substantive norms that would be applied. It is nevertheless clear that, in practice, by giving access to the courts and by granting certain remedies in certain cases but not in others, the king substantially modified the existing normative order. Each time his chancery issued a writ allowing litigants to seek a specific remedy, it also implicitly recognized the existence of a right. And if allowing litigants access to the court created new rights, denying a writ was the same as the suppression of a right or an obligation. These rights and obligations theoretically continued to exist, but in practice they were no longer available because there was no writ enabling the interested party to request their implementation.

This relationship between remedies and rights was to become the most salient feature of common law. This important characteristic was already present in the formative period. In the twelfth, thirteenth, and fourteenth centuries, writs recognized (and thus created) such important rights as the right to inherit land (given by the *assize of mort d'ancestor,* a writ enabling a plaintiff to sue a defendant for taking land that the plaintiff had inherited after the death of his kinsmen) or the right not to be charged with a crime unless there was an official indictment or presentment (established by the assize of Clarendon, 1166). The linking of remedies to rights became more pronounced as time passed. By the early modern period it occupied such a central place that many began arguing that common law was nothing other than a system of rights, which they identified as the rights of Englishmen (see Chapter 8). During this period, old writs such as *habeas corpus* ("have the body") regained particular prominence. It was now suggested that this writ, which ordered authorities to present the judge with the body of the person in custody, constituted a remedy against unlawful imprisonment. It was further argued that, by supplying this remedy, *habeas corpus* indirectly recognized the right not to be imprisoned without cause.

Eventually the idea that remedies created rights would be so important that it could lead to decisions that otherwise could be considered peculiar. This happened, for example, in 1704 when the House of Lords, sitting as an appeal instance, reversed a decision by the Queen's Bench denying recourse to an individual deprived of the right to vote in parliamentary elections. The denial was based on the commonsense observation that the individual required no remedy because his preferred candidate won the election even without his vote. The House of Lords disagreed because "if the plaintiff has a right, he must of necessity have a means to vindicate and maintain it and a remedy if he is injured." It was a vain thing, the lords argued, "to imagine a right without a remedy, for want of right and want of remedy are reciprocal."[11] The lords' conclusion was straightforward: though the inability to vote made no difference because the candidate preferred by the plaintiff won the election anyway, the petitioner must receive a remedy because, under common law, the lack of remedy implied the lack of right. Thus, if the court did not grant the petitioner a remedy, it would be as if it did not recognize his right to vote.

The Centrality of Procedure

If common law was particular in its insistence on the relationship between remedies and rights, it was also special in focusing attention, not on ensuring material justice (as Continental courts did), but on controlling the way the courts functioned. Because it was founded as a system of licenses (writs) allowing litigants to plead before royal officials, common law was extremely attentive to procedural issues. It did not ask what the proper result should be but whether the right procedure would be followed.

Pleading—how the parties translated their agreements and disagreements into legal formulas that could be used at the court—was often considered the most important issue. This translation began when the plaintiff chose to invoke a specific writ, the defendant responded to it, and the plaintiff replied. Because pleading was crucial to defining the issues at stake, experts of common law insisted that it was essential to verify that it was done correctly. In the late Middle Ages this became the main task of royal justices who presided over these exchanges and ensured that the parties followed an acceptable script. Because by that stage knowing which writs existed and how to employ (and answer) them became a sophisticated pursuit, most legal literature was dedicated to describing the complex ceremonies and formulaic exchanges that ruled over the working of royal courts and advised practitioners on how to channel cases through them. The preparation of lawyers followed this route, mostly centering on teaching candidates the art of pleading and procedure. Yearbooks that reported on what happened in courts did the same. Rather than describe rules and principles or narrate the decisions reached by the judges, they reproduced the dialogues between the parties and the judge, which led to the adoption of a commonly acceptable question. The issue for them was how cases were actually formulated and argued (that is, how the facts of the conflict were transformed into legal arguments), identifying what good claims were and how they could be presented.

Procedural rules were at the center of how the common-law courts operated, but they were also important for safekeeping the prestige of royal justice. For the royal system to operate well and compete successfully with local, feudal, or ecclesiastical courts, it was essential to guarantee its reputation. This could be done by, among other things, ensuring litigants that a certain procedure would be followed without making exceptions because of the identity of the parties or the nature of the case. Among the instruments devised to do so were the many rules we now identify as embodying "due process." These rules were designed to make sure that judges would be impartial umpires whose main task would be to give the same opportunities (that is, procedural rules) to both sides, allowing them to plead their cases as if on equal grounds.

Because the task of common-law judges was mainly to oversee the exchanges between litigants at the court, not to verify the making of justice, common law left almost no room for appeals. "Writs of error" allowed a superior court to review and correct the proceedings of lower courts, but these were mostly restricted to procedural errors that were evident in the record and did not extend to challenging, for example, the factual or legal basis for the decision. In exceptional cases, rather than allowing to appeal, common-law courts allowed revisiting a case by ordering a new trial.

It is therefore not surprising that even as late as the fifteenth century, common law judges often refused to depart from the traditional system of rules in order to ensure material justice. The contrast with the rest of Europe could not be greater. Continental judges were charged with doing justice. How they arrived at a just decision was not particularly consequential. Although litigants in most countries had to follow a certain procedure in order for their cases to prosper, for much of the medieval and early modern period, this procedure was based on the "practice of the court." Rather than prescribing a strict formula, it could be abbreviated if the judge considered it beneficial, or prolonged, if justice so required. Suspects of criminal offenses, for example, had a right to trial, that is, the right not to be sentenced without a court reviewing their case, but judges had a huge discretion as to what would actually happen once the case was brought to their attention.[12] Until the sixteenth and even the seventeenth century, Continental judges could render decisions "following their conscience" rather than the law. As a result, while common law mostly admitted appeals on procedural issues, European courts did not. There, appeals were always based on the allegation that the decision was unjust, the question whether a specific procedure had been followed or not being considered almost irrelevant.

Professionals of the Law

During the formative period of common law, members of the higher echelons of royal administration, judges included, were often trained professionals who had studied canon or Roman law at universities or cathedral schools. Ranulf de Glanvil (ca.1112–1190) was an important and influential judge during the reign of Henry II. He was said to have written the *Tractatus de legibus e consuetudinibus regni Angliae* (ca.1187–1189), which was a manual that surveyed the work of the English royal courts. Meant not only to reproduce the practice followed by these courts but also to give it intellectual coherence and authority, the manual was composed in Latin rather than in French (the language of the court), probably to bring it to European-wide scholarly attention and have it taught in schools and universities.

Henry of Bracton (Bratton) had a similar profile. The alleged author of *De legibus et consuetudinibus Angliae* (ca. 1220s–1250s), a work most scholars now attribute to several authors rather than to a single individual, and not necessarily to Bracton, he too was a royal official who was university trained. Although his participation in the writing of *De legibus* is currently questioned, it is nevertheless clear that whoever authored this text was extremely familiar with Roman law. *De legibus* collected the norms of common law while constantly referencing Roman law in ways that echoed contemporary discussions in universities. Among other things, it appealed to *ius commune* categories and to Scholastics in order to lend coherence to the English records. This was done by drawing similarities and distinctions between different texts in order to demonstrate that they did not contradict each other. *De legibus* also emulated the order and divisions employed in the Justinian *Corpus Iuris Civilis,* and it cited numerous passages of it as well as canon law texts.

It is now believed that these two cases, particularly notorious, were not unique and that in the twelfth and thirteenth centuries common-law experts looked to and often adopted Roman law solutions much more frequently than we have imagined in the past. It is also clear, though, that beginning in the fourteenth century, successive English monarchs began appointing to the bench laymen with no university training. Instead of preferring jurists, as has been the case before, the main qualification of royal judges was now that they were obedient servants. Because by that time great practical knowledge was required to discern, for example, which writ was appropriate to which case and how it functioned, eventually most royal judges were selected from among the advocates working at the king's court.

By the fourteenth century not only royal judges needed a particular set of skills, mostly acquired by working at the courts; so did the parties who had to identify the correct writ, understand which procedural and evidentiary rules were associated with it, and know how to plead affectively. Adjudication in royal courts also required knowledge of French and Latin, as French remained the spoken language of the English royal courts, and Latin (alternating on occasion with French) its written language, until well into the early modern period.

The need for growing expertise led to the emergence of legal specialists. These included a variety of professionals such as procurators (who could stand for an absent party), barristers (who specialized in the actual pleading in the courts), and attorneys (who counseled clients). Barristers eventually organized themselves into guilds and began frequenting certain places. These places, identified as "the Inns," mostly began as residence halls but soon emerged also as spaces for socialization and training, where young apprentices heard and observed masters perform different tasks. There were four "Inns at Court" where barristers trained, and an Inn of Chancery, where aspiring attorneys watched how writs and other documents were drawn up. By the fourteenth and fifteenth centuries, most Inns also offered apprentices sessions of mock trials focusing on the process of obtaining evidence and following procedures, lessons in argumentation of the law ("moots"), and lectures ("readings"). Lectures required students to analyze written texts, mostly statutes. These texts were often accompanied by factual cases, which were meant to exemplify their meaning and extension. Moots were centered on watching courts in action and conducting exercises mainly focused on procedure, the selection of writs, and pleading.

How Common Law Functioned

The particular way common law functioned can be exemplified by observing how it developed the distinction between English subjects and foreigners. Most historians point to a pivotal ruling in which this distinction was clarified. In a decision known as "Calvin's Case," judges declared in 1608 that birth in a territory under allegiance to the monarch was the condition that rendered individuals English. Why the judges addressed this issue and how they reached their decision is a fascinating story that illuminates the complex procedures by which common law operates.

Calvin (whose true name was Robert Colville) was a Scot born after the ascension of King James of Scotland to the English throne (1603). The question the court had to answer was whether, having been born in Scotland after the union of the crowns, Calvin could be considered an English subject. The importance of answering this question was that, if declared English, Calvin would be entitled to inherit land in England, but if he was a foreigner, he would not. The answer the judges gave was positive because they reasoned that Calvin was born under allegiance to James. Allegiance, the judges stated, was owed to a physical person (James), not to a crown or a kingdom (the English crown or England). As a result, those born under allegiance to James in one kingdom were subject to his royal jurisdiction everywhere. Thus, a Scot born in Scotland under allegiance to James could be considered an English subject in England as long as James also reigned there.

Today we know that Calvin's case was a fabricated lawsuit. It was sponsored by a group of individuals who wanted to force a decision regarding the status of Scots. This question had preoccupied James after he ascended to the English throne. He appointed a commission that concluded that Scots should be treated as English subjects, and he insisted that such was legally the case. Yet the English Parliament refused to accept this solution. Because under common-law remedies created rights, the only way to unblock the situation was to bring a case in which, by giving a remedy, the judges would recognize a right, namely, the right of Scots to be treated as English subjects in England. For this to happen, those interested in obtaining this recognition had to find a person who was in need of remedy.

The person they found was a young child born in Scotland after the union. This child had inherited properties in England but his right to them was denied because, according to common law, foreigners could not inherit land in England. This child, who claimed to be a Scot in Scotland yet an English subject in England, thus had a reason to bring an action against those who refused him his rightful inheritance. For the court to grant him the requested remedy, it would have to recognize him as an English subject. This was precisely what happened. The court gave Calvin a remedy allowing him to inherit in England, thereby recognizing him as an English subject. Thereafter, Scots born after the union would be identified as such without the need for Parliament to acquiesce to that result.

This example makes it clear that even as late as 1608 basic questions such as who was an English subject and who a foreigner could be resolved in England not by a royal decree or a parliamentary act, but by appealing to the courts and requesting a remedy. But Calvin's case was also exemplary in other ways. The judges reviewing it tied the right to inherit in England to the status of English subject. According to them, only English subjects could inherit land in England; foreigners could not. But this rule too had developed because of the particular characteristics of common law: its unique insistence on the relations between remedy and right as well as on procedural requirements that were often tied to the specific writ that was employed.

Today we know that the distinction between those who could and could not inherit land in England probably had nothing to do with foreignness and that, initially, birth outside the kingdom did not make people alien. A question therefore arises: Why and how did the rule connecting land inheritance with foreignness and foreignness with foreign birth come about?

According to historians, the reason may have been procedural requirements. The common-law writ that regulated succession determined that, in order to inherit land, petitioners had to prove their genealogy by supplying local witnesses. In cases of petitioners born outside the jurisdiction of the court, the king could order the sheriff of their hometown to send a group of local men as witnesses. However, this solution was impossible when petitioners were born abroad. As a result, those born abroad were eligible to inherit land, but because of the particular procedural requirement tied to the writ regulating land inheritance, they faced real difficulties in proving their right to do so. Initially, whether they were or were not English was completely irrelevant. Nonetheless, over time, because of the tight connection in common law between remedy and right, the practical difficulty in proving genealogy (and therefore securing a remedy) was interpreted as inability to inherit (the absence of right). Thereafter, because there was no remedy (foreign-born individuals could not prove their genealogy and thus their right to inherit), there was no right. The circle was now closed: foreign-born individuals no longer had the right to inherit land in England, and those who could not inherit because born abroad were identified as foreigners.

The Backlash

The proliferation of writs and the growing presence of royal jurisdiction were not always appreciated by the lords and barons who saw their powers and privileges diminish. Protests against this state of affairs led to a rebellion that ended with the adoption of the Magna Carta (1215).[13] Contrary to what is commonly believed, the Magna Carta sought to guarantee mainly the privileges of the barons and freemen, not the rights of all Englishmen. It was concerned with ensuring feudal control over land and feudal inheritance, which legal developments in the late twelfth and early thirteenth centuries seriously threatened.

Because the Magna Carta failed to resolve these issues, King Henry III (r. 1216–1272), under renewed pressure from the barons who again rebelled, in 1258 ordered his officials to halt the creation of new writs. In 1285 his son, King Edward I, made a similar promise that no new royal courts would be established and none would extend its jurisdiction to new subject matters.

Because the pressure to extend royal jurisdiction continued and litigants persevered in requesting royal intervention, in the late fourteenth century a new system came into being. Its creation was justified by the argument that although no new common law writs were to be established, the monarch still had to attend to special circumstances that justified his attention. Royal conscience, it was alleged, could be discharged only if the king did what he ought to do, that is, defend the weak and dispense justice. To comply with this duty, presented as a moral obligation, the king would institute new procedures. In exceptional cases, because justice so required, he would allow his chancellor to hear litigants and grant them an extraordinary remedy if existing common-law writs supplied none.

As a result of these developments, litigants who could use writs already recognized by the Chancery took their cases to the ordinary royal courts (common-law courts). Those who could not find an appropriate solution in the registry of writs addressed the Chancery and requested its extraordinary intervention.

This development introduced a new system of conflict resolution. This system was distinguished from common law because its operation, at least initially, was divergent. While by that stage (the fourteenth century) common-law courts were routinely open to all those who could find an appropriate writ in the registry of writs, the new system gave remedies only in exceptional cases and it had no preset list of causes of action.

This new system, emerging in the fourteenth century, was called "equity," and the court that adjudicated these extraordinary remedies was identified as the Chancery court. Meant to deal with exceptional situations, equity was intentionally fashioned as a flexible system with fluidly defined rules. It depended on the discretionary powers of the chancellor, who was empowered by the king to solve difficult cases in which common law supplied no appropriate solution. This, however, did not mean that equity was a completely arbitrary system. Initially most Chancery officials were university trained and many of them were ecclesiastics. As a result, they frequently, directly or implicitly, adopted the criteria, doctrines, and procedure of canon and Roman law.

In the fourteenth and fifteenth centuries, equity was where the most exciting legal developments took place. Filling the vacuum left by the institutionalization of common law, equity fostered the creation of new instruments. Among them was the issuing of injunctions—remedies that forbade the defendant from taking certain actions otherwise allowed. Equity courts also elaborated means to enforce judicial decisions, for example, by way of sequestration, authorizing the interested party to seize the properties of the opponent who refused to obey a court order. Another important remedy created by the Chancery court was the prohibition of enforcing unreasonable, even if legal, contracts. Equity also developed important new areas such as trust, mortgages, guardianship, bankruptcy, commercial partnership, and corporations, and included doctrines defining honest mistakes as well as fraud.

Despite its original malleability, over time equity also became more institutionalized and more rigid. As with common-law writs, it evolved into a system of permanent solutions. These solutions would find their way into lists of (equity) remedies that the parties could invoke. By the late fifteenth century, equity thus clearly evolved into a second system of royal adjudication that ran parallel to the older system of common law, often interacting and influencing it and vice versa. Thereafter, equity and common law began integrating. This happened in part because individuals trained in common law became chancellors; that was the case of Thomas More (1478–1535). But the integration of equity with common law was also the result of changes in the Chancery itself. By that time, rather than adopting ad hoc decisions justified as exceptional because meant to discharge royal conscience in particularly difficult situations, chancellors began applying the same principles of fairness to all similar cases. This tendency for repetition became the rule in the second half of the seventeenth century, when the principals of equity were formally systematized and classified. Thereafter, the royal conscience that equity guarded became civil and political rather than natural and internal.[14] No longer focused on discharging a subjective royal sense of right and wrong, it now aimed at guaranteeing an objective fairness and providing comparable solutions to similar conflicts.

Royal Legislation

Coinciding with the institutionalization of common law and the formation of equity, English monarchs proceeded to legislate. From as early as the reign of Henry II and throughout the Middle Ages and the early modern period, successive kings intervened in the legal order by enacting important statutes touching upon a diversity of subjects. In the Assize of Clarendon (1166), Henry II modified criminal procedure, instructing that all criminal accusations were to be made by a jury of twelve men (presentment). The assize also established that criminal jurisdiction would be in royal hands as would be the execution of convicted felons.

Equally famous were the statutes of Edward I that made trial by jury compulsory in criminal cases, extended the scope of actions for damages, and modified various aspects of land regimes. Several edicts by Henry VIII, such as the Statute of Uses (1536), which regulated ownership and taxation, and the Statute of Wills (1540), which allowed owners to determine who would inherit their land, were of importance for property law. The Statute of Frauds (1677) conditioned the validity of certain legal transactions in real estate on these transactions being recorded in writing and the documents being appropriately signed.

From the late thirteenth and fourteenth centuries, Parliament, which had begun as an advisory council and a court, began acquiring additional powers. Among them was the hearing and presentation of petitions that sought to address questions of legal, economic, political, or administrative nature. The king's response to these petitions was considered a legislative act, most particularly when it included instructions regarding applicability in the future. By the mid-fourteenth century, a substantive amount of royal legislation was enacted in this way. Although initiated by Parliament and often almost automatically granted, the power to enact remained exclusively at the hands of the king.

Historians have long debated the importance of royal enactments. Some suggest that because royal courts habitually assumed that royal legislation could not contradict existing arrangements, they took great liberty in interpreting it, on occasion even making exceptions to it, expanding its instructions, or, on the contrary, ignoring them altogether. These observers also conclude that common law was superior to royal legislation because legislation mainly repeated rather than changed existing norms, and statutes were not very numerous if compared to the quantity and importance of other legal sources. As a result, even if statutory law was important, it was responsible only for a small fraction of the growth of law, and it mainly functioned in particular areas of law such as criminal law or real property, but not others.

Other scholars point out that even as early as the thirteenth century judges habitually discussed what the statutes prescribed. They suggest that lawyers training in the Inns of Court were taught to comment on royal legislation and that statute books were copied for their use. Some even argue that the study of statutes was the centerpiece in lawyer's education. If legislation was such a marginal component of the legal system, how could this be explained? Is it possible that our image of early common law was influenced too much by seventeenth-century developments that sought to decenter the king and make this law customary?

Was England Exceptional?

The system we now recognize as common law thus consisted of a collection of remedies and procedures for settling disputes that developed as a result of the growing preeminence of royal jurisdiction. It was based on the belief that royal courts would be more just or more efficient than feudal or local courts, and it was enabled by the success of English monarchs in central-izing the administration of justice and affirming their superiority vis-à-vis both lords and local communities. Although gradually triumphant, until the seventeenth century (if not later) common-law courts nevertheless competed with local, feudal, and ecclesiastical courts, which continued to exist, as well as with the Chancery court, which developed a system of its own (equity). Was the situation in Continental Europe dramatically different?

Historians who concluded that England was exceptional tended to con-centrate on the impermeability of its legal system to the influence of Roman law. They argue that, although spreading throughout Europe, *ius commune* failed to penetrate England, at least to the extent to which it influenced other European countries. They suggest that such was the case because, contrary to other European monarchs, the Normans who controlled England had no reason to permit, let alone encourage, the penetration of the new legal method into the realm. According to these narratives, *ius commune* was unnecessary in England because by the time it became available, the English already had a new, modern, centralized, and efficient legal system that, contrary to those operating elsewhere in Europe, needed no improvement. Hence, while the authorities and inhabitants of other European territories looked to *ius commune* for inspiration and perfection, no such thing happened in England.

This narrative dominated much of the scholarship for many centuries, but it has been criticized since by historians who point out that during the Middle Ages no modern, centralized, or efficient English system ever existed. During this period, the English normative order was divided among royal, feudal, and local courts, and it contained rules originating in Roman, canon, Germanic, feudal, and local law. Royal courts adjudicating according to common law included only a small number of judges, and until the eighteenth century the number of cases they saw was relatively small, if compared to the quantity and importance of cases adjudicated by other courts.

Furthermore, in the last two to three decades historians have also stressed that common law was developed by a French dynasty that used the services and advice of Roman and canon law jurists in order to ensure the supremacy of royal jurisdiction. These jurists, whose work was essential in the formative period of common law, employed *ius commune* terminology, concepts, and methodology. In some areas, such as guardianship and defamation, common law was highly influenced by the work of ecclesiastical courts, and even as late as the fifteenth century allowed Roman jurists to plead. It is also possible that common-law judges might have continued to consider Roman law as an important point of reference even as late as the eighteenth and nineteenth centuries, most particularly when they searched for new insights or desired to create or clarify categories. As far as they were concerned, Roman law was not binding, but it included a collective wisdom that was worthwhile considering, even adopting. During the same period, lawyers and judges might have used Roman law as a means to better comprehend common law in ways that were not vastly different from how Continental jurists used it to solidify and support their own *ius proprium*.

It is also clear that by fostering royal courts and developing procedures that sanctioned their activities, English monarchs sought to achieve what most of their European peers also desired, namely, affirmation of royal superiority vis-à-vis (mainly) feudal lords. The way they justified the extension of royal jurisdiction, by appealing to their obligation to guarantee peace, was not radically different from what happened elsewhere in Europe, where other monarchs also referred to their duty to ensure concord. Yet, while the Norman monarchs proceeded to create their own courts, other monarchs used *ius commune* for the same purpose. They believed that because of its combination of Roman and canon law it was sufficiently universal to assist them in solving conflicts among communities whose laws were radically distinct. The penetration of *ius commune* to the territories we now identify as Germany, for example, is currently interpreted as the result of the urgent need felt by emperors for coordination and peacemaking among rival German polities.

If all of the above is true, then England diverged from Europe only gradually. Divergence may have become particularly noticeable in the fourteenth and fifteenth centuries, which was when the English monarchs at last succeeded in efficiently extending their royal jurisdiction throughout the realm. Also determinant was the fact that by that stage most monarchs had ceased appointing clerics and jurists to their courts and instead selected laymen who were no longer trained in Roman or canon law. With the absence of university-trained personnel and the preference for practical training mostly acquired by pleading before the king's court, common law (though not equity) gradually parted from the rest of Europe.

Adding to the distance that gradually appeared between England and the Continent was the growing prominence in thirteenth- and fourteenth-century England of lay juries. Juries began as assemblies of local men who answered collectively under oath to questions asked by royal officials. Used in the eleventh and twelfth centuries mostly as a means to collect information locally, in the thirteenth century their employment greatly expanded. During this period, juries were introduced in England in both civil and criminal litigation as a means for fact-finding when other mechanisms, such as oath taking, trial by battle, or ordeal, became unavailable or were considered untrustworthy. Initially testifying on knowledge they already possessed as members of the local society, by the fifteenth century jurors could also consider other types of information that was brought to their attention.

Although juries also existed in the Continent and their tasks were similar—to collectively testify to local circumstances—after the Continent moved to adopt the inquisitorial process in the thirteenth century, identifying the relevant facts and deciding the case was reserved to judges, not juries. Eventually these distinct paths would lead the English and the Continental systems in different directions. In Continental Europe, judges would be charged with the implementation of justice and, in criminal cases, would decide whether to investigate, whether to bring the suspect to trial, whether the proofs were sufficient, and what a just resolution would be. In England judges would oversee procedure, yet juries would decide whether to prosecute, which were the fact of the matter, and whether a conviction should follow. Though less notorious, in civil cases the same distinction between a judge charged with ensuring justice (the Continent), and a judge that oversaw procedure (mainly pleading) and delegated decision making in juries (England), held true.

These differences, however, did not imply that the system that emerged in England was completely new. Many historians point, for example, to the striking similarities between common and ancient Roman law. They suggest that in both places conflict resolution and the courts were at the center of the legal system. In both places, trials were conceptually divided between a first stage, in which the debated question between the parties was framed (before a praetor in Rome, and during pleading before a judge in England), and a second stage, in which nonprofessionals (*iudex* in Rome, jurors in England) evaluated the facts of the matter and rendered judgment. In both places, by granting remedies, praetors in Rome and the king's officials in England, created rights. These remedies—which took the form of writs in England, formulas in Rome—were initially ad hoc solutions to particular problems but, over time, praetors and officials tended to repeat them. Repetition eventually led to the creation of a closed list of remedies, which in Rome found expression in edicts elaborated by praetors and in England in a public registry of writs. After formulas and writs fossilized, legal creation was channeled through other means: jurisprudence and legislation in Rome, legislation and equity in England.[15]

As a result, despite what is commonly assumed, *ius commune* and common law were perhaps not twins, but they were certainly siblings. As one historian put it, taking into account the "basic principles, organizing ideas, techniques of argumentation, and habits of thought," one "might want to call the common law simply a variant, admittedly an eccentric variant, of the multitude of legal systems that ultimately derived from *ius commune.*"[16] Said differently, Norman monarchs might have been successful at promoting their own jurisdiction in unprecedented ways, but the legal system they instituted was heir to a European past and engaged in their European present. As will be argued in Chapter 8, if England seriously parted ways from Europe, this may have happened not during the Middle Ages but instead during the sixteenth and seventeenth centuries, when common law was reinvented by legal experts who sought to curb royal ambitions.

PART FOUR

The Early Modern Period

7

Crisis and Reaffirmation of *Ius Commune*

THE PREMISE OF *ius commune* was the existence of a single community, Christian and Roman, identified as Latin Christendom. In the twelfth and thirteenth centuries when *ius commune* came into being, this community was Catholic, that is, it sustained the fiction that its tenets included that which has been believed always, everywhere, by everybody.[1] Heirs to the Roman Empire, and upholding its traditions, the members of this community shared submission to a single central authority (the pope), a common Roman and Germanic heritage, and, with the emergence of *ius commune,* also a single overreaching legal system that harmonized to some degree the enormous differences between the normative order of one place and the next. Despite internal divisions and extreme localism, which often led European Christians to confront one another bitterly, as far as contemporaries were concerned, they all lived in a single *ecumene*—a common inhabited world.

These convictions came under pressure in the fifteenth and sixteenth centuries. Political divisions in Europe grew stronger as monarchs gradually affirmed their supremacy vis-à-vis both local lords and universal powers such as the pope and the German emperors. These monarchs strove to control territories they now defined as kingdoms and fought to establish themselves as sovereigns—that is, superior—not only with respect to other authorities, but also with respect to the law. These processes became particularly acute in the sixteenth century with the coming of the Protestant Reformation and the secession of a great variety of reformed denominations from the Catholic Church. With political and religious fragmentation, it was only natural that the idea of a common European / Christian law would also come under attack.

Legal Humanists and the Contextualization of Roman Law

Although political and religious strife in Europe justified growing disbelief in the shared heritage of a community that was once thought to be united culturally, religiously, and (to some degree) politically and legally, the first signs of fissure were intellectual, and they found expression in a current of thought we now identify as humanism.

A product of the Renaissance, humanism was an intellectual, political, and artistic movement that began in Italy in the fourteenth century and soon spread throughout most of Europe. The Renaissance glorified antiquity but it also sought to place man at the center of its attention. Those scholars who shifted their focus from law, medicine, and theology to the study of the arts (grammar, logic, arithmetic, geometry, music, astronomy, and rhetoric) became known as humanists. Some among them embarked on philological studies and devoted themselves to the vernacular languages of Europe. Others were interested in history and material culture. They developed a taste for antiquarianism and surveyed how techniques, preferences, and meanings changed over time and according to location. Human experience, humanists insisted, was always circumscribed by the period and place in which it transpired, and an understanding of it could never be disconnected from the where, when, and how.

These beliefs, which questioned both the unity and the permanence of culture, placed humanists in a perfect position to stress differences and disjunctions across Europe. They encouraged them to appreciate the particular practices they observed around them and to insist not on commonalities but instead on divergences.

Applied to the study of law, these beliefs led humanists to criticize *ius commune* scholars for disregarding context and employing no historical perspective. University-trained jurists, humanists argued, abused rather than used Roman law. They employed it to solve present-day conflicts but had not attempted to understand it properly. Criticizing this treatment, humanists insisted that law was always a product of the particular circumstances of the society that created it. To understand what it instructed, it was vital to historicize the law (to study change over time) as well as to contextualize it (to study it in context).

While criticizing jurists for failing to account for how society and language had changed since Roman times, humanists also censored them for misunderstanding the nature of the legal sources they analyzed. *Ius commune* jurists were mostly interested in harmonizing different pieces of Roman law. Their methodology, Scholasticism, was based on the assumption that these sources were coherent rather than contradictory. Even though this method had proved useful to the development of *ius commune,* humanists insisted that it was nevertheless very wrong. The *Corpus Iuris Civilis* that *ius commune* jurists studied, and most particularly the *Digest,* which included the opinions of Roman jurists, in fact comprised a wide, almost accidental, array of fragments. Written by different people at different points in time, these fragments were not consistent. Instead, each obeyed the logic of its time, place, and authors, and the different fragments often contradicted one another.

Humanists therefore argued that the basic methodological assumptions of *ius commune* jurists could no longer hold water. To truly understand Roman law, what jurists needed to do was historicize and contextualize it. They would have to account for the differences between Rome and their society and consider Roman law as a historical phenomenon that had undergone constant changes and mutations. This would require that jurists divide Roman law into several periods and distinguish the different places in which the various fragments were produced and the identity of their authors. Jurists would also need to acknowledge the existence of multiple schools of thought and the presence of contradictory solutions.

The Emergence of a French Method of Law

Historians have long debated whether humanists' criticism made a difference. Those who suggested that it did point to the emergence of a new legal method. Identified as *mos gallicus* (the French manner) to distinguish it from the existing method (now baptized as the *mos italicus,* the Italian manner), this new method was practiced mostly by French legal humanists.[2] These humanists adopted a historical and philological approach to Roman law. Not unlike eleventh-century jurists, they began by reconstructing the texts they wished to study. Seeking to purge existing versions of the many errors they allegedly contained, they published critical editions and tried to eliminate or at least discredit defective copies. Some humanists even reorganized the Roman compilations that eleventh-century jurists had composed, reordering them according to genealogy rather than subject matter.

After humanists were satisfied that they had reconstructed an accurate body of Roman law, they proceeded to study these revised texts. Applying a new approach, they made contradictions consequential—because they believed that they encapsulated disagreements, proved the development and change of law over time, and showcased regional differences. Presenting their work as an archeology of sorts, humanists labored to rediscover what Roman law instructed at each given moment. They dug under centuries of accumulated juridical exegesis that, according to them, obscured rather than clarified what this law was. Contextualizing Roman texts, determining the original meaning of terms, inquiring how they had changed over time, and considering each fragment separately, humanists thus strove, not to reconstruct a coherent message (as eleventh- and twelfth-century jurists did), but to discover an evolving and living normative world.

Legal humanists relied on a close reading of texts, but they also applied their knowledge of the past to their analysis. They read nonlegal sources and integrated into their understanding the study of material culture and material remains. Humanists also considered Greek texts that predated Roman law, as well as Byzantine legal sources. Mostly applying their energy to Roman law, some studied feudal and canon law. Their work ended up portraying much of medieval jurisprudence as being a gross misinterpretation because those who elaborated it were ignorant of classical culture, dismissed change over time, and adopted the false assumption that law was always homogeneous and wise.

The Protestant Reformation

The propositions advanced by legal humanists would eventually find their widest implications with the coming of the Protestant Reformation. Standard narrative suggests that the Reformation began in 1517 when Martin Luther published his ninety-five theses against indulgences (reduction of time in purgatory in exchange for payment of fees). Luther was neither the first nor the last to criticize this practice, but his claims unleashed massive reform and counter-reform movements within Christianity. Regardless of why his particular protest became powerful enough to divide Christians into Catholics and Protestants, a question historians still debate, from a legal-history point of view the Reformation was an important point of rupture. First and foremost, it made people ask whether a single community of belief indeed existed in Europe and whether this community could be administered by a single shared *ius commune.* By the mid-sixteenth century the answer was mostly negative. Following this conclusion, the new religious denominations (now identified as Protestant) began elaborating their own laws. No longer was there a common canon law, and by implication it was unclear that *ius commune* could survive this crisis.

The Reformation also had indirect implications for whether law could guide Christians, and if so, which law. The Reformed denominations of course believed in a lawgiving God, but in most Reformed churches salvation became an individual affair that did not require legal mediation. Jurists were enemies of Christ rather than his helpers, and law should not mediate between a believer and his faith. It was the task of secular, not ecclesiastical, authorities to elaborate sanctions that would deter sinners and guide the righteous. At any rate, faith, as Martin Luther argued in his famous essay "On Christian Liberty" (1520), depended on God's grace, not on a blind, mechanical obedience to legal precepts. Because the Scriptures contained everything Christians needed to know, all that was required to obey God's will was to translate the Bible into the vernacular and ensure that each household had a copy.

The Reformation thus proposed interpretations that could potentially affect the normative world. It negated the existence of a single community of believers in Europe and the possibility that all Christians would share a single canon. It also decentered the normative system altogether by arguing that neither law nor legal experts were required to guide Christians to salvation. Politically the Reformation brought about a division between Catholics and Protestants and among the various Protestant denominations. Rupture led to a century of religious wars, which sometimes focused on doctrinal disagreements but also were fought to obtain economic, political, and social goals. Characterized by extreme violence, these wars, which divided families, cities, regions, and kingdoms, further diminished the belief in a unified Christian *ecumene.*

The Combined Effect of Humanism and Reformation

The combination of humanism and the Reformation was extremely subversive. *Ius commune* depended on religious unity, now broken, and it was also tied to the prestige of Rome. It had an authoritative appeal because it was a useful instrument for solving disputes and harmonizing the distinct laws of Europe, but also because it was backed by the Church and was said to have originated in an exalted past. If the backing of the Church no longer mattered because many believers no longer followed its teachings, and if medieval jurists had erred and their method was a distortion of the truth, then the status of *ius commune* had to be questioned, too.

Although this subversive potential was not apparent everywhere—protestant Germany and the Netherlands, for example, continued to adhere to and even enhanced their dependence on Roman law[3]—it is not surprising that in the mid-sixteenth century a particularly virulent strand of legal humanism became associated with the Reformation. While Church reformers disputed the authority of the pope and advocated a return to an early (and thus more authentic, according to them) Christianity, legal humanists argued the same with regard to law. They wished to free themselves of the work produced by generations of jurists and instead revert to a so-called genuine Roman law. Both Reformed ministers and legal humanists insisted that this return to an early yet authentic past could be achieved by better understanding the texts that survived from antiquity. John Calvin's commentaries on the Bible (1540–1557) demonstrated this point. Calvin was greatly influenced by his years as a law student in universities that ascribed to *mos gallicus*. It was as a law student that he first formed his vision of the differences between present and past, as well as his ideas regarding how the Scriptures should be read and interpreted as a result.

Reimagining Local Laws

While many legal humanists challenged the established religious and legal canon, some also extended their criticism to the political sphere. They mostly reacted against the growing assertion of supreme power by kings and their gradual claims for sovereignty. In France, the stronghold of *mos gallicus,* opposition to the extension of royal sovereignty led some legal humanists to turn their attention to local law. According to their claims, if it was correct to assume that all laws were products of the society that created them, then France must have an authentic law distinct both from the law in other areas of Europe and from *ius commune.*

Following these convictions, French humanists proceeded to imagine what this particular French law was. They collected local laws and attempted to understand their commonalities and differences. The message they sought to convey was both legal and political. If there was an authentic law of the land, anchored in France's particular traditions, then this normative order was superior to all others, including royal mandates, and all inhabitants of the kingdom, including the king, must obey it.

In trying to affirm the specificity of French law, humanists also turned their attention to feudal law. There they found elements that were surprisingly useful for advancing their political and religious agendas. Most important among them was the idea that relations between lords and vassals depended on a pact. This pact was perhaps established between two radically unequal partners, but it nevertheless included mutual obligations. Because political subjection was based on a pact, it was possible to claim that monarchs who did not fulfill their end of the pact were tyrants and could be legitimately resisted and replaced. This theory would eventually become a radical philosophy validating both resistance and revolution. Among other things, it would justify, in seventeenth-century England and eighteenth-century France, the execution of kings.

The Customs of France

The work of the French Protestant legal humanist François Hotman (1524–1590) was emblematic of these currents of thought. Hotman studied at the University of Orléans and taught Roman law in Paris. After a period of exile in Geneva and Lausanne, he returned to France, where he continued to teach Roman law. Throughout his career Hotman harbored the idea of writing down the laws particular to France. Identifying these laws as "customary," he insisted that they were Germanic rather than Roman in origin.

In one of his most famous essays, titled *Anti-Tribonian* (1567), Hotman argued in favor of purging French law of the influence of both canon and Roman law, which he considered foreign elements. Also advocating educational reform, he criticized universities' monopoly over juridical training and suggested that, rather than teaching Roman law, university professors should impart classes on French law. Hotman also firmly believed that the notion of uncovering Roman law by studying the *Corpus Iuris Civilis* was ridiculous. The *Corpus* was enacted late (in the sixth century) and on the periphery (in the Eastern empire). It was therefore hardly indicative of what Roman law was genuinely like.

In his later work, such as *Francogallia* (1573), Hotman further advanced these ideas. Striving to uncover the origins of French institutions, he concluded that they pointed to the existence of a political pact that was particular to that country. This pact, he argued, delegitimized royal claims for absolutism.

Instead it guaranteed the continuation of several liberties that Frankish subjects enjoyed before the establishment of the monarchy. Because the pact between kings and subjects was anchored in customary law, monarchs could not violate it by citing Roman law, because the only legitimate frame of reference in France was local, French law.

How Customs Obtained This Status

Legal humanists such as Hotman were not the first scholars to understand the potential power of customs. As described in Chapter 1, after the extension of Roman citizenship (and thus law) throughout the empire, Roman jurists allowed the previous native legal systems to persist by reclassifying and recognizing them as permissible "local customs." Yet it was under *ius commune* jurists that customs found their new prominence. From as early as the twelfth and thirteenth centuries, these jurists engaged in transforming local norms from oral and flexible to written and formal. Eventually, in the fourteenth, fifteenth, and sixteenth centuries, campaigns to verify, clarify, consolidate, and write down the laws particular to villages, towns, regions, and kingdoms swept through large parts of Europe. In theory these campaigns were meant to register the law that already existed. In practice, they greatly modified it.

The processes introducing these changes were extremely slow. In the early Middle Ages, village assemblies or jurors (witnesses under oath) decided how conflicts would be resolved. Although most historians agree that their decisions must have hinged on a particular understanding of what was right and what was wrong, what was possible and what not, discussions rarely invoked abstract principles or rules. From the little evidence we have, it seems that most decisions either were adopted after some negotiation between community members or were imposed by powerful individuals in pursuit of their own interests. There is no indication in the record that they replicated earlier decisions or made reference to preexisting norms.

While this was the original character of local law, from the thirteenth century onward, mainly through the work of *ius commune* jurists, this law was subjected to a profound transformation. Arguing that local decision-making depended on "customs," that is, on practices that had existed in the community long enough to have become prescriptive, jurists now stated that village assemblies or juries that ruled on how conflicts should be resolved did not create the law. Instead, they only discovered and then applied the norms that already existed within the community prior to the conflict. According to this vision, local law was not the product of negotiated solutions to particular problems that were reached when necessary, but instead it was made of a series of norms (customs) that had evolved in the community over time.

This interpretation changed the essence of what village assemblies and juries did. Rather than searching to adopt a practical compromise that would preserve the peace as has been the case in the High Middle Ages, these assemblies were now reimagined as bodies responsible for identifying and applying preexisting norms. From the fourteenth century onward, instead of asking what the correct solution to a particular case should be, or whether the solution was just or consensual, jurists observing or advising village assemblies began inquiring what their customs mandated. They asked whether the jurors or the members of the assembly were sufficiently familiar with communal arrangements and whether their telling of these arrangements was true and accurate. To decide on such issues, jurists considered the statements collected from different people and, contrasting one with the other, they reached a conclusion regarding what the local customs "truly" prescribed. The law that they searched for was a stable, old, and permanent law, which they believed was part of communal heritage, even communal property. This law contained privileges that belonged to all communal members.

Following their conviction that local law represented enduring, even immemorial, customs, jurists began formalizing this law by using increasingly abstract and general categories. They systematized a wide range of solutions and began arguing that these solutions had always existed in precisely the same manner. The aim was to distill a local law that could exist independently of the circumstances of the case and time and that could fit any number of similar situations. The road from abstraction to centralization was swift but meaningful. By the late fourteenth and fifteenth centuries, the geographical projection of certain norms, now identified as customary, was expanded from a single locality to entire regions.

The influence of *ius commune* jurists on these developments was substantial, but equally important was the emergence of royal bureaucracies and the redefinition of relations between local and central powers. As smaller units such as villages became integrated into larger polities such as kingdoms, the identification of what these smaller units consisted of, and what were the privileges of their inhabitants, became matters of concern. It was now necessary for locals to obtain recognition of what they thought were their traditions and for central powers to know what the limitations on their freedom to act would be. As a result of these requirements, policies were devised to identify and register the local normative order, sometimes in order to conserve it, sometimes in order to change it. Efforts were also invested in facilitating the work of royal and regional governments by standardizing customs and expanding their reach, in order to diminish the complexity of a legal system in which each village had its own practices and norms.

If politics mattered, so did the availability of jurists and of new techniques of recording, mainly, the passage from orality to written forms. But if customs seemed to vindicate the importance of a popular law, created without the intervention of jurists or kings, they also paradoxically testified to the powerful presence of *ius commune*. Although German historians once argued that Germanic territories turned to Roman law only in the fifteenth and sixteenth centuries, a period they identified as "the Reception," and explained this reception by suggesting that Germanic customary law was far too chaotic and fragmented to be useful, it is now clear that many Germanic territories were deeply influenced by *ius commune* long before the sixteenth century. In the fourteenth and fifteenth centuries, *ius commune* jurists indeed collaborated in the formation and formalization of Germanic customary law, which scholars no longer believe was the expression of popular wisdom. Rather than two regimes in opposition, in the late medieval period, in Germany and elsewhere, customary law and *ius commune* merged together as *ius commune* jurists labored to collect, register, but also change and modify the local law. This legacy of collaboration would again become crucial in the nineteenth century, when German jurists codifying their laws would turn to Roman law in order to develop mechanisms that would allow them to comprehend and describe the so-called customary law of the various German states and territories (see Chapter 12).

Monarchies and the Writing Down of Customs

Although the writing down of customs was common across Europe, the French tradition from which Hotman emerged was particularly emblematic of such processes. From as early as the thirteenth and fourteenth centuries, several French jurists drew up compilations of local law. Written in the vernacular, though structured by reference to the Roman *Corpus Iuris Civilis,* these compilations were widely followed. In the fifteenth and sixteenth centuries, French royal authorities began fostering these processes by initiating campaigns to write down the customary law. Organized regionally, these campaigns called for a meeting of the representatives of the three estates (noblemen, ecclesiastics, and commoners) with royal commissioners and lawyers. These assemblies were to agree on what the local customs were and prepare written texts that enumerated and explained them. As a result of these projects, by the late sixteenth century much of French customary law had been written down.

The writing down of French customary law allowed experts to imagine the country as a territory divided between *pays de droit écrit* (areas of written law), which allegedly followed Roman law, and *pays de droit coutumier* (customary law), which did not because their legal order was said to be customary. Yet, considering how customs were written down, it becomes evident that this opposition between customary and Roman, oral and written, was mostly rhetorical. Among other things, although the customary laws of France were said to have been created in a distant past, records demonstrate that such was not the case. Commissions charged with identifying customary law in the sixteenth century left ample evidence proving that their members mostly negotiated with one another and with locals. Rather than considering themselves recorders charged with locating and identifying existing norms, they sought to influence these norms by deciding what would be written down and how. By the end of this process, not only were customs invented anew—because, among other things, they were greatly influenced by the work of Roman law jurists who collected them—but also they were no longer oral.

If there was no reason to assume that some parts of France had an old authentic oral law while others did not, it was equally wrong to conclude that the French customary law stood in opposition to Roman law. As happened elsewhere, French jurists employed Roman law terminology, criteria, and doctrines to register customs. After customs were codified, they became subject to academic comment and interpretation by professional, university-trained jurists. Thus, even if one could ever imagine a pure custom untouched by Roman law, which would be extremely difficult, such a custom did not exist in France, at least not in the late medieval and early modern period.

A Last Word on the Political Utility of Customs

Hotman hoped that the writing down of customs would limit royal claims for sovereignty by producing norms that the king could not violate. But the French kings who encouraged these processes sought to achieve the contrary.

By reducing customs to written texts, these kings aspired to control the local normative order and indeed change it. Royal commissioners who engaged in this task understood what was at stake. They constantly imposed their opinion on locals as to how norms should be identified and written down, what should be added and what subtracted. Royal officials also favored the unification of various customary regimes and selected those customs that should be applicable everywhere in the kingdom. The writing down of customs, royal jurists hoped, would also stop their evolution by fixing them conclusively. No longer would customs change, no longer would negotiations be possible. Most importantly, the local norms that became royal law after they were written down would no longer depend on the community. Instead, they would obtain their validity and would be legitimized and obeyed because the king had so willed.

In the long run, rather than being an instrument for preservation, the writing down of customary law was a means to introduce change. It ushered in, not the preservation of communal privileges and liberties, as Hotman had wished, nor the permanence of orality, but the beginning of a new age that featured the growing intervention of kings in the normative order. In the aftermath of its official recording, local law would no longer depend on the community. It would instead be imposed on locals by outsiders who would tell them what their own customs dictated. Paradoxically, the one point on which both humanists and kings converged was the hope that customary law would replace *ius commune*. For Hotman this would be a means to return to a genuine French law and resist royal intervention in the normative order. For kings, this would be a way to augment their powers under the pretense that they conserved the ancient law rather than created a new one. But the hope that customs would replace *ius commune* were frustrated. Not only did *Ius commune* survive the fifteenth- and sixteenth-century crisis, but the writing down of customs manifested its hegemonic presence.

8

Crisis and Reinvention of Common Law

IN THE SIXTEENTH CENTURY, England experienced a particularly virulent period of religious, political, social, and economic strife. A confrontation with the papacy led to the creation of the Anglican Church. Because King Henry VIII had no male descendant, the country endured several succession crises, with various factions each supporting a different contender. Disagreement regarding the identity of the rightful heir entailed questioning not only who the correct successor was but also who had the authority to decide on such matters. The Reformation, which divided the English into Catholics and Protestants, also produced multiple Protestant denominations, and political struggles often became confessional rivalries and vice versa. In the seventeenth century these problems were accompanied by debates regarding the legal consequences of a union between Scotland and England (1603), mostly whether the ascension of a Scottish king to the English throne should bring about legal unification. It also required deciding how to react after the king, upon his coronation, declared that all ancient laws were *ipso facto* null and void. The king (James I) also determined that monarchs were above rather than under the law, and were accountable only to God. Rather than receiving their authority from the people, and rather than being bound to these people by some sort of pact for which they could be held accountable, they are divinely appointed.

Adding to this complex constellation, there was growing confrontation between the monarch and Parliament. Because in 1611 King James dismissed

Parliament, in the following years the struggle against James's pretensions was mostly channeled through the common-law courts, where Chief Justice Edward Coke, but also many others, believed that because kings were under rather than above the law, they, the judges, could censure their activities. The power struggle that ensued continued into the reign of James's son Charles. It led to the dismissal of various prominent judges (including Coke), the impeachment of others, and the abolishment of certain courts. It also produced tensions within the judicial system itself as common-law courts were seen as supporting Parliament, whose allegations they backed, whereas the equity judges were perceived as associated closely with the monarchy. Contrary to common-law justices, equity judges were mostly trained in Roman or canon law. Dispensing extraordinary remedies where common law was otherwise silent or inadequate, by definition they exercised a jurisdiction that enabled the extension of royal powers beyond the realm of common law.[1] These characteristics allowed many common-law lawyers and judges to view equity judges as allies of royal pretensions. They argued that equity judges followed a foreign legal system (Roman and canon law) that was dangerous, not only politically but also religiously and culturally. James's 1616 declaration, that whenever equity and common law conflicted, equity should prevail, did not improve these ailing relations.

Compounded with Scottish and Irish revolts and a foreign invasion, this entanglement produced a civil war, in which armies representing King Charles I clashed with those representing Parliament. In 1648, after a period of sheer anarchy, Parliament, accusing the king of breaking his pact with the people, convicted him of high treason and sentenced him to death. The monarch was executed in 1649, the monarchy and the House of Lords were abolished, and a republic (the Commonwealth of England) was instituted under the leadership of Parliament's military commander, Oliver Cromwell. The monarchy was restored in 1660 in the person of Charles's son, yet the relationship between the king and his subjects had changed forever.

Though the English civil war ended with victory for Parliament, the issues that haunted political and religious life before 1649 were not resolved. In 1688, in response to fears that a Catholic contender would inherit the crown, Parliament invited the Dutch Prince of Orange, William, who was married to Mary, the Protestant daughter of the king, to rule over the country. Accusing the monarch of abusing his powers, William set out for England and confronted King James militarily. Defeated on the battlefield, James left the country. Parliament declared the crown vacant and called upon William and Mary to occupy it. The invitation, however, was conditional. The terms under which the kingship of William and Mary would be accepted were detailed by Parliament. The 1689 document that came to be known as the Bill of Rights, listed, among other things, important checks on what the kings could do.

Historians look back to this period to explain the origin of a new modernity that was said to have emerged in England in the sixteenth and seventeenth centuries. They explain the ideologies, strategies, interests, cultures, and practices that justified this upheaval and trace the individuals and networks that were responsible for their genesis. In what follows, I ask which legal structures facilitated these developments and how law changed as a result.

Dissatisfaction with the Legal System

As we have seen, the emergence of common law in the twelfth and thirteenth centuries was a direct result of the development of a royal system of adjudication. The expansion of royal jurisdiction throughout the realm required the adoption of rules as to who could access royal courts, in which types of cases, and what the procedures would be. These rules were embodied in royal orders identified as writs that instructed royal officials to listen to certain litigants in certain ways. Although in theory royal officials were to implement a preexisting law, as writs multiplied they became an important tool for legal creation. The grant of remedy—the ability to sue in court—was thought to generate a right, and inversely, inability to find redress was understood to be denial of entitlement.

Growing exponentially during the twelfth and thirteenth centuries, this system of royal jurisdiction we now identify as common law came under pressure in the fourteenth century. Fierce opposition by barons and feudal lords to the continuous expansion of royal powers led successive monarchs to promise to halt the creation of new writs. Yet royal officials found it difficult to adapt available remedies to the requirements of a constantly evolving society. Pressure to reform the system led kings to authorize the Chancery to intervene in new cases (where writs did not exist) by giving exceptional remedies because justice so required. Royal legislation in the forms of statutes also intervened in the legal system, creating new rules and procedures.

The growing complexity of these legal arrangements, made of a great variety of legal sources, led some scholars to complain in the sixteenth and seventeenth centuries that the legal system was far too rigid. Others suggested that it was far too opaque. Existing remedies and procedures, they argued, were not obvious to the uninitiated and were often hard to understand even for trained professionals. The use of Latin and French instead of the vernacular English and the adoption of a particular style of annotation in the courts (identified as "court hand") made the work of judges particularly difficult to follow. Too many piecemeal changes were introduced without systematization. All this resulted in a legal system that was characterized by great uncertainty and was extremely expensive, inefficient, and often inaccessible to the point of being dysfunctional.

Contemporaries also complained about the coexistence of a multiplicity of dramatically different jurisdictions, courts, and normative systems on the island. Common law and equity were the systems followed by royal courts, but parallel to them were hundreds of feudal, ecclesiastic, and municipal courts, each obeying radically different rules, procedures, and norms. This multinormativity was considered normal in the Middle Ages, when the royal system of courts was first established. During this period, most lawyers, judges, and intellectuals believed it was advantageous because it allowed flexibility and correctly reflected the complexity of a society in which kings were considered superior to urban and feudal powers that nevertheless remained (almost) untouched. Yet, with the coming of modernity, the acceleration of economic activity, and growing immigration, many began insisting on putting some order into what was now perceived as chaotic. They suggested the need to rationalize the law, systematize accumulated knowledge, and clarify hierarchies between norms and jurisdictions with the aim of guaranteeing greater legal certainty and legibility.

Questioning Royal Justice

Although it was substantial, the criticism of the opacity, difficulty, and multinormativity of the legal situation initially did not strike at the heart of the common-law system. Most judges, lawyers and intellectuals suggested that some measure of reform would be sufficient to render the situation more tolerable. In the sixteenth and seventeenth centuries, however, a potentially far more dangerous element was added, namely, the growing criticism against the monarchy in the midst of an acute religious and political upheaval. This was a serious threat to common law, whose expansion during the twelfth, thirteenth, and fourteenth centuries was directly tied to the prestige of the monarchy. This expansion was based on the assumption that litigants would find justice more fair, impartial, and efficient in royal courts than in all other judicial and administrative instances. If royal jurisdiction grew during this formative period, it was because the king was willing to engage in dispensing justice and because he was asked to do so by his vassals. The more they turned to royal jurisdiction, bypassing feudal and urban courts, the faster writs were created, and the greater was the reach of common law.

In the sixteenth and seventeenth centuries, however, who the king (or queen) should be became a matter of debate. Growing discord regarding how to identify the legitimate claimant to the crown was accompanied by disagreement over whether the reigning monarch acted as he should, or whether he had abused his powers (a question asked with regard to both Charles I and James II). Also discussed were other essential questions such as whether kings were subject to the law or superior to it, and whether they could change the law or required the consent of Parliament. Conflicts between common-law and equity judges added to these tensions, as they brought royal officials into conflict with one another, allowing for interpretations that were often outright contradictory and that moved much of the political debate into the realm of the courts. Should common law, which had its own professionals and rules that mostly backed Parliament, prevail over equity—mostly manned by Roman and canon-law jurists who backed the king—or should the inverse be true? Could a king who was dissatisfied with the legal system overhaul, or even replace it? Would such a move be permissible or completely illegal? During the seventeenth century, the conclusion that the monarch was a tyrant led to the execution of one king (Charles I) and the removal of another (James II).

These developments questioned some of the basic assumptions regarding the superiority of royal justice. With the monarchy discredited, legal experts searched to rescue common law from its traditional dependence on the crown so that criticism against the monarch would not harm the reputation of the legal system. They also sought to subject equity to common law. In order to obtain these results, they set out to reinvent what common law was and why and how it was important.

Juridical Response to the Crisis

Responding to these pressures, in the sixteenth and seventeenth century legal experts adopted three measures to reform and safeguard common law. Although initially these measures were not consensual and proponents of their various parts did not agree about what they meant, in the long run they succeeded in winning acceptance and in changing contemporary (and posterior) views to an astonishing degree.

The first move was to distance common law from the king, arguing that, rather than being the product of royal intervention, this system was based on a customary law that predated the Norman Conquest. Although discovered by royal judges as they adjudicated conflicts and although commanded by the king, this law was created by the community and it reflected its ancient norms. The second move was to conclude that common law was the only significant system that had ever existed on the island, all other jurisdictions and courts—equity included—being inferior and subject to it. The third move affirmed that common law included rules that supported royal power but also limited what the king could do. Communal agreement to obey the king, legal experts maintained, was given only as long as he respected the customary privileges and rights of individuals and communities.

Together, these moves, which are explained in greater detail below, considerably changed the significance and substance of common law. Even though they required an extensive rewriting of English legal history, their success was so spectacular that by the eighteenth and nineteenth centuries their reinterpretation was no longer contested. By that time, legal experts both in England and abroad referred to common law as the only legal system of significance in England, and they determined that it reproduced a customary law that included constitutional arrangements.

Only in recent decades have historians begun challenging these conclusions. They question whether common law was customary, they point to the importance of the local, urban, feudal, and ecclesiastical jurisdictions that operated in England side by side with royal courts and the yet relative independence of equity, and they demonstrate the degree to which the constitutional arrangements that seventeenth-century authors vindicated were based on a restrictive and often misguided (yet always interested) reading of the past.

The First Move: Making Common Law Independent of the King

Awareness that political events in the sixteenth and seventeenth centuries potentially endangered the very basis of common law led English legal experts to propose a new, ingenious and, to some degree, self-interested reading of the English legal tradition. In accordance with the needs of the period, their aim was to make law independent of the king, place checks on royal activities, and position the judges of common law at the center of the political system. Although this reading included a fairly fictitious story that reversed the most basic understanding of what the law was, because of its enormous political utility and its intellectual sophistication it soon became the standard account of how common law emerged and what it included.

Mainly attributed to Edward Coke (1552–1634), although certainly beginning before him and continuing after, as well as shared by many of his contemporaries to some degree or the other, this new narrative suggested that common law was not created by the king through writ-giving. Instead, at the heart of this system was a customary law that predated the Norman invasion and the institutionalization of royal courts and writs in the twelfth and thirteenth centuries. Ancient to the degree that it was immemorial, that is, its beginning was no longer recalled, this customary law dominated the island before the Normans arrived. Anglo-Saxon (that is, Germanic) rather than Roman in origin, this customary law was recognized by the Normans, who in a series of successive confirmations promised to adhere to it. As with all customary laws, rather than having been imposed by kings, this law was created by the community; and rather than having been fashioned in royal courts, it was only discovered and then upheld by judges. Common law, in short, was not a Norman imposition. It was instead an authentic autochthonous law.

This reinvention of what common law was enabled the envisioning of a legal system that no longer depended on the king. According to this narrative, English monarchs and their judges had to obey this law not only because it was customary but also because they had constantly promised they would. Indeed, the seventeenth-century upheavals were a demonstration of what happened when kings suddenly refused to continue respecting this old, customary law and instead sought to introduce legal changes. Kings who violated customary agreements with their subjects were tyrants and deserved removal, even death.

The final aim of this new reinterpretation was not only to disassociate law from the king, arguing that he was not charged with its creation, but also to place common-law judges at the heart of the juridical system. According to this understanding, these judges were no longer royal servants who dispensed justice for the king by following his instructions (the writs). Instead, they were charged with identifying preexisting norms (customs) and applying them. They were a bastion both ensuring the survival of the authentic law of the land and resisting royal pressure to change it (when such royal pressure existed). Common-law judges were also members of an autonomous body that was perhaps administratively dependent on the king but that legally obeyed only the law.

To sustain this amazing transformation and create this fiction, Coke and other legal experts had to modify not only the character of common law but also their understanding of history. The argument that common law was a customary law that predated the arrival of the Normans required, among other things, rewriting the history of the Norman Conquest. In their effort to do so, these experts suggested that there was no real conquest, either because the Normans were (or could be seen as) legitimate heirs to the throne or because they never acted as true conquerors. Rather than abolish the rights of natives, as was customary in cases of conquest, the Normans were willing to submit to the existing normative order, acting as lawful heirs who continued rather than disrupted the normal state of affairs. Converting the Norman Conquest into a "non-event," these experts thus argued that from a legal point of view it marked no transformative moment. Legally, it was as if it had never happened, because it had not changed the basic tenets of English law.

In some odd way, this reinterpretation reiterated the assertions already made by the first Norman kings, who indeed suggested that their principal aim was to guarantee the continuation of the legal order. Yet it ignored the legal revolution that had taken place in England in the twelfth, thirteenth, and fourteenth centuries, indeed the birth of common law. It suggested instead that the institution of royal courts and the development of a system of writs featured a continuity with ancient times rather than introduced a profound change.

If negating the conquest upheld the antiquity as well as the continuity of common law, it was also a powerful argument against the ambitions of seventeenth-century monarchs. Upon his ascension to the English crown

(1603), James I of Scotland hoped to unify both kingdoms by imposing a new legal regime or at least substantially modifying the existing one. The response of English legal experts who opposed such measures was that even the Normans had not dared do that. Nor had the many rulers and kings who had successively invaded the island from Roman times until the Normans arrived. Instead, they preserved the existing law.

The new fiction, according to which common law was not a conglomerate of writs and court procedures followed by lawyers but instead a customary law that predated the arrival of the Normans, facilitated profound ideological transformations. Common law was no longer "common" because it was instituted by the king and applied equally to all his vassals or because it was created by the judges and lawyers working in common courts. Instead, it was "common" because it was said to have originated in the community. Like all other customary regimes, it emerged spontaneously from community members. Typical of them and representing their spirit, it was by necessity profoundly different from all other legal systems elsewhere. It represented not the will of a single individual (the king) but the experience and wisdom of many generations and was said to match perfectly the needs of society. This customary law was essentially oral because it was based on the way community members behaved and what they believed was normative.

Because it originated in Anglo-Saxon rather than Norman times, this law formed part of a Germanic rather than a Roman tradition. Created in the early Middle Ages long before the rebirth of Roman law in Europe (in the eleventh and twelfth centuries), it was (or should be) immune to the influence of canon law and Roman law, which were now presented as profoundly foreign. These characteristics explained Coke's rejection of suggestions to introduce parts of Roman law in England and the facility by which he could criticize the Chancery court, where experts of this now seemingly foreign law sat. Reimagining English law as Germanic allowed presenting common law as an instrument different from and capable of resisting papal power, mainly the encroachment of royal prerogative by the Church.

Although extremely radical, even revolutionary, when first proposed, these ideas nevertheless found ample support among legal experts. For example, William Blackstone (1723–1780), author of the *Commentaries on the Law of England* (1765–1769), the most popular legal manual in the eighteenth and nineteenth centuries, agreed with this analysis. He too swore by the hypothesis that common law was essentially made of unwritten customs that originated in Anglo-Saxon times, before the arrival of the Normans in the eleventh century. These customs, according to him, were "as old as the primitive Britons" and continued "unchanged and unadulterated." Blackstone also agreed that, despite conquests, invasions, and immigration by Romans, Saxons, Danes, and Normans, England never experienced "any formal exchange of one system of laws for another."[2] The identity of its inhabitants constantly changed, and so did their governments, but its laws persisted unaltered.

Paradoxically, historians suggest that despite belief in the orality of the law, Coke's reinterpretation of common law was particularly successful because it was published and circulated in written form. Coke used printing—mainly publishing reports on selected court cases—to advance his reform agenda. Deliberately addressing lawyers and hoping to contribute to both their knowledge of the law and their identity as a group, Coke supplied a set of rules and explained their reasoning in order to propagate among his readers the view that common law was both ancient and superior. His reports were extremely influential in the inns where lawyers met to discuss legal issues and among law students. They allowed Coke to transform his personal opinion into a public record of what the common law was. Through these publications he became an authority to such a degree that it seemed that "common law was what Sir Edward Coke said it was."[3]

In the seventeenth century, therefore, English legal experts elaborated a theory that allowed them to protect common law from the contemporary political upheaval or even use this upheaval to bolster its importance. Liberating this law from dependence on the king and his writs, these experts placed the courts at the center of the normative system because they believed that judges exercised the power to identify what it included. Thus, although law was made by the community in a slow, spontaneous, and hardly perceptible process that took centuries to complete, judges, now charged with implementing this law, became responsible not only for the discovery of this authentic customary normativity but also for its safekeeping.

This reinterpretation of what common law was also potentially solved another thorny issue that haunted many in England at the time, namely, what would happen to common law if the throne were vacant. The response was that perhaps the courts required a king, but law could exist independently of him and indeed had done so for many generations. By upholding these fictitious arguments and by propagating them, sixteenth- and seventeenth-century legal experts disguised a profound change under a mask of continuity, arguing that rather than innovating (as they have) they were simply restoring what the king had unjustly and illegally taken.

Questioning the First Move: Was Common Law Customary?

The easiest way to question whether common law was indeed customary is by examining how it emerged over time. This examination would clarify the essential role played by the monarch and his officials in the creation of writs and remedies. But beyond questions of genealogy that clearly tied common law to the king rather than to the community, it is clear that customary law the way English legal experts described it in the sixteenth and seventeenth centuries was a twelfth-, thirteenth-, and fourteenth-century invention. *Ius commune* jurists who were responsible for this invention (see Chapter 7) strove to systematize the legal order by suggesting that the wide array of local arrangements in Europe could be considered "customs." They portrayed this customary law as including principles that were repeatedly applied to a variety of cases by communal assemblies, which discovered rather than made them. According to this narrative, habits, which emerged spontaneously among community members, became customs when a sufficient number of individuals began considering them normative.

By the fourteenth, fifteenth, and sixteenth centuries, *ius commune* jurists began writing down the so-called customary laws of their communities with the aim of systematizing them. Eventually jurists suggested that the most important function of customary law was that it could be used as an instrument to resist royal jurisdiction. It could do so because it included constitutional arrangements that restricted what governments could do.

These claims by Continental jurists involved a fabulous recreation of what early medieval local law had been. If this law was dramatically different from how *ius commune* jurists described it, it was also radically distinct from how sixteenth- and seventeenth-century English lawyers imagined it. In both cases, the newly proposed understanding was driven by a similar aim: to control, even modify, the normative order. By appealing to customs, what jurists (and eventually rulers) sought to achieve was not to confirm the good old laws but to change them. This was true in both England and the Continent and, indeed, this interpretation that made law "customary" is likely to have appeared in the Continent first.

There is ample evidence, for example, that the Norman kings who invaded England followed these strategies that, under the guise of continuity, initiated a process of change. Most noteworthy in this regard were the "Laws of Edward the Confessor." These laws, which were said to reproduce the "laws of the land" in writing in order to preserve them, assert that in 1070 the Normans decided to write down the existing norms by asking a group of local jurors to declare what they included. Historians, however, conclude that this description of how this legislation came about was completely fictional. Instead of being the result of public participation, the Laws of Edward were probably authored in the twelfth century by a single jurist, contracted by the king. Despite claims to the contrary, their aim was not to guarantee continuity but to capture only those laws that favored the Normans. Glanvil's and Bracton's description of common law as customary might have responded to similar impulses.[4] Like their colleagues working on the Continent, whose juridical culture they shared, Glanvil and Bracton most probably perceived English law as "customary" not because it was created by the community—both Glanvil and Bracton clearly credited the king—but because it was shared among royal councilors and legal professionals. The customs they described, in short, were those created by the courts, not the community.

It is possible that the idea that common law was customary, in the sense that it was created by the community and predated the Norman Conquest, emerged in England in the mid-fifteenth century. It can be traced back to specific authors who suggested that the true *lex terrae* included the customs of the land.[5] From there to the conclusion that the English "had made their own laws out of their wisdom and experience" was a short but meaningful step.[6]

The Second Move: Making Common Law the Law of the Land

If common law had to change its nature to fit the narrative of continuous confirmations of a customary law, of equal importance to the theory proposed by seventeenth-century legal experts was the obligation to make common law the law of the land. This move required classifying canon, local, urban, and feudal law, even equity, either as inferior to common law or sufficiently influenced by it to form part of its system. Or it proposed that common law was authorized to oversee other jurisdictions. After all, it represented royal justice, and the king was superior to all other powers.

Thereafter, legal experts began arguing that common-law courts were the most important courts of the land and that common law itself was the most important legal system in existence. Coke referred to this point when, having admitted that more than one hundred courts existed in England, each responding to a different set of rules and principles, he nevertheless concluded that common law was the most important because it was "the law of the land" *(lex terrae)*. He might have meant that this was the only law common to the entire realm (which it was), but in the following years his words were credited with a new meaning—literally, that common law was the only law in the land.

This interpretation was followed by subsequent scholars. In the nineteenth century, Frederic William Maitland (1850–1906), a notable lawyer, professor, and legal historian, went so far as to conclude that by the end of the Middle Ages most feudal courts had adopted the procedures of royal courts, as well as borrowed substantive solutions from them. According to his understanding, by that time feudal courts were but mere local projections of a general common law. Reaching a somewhat similar conclusion, the English Ecclesiastical Courts Commission stated in 1883 that the work of ecclesiastical courts was "guided" but not "determined" by canon law. According to this version, as early as the fourteenth century kings and barons had subjected canon law to the "laws of England." As a result, since that period English customs had acted as a constitutional check of sorts, ensuring that canon law, now identified as a foreign law, would not penetrate the island if its instructions contradicted common law.

Questioning the Second Move: Was Common Law Superior?

The degree to which common law either was superior to or at least greatly influenced all other jurisdictions in England is currently under debate. Some historians conclude, for example, that most English peasants had no understanding of, need for, or access to royal courts, as they were mostly dependent on feudal jurisdictions and their particular normative order. These historians find no reason to assume that feudal courts were but mere local "clones" of common-law courts. Instead they suggest that these seigneurial instances, meant to regulate relations between lords and their vassals, were mainly geared toward keeping other powers out and therefore had absolutely no reason to emulate royal jurisdiction or allow royal norms and standards to affect the rulings of their judges. Local regulations often forbade using courts other than the feudal court, though some historians suggest that these prohibitions are evidence that people were doing just that.

Scholars also assert that if there was on occasion similarity between what feudal courts determined and what common law mandated, it could well be the case that, rather than one imitating the other, they responded to similar social, economic, and political constraints. Furthermore, judges in feudal courts sought to identify the most convenient and consensual solution to the specific problems they were called to resolve. Their rulings were not motivated by some preexisting system of rules, not even customs, but instead depended on place, parties, and time. There were hundreds of feudal courts in England, each of them dissimilar to the others. If there was no uniformity within each court or across the many feudal courts, why assume that they were all part of a common-law system? If influence flowed at all, it flowed from feudal courts to common-law courts. After all, each time feudal or local norms were upheld by royal courts, royal jurisdiction perhaps won additional legitimacy, but so did local legal arrangements. These cases, in which the declaration of witnesses or the presentation of collections of customs (identified as *custumals*) were integrated into royal jurisprudence, showed the endurance and resilience of a local system of norms that dictated solutions different from rather than similar to those proposed by the royal courts.

Because local norms maintained their power, during the early modern period locals often struggled to identify what these norms were; they destroyed evidence such as collections of customs or attempted to rewrite them. Although they were not always successful, on many occasions they managed to influence legal arrangements that were said to have existed from time immemorial but could be entirely new. These struggles were extremely local and produced a radically diverse system of norms, yet for those who upheld those norms, they were just as valid, perhaps even more so, than common law.

Similarly, research on English ecclesiastical courts suggests that until the Reformation these courts followed canon law. After the English monarch broke with Rome and instituted a national Church in England, canon law was presented as a foreign law imposed on the English by the pope. Yet it continued to operate. The only immediate, noticeable change after the Reformation was the establishment of new appeal procedures that replaced the traditional plea to the pope with a local instance. A separate English ecclesiastical law never came into being, nor was the jurisdiction of the Church, which continued distinct from the common-law courts, ever abolished.

As for equity, it is currently argued that it had begun converging with common law in the sixteenth century, but that in the seventeenth century while these debates took place it was still considered a separate system. Indeed, it was separate enough to bring about the wrath of Parliament and common-law courts or, on the contrary, to lead monarchs such as James to instruct that equity should be superior to, rather than subjected to, common law.

Common law, in short, might have been an important, even essential, component of the English legal system, but until the seventeenth century, at least, it never operated on its own. It was not superior to other jurisdictions, and was not placed hierarchically at the top of the judicial system. Common-law courts, for example, could not see appeals on other jurisdictions. Furthermore, there is reason to believe that influence between the various parallel systems that existed in England must have flown in all directions rather than only (or even mainly) from common-law to other courts, leading historians to the conclusion that common law neither absorbed nor affected all other jurisdictions.

The Third Move: The Ancient Constitution

Seventeenth-century legal experts argued that an important component of so-called English customary law was the norms that governed the relationship between individuals, the community, and the king. According to this proposition, in a long succession of formal and ritual confirmations the Norman kings promised to respect the existing Anglo-Saxon legal system. These confirmations were now reinterpreted as including a solemn pact, or an "ancient constitution." This pact encompassed a royal promise to abide by existing structures and laws and a communal agreement to be loyal to and obey the monarch. Although this argument supported royal authority in some ways—it included the duty of subjects to obey the monarch, and it legitimized royal commands—it also limited what the king could do. If the king failed to comply with his promise, he broke the pact, became a tyrant, and conferred on his vassals the right (even the duty) to oppose him. And because these arrangements were customary, the king could not modify them.

The myth of continuous confirmations, however, did not say much about the contents of the alleged pact. To identify what it included, seventeenth-century legal experts who believed in the orality of customary law nevertheless looked for documentary evidence. They located many historical texts that, according to them, contained elements central to this pact. Most emblematic among them was the Magna Carta (1215). From the seventeenth century onward, the Magna Carta would come to symbolize the monarchy's promise to uphold the existing law and agree to limit its powers by providing trial by peers, prohibiting arbitrary arrest, and securing the consent of the kingdom for the levying of new taxation.

Questioning the Third Move: Why the Magna Carta?

The Magna Carta was a feudal charter. Written in Latin, it contained a peace treaty or a compromise between the king and his barons at the end of a civil uprising. Mainly centered on the barons' desire to remedy what they perceived as royal abuse, the Magna Carta did not represent the interests of "the people." Instead it referred to some of the most important aspects of feudal relations such as the right to land, inheritance, debt, and taxation. Enacted in a colonial situation in which both the king and the barons were Normans and most of their subjects were Anglo-Saxon, the last thing the charter was interested in was guaranteeing the rights of subordinates. It aimed instead at ensuring the continued collaboration between the monarch and his barons and freemen, who together conspired to maintain the subjugation of the local population.

Worded as a royal response to a series of complaints, the Magna Carta was long and casuistic. It included no declaration of principles and no enumeration of norms, customary or otherwise. When it was promulgated, and even in the following centuries, no one pretended it had constitutional significance or that there were remedies available when it was infringed. Rather than enabling legal proceedings, it was considered a political document that first barons and then Parliament could use to pressure the king.

Nevertheless, in the seventeenth century authors identified the Magna Carta as the best proof of what the customary ancient constitution of England included. Ignoring most of the document and refusing to contextualize or historicize it, these experts centered their attention on only a few paragraphs that best suited their seventeenth-century needs. These included chapter 39, which declared that no free man shall be captured or imprisoned except by the lawful judgment of his peers or by the laws of the land. In this paragraph, early modern legal experts found confirmation for the idea of jury (trial by peers) and due process (adjudication according to the laws of the land). They stated that these rights were granted not only to the barons but to all Englishmen, whatever their status. Some went so far as to indicate that this chapter constituted a precedent and justification for the *habeas corpus* writ that protected individuals against arbitrary arrest. Of similar importance was chapter 12, which said taxation could be levied "only by the common counsel of our kingdom."

Not only was this reading highly selective, it also introduced into the Magna Carta ideas that mostly originated in the sixteenth and seventeenth centuries. Initially the Magna Carta was not understood to include the promise of jury trials or *habeas corpus,* to mention just two examples. Neither is there reason to believe seventeenth-century interpretations that saw in the Magna Carta an instrument by which the king, facing the discontent of the nobility, promised to limit his powers by restoring the laws of the land and the liberties of his subjects.

Many historians have asked why and how the Magna Carta was chosen to carry this enormous symbolic weight. They traced its rise to prominence to the fourteenth century and its growing fame to the sixteenth and seventeenth centuries. Some suggested that because it was such an odd and confusing document, it was fairly easy to read its different parts out of context. Others argued that it was chosen because it was written in the formative period of common law and because it expressed the barons' protest against the establishment and expansion of royal jurisdiction. But most historians believe that, above and beyond these considerations, the Magna Carta was simply a perfect document to serve the purposes of seventeenth-century actors. It was perfect because it was constantly mentioned in negotiations between the king and the nobility and because it was interpreted by different acts of Parliament and confirmed by successive monarchs. It was malleable and its understanding mutated constantly long before it was taken up by seventeenth-century legal experts and made into a symbol of English liberties.

Regardless of why the Magna Carta became so central to the narrative of successive confirmations of a political pact, the final message was clear: If England had an ancient constitution that was customary, the king was obliged to respect it. These customary laws that framed the relations between kings and their subjects now protected the lives and properties of all Englishmen. They were an inheritance that the present generation must enjoy, preserve intact, and pass on. That the Magna Carta included none of the elements that were read into it no longer mattered.

Parliament as Guardian of Customary Law

England thus had a customary law that predated the Norman Conquest and was subsequently upheld by the English monarchs as part of a pact between them and their subjects. This pact included many arrangements fundamental to the political constitution of the kingdom. But who was to ensure that the pact was respected and followed?

In the seventeenth century, the English Parliament appropriated this task. English customary law, it was now argued, was gradually revealed by judges who, as they adjudicated conflicts, also declared what the law was. But judges could not guard against infringement of this law, only Parliament could. Parliament was best suited for this task because it was an assembly that represented the kingdom. Thereafter, Parliament, which had begun as a gathering of individuals residing at court who undertook a wide range of activities including responding to petitions, issuing orders, and deciding on taxation, was refashioned as a legislative body. It was now charged with introducing, articulating, and passing laws meant to ensure the primacy of the existing legal system, theoretically in collaboration with the king. Also asserted was the idea that the king could no longer legislate on his own but must do so in collaboration with Parliament.

The gradual affirmation of Parliament and its assertion of power were evident, for example, in the transition from the Petition of Rights (1628) to the Bill of Rights (1689). The former was a request submitted to Charles I in exchange for Parliament's assent to additional taxation. Formulated as a plea, the petition noted royal agreement, which was presented as a grace. The petition cited various authorities to demonstrate that certain rights and liberties that had been enjoyed in the past—such as no taxation without representation and no trial without jury or due process—were being violated.

By 1689 (the Bill of Rights), political dynamics had dramatically shifted. Rather than being a one-sided grant by the king like the Petition of Rights, the Bill of Rights was a solemn proclamation by Parliament presented to William and Mary upon their ascension to the throne. An ultimatum of sorts, it placed Parliament at center stage, stating that Parliament was a legitimate assembly legally representing the people (a question that was not at all settled at that point). The bill censored the departing king (James II) for behavior that violated the true, ancient, and indubitable laws and liberties of the land, and it agreed to accept the new monarchs on condition that they promise not to do the same. The liberties enumerated included the traditional list (jury, due process, taxation), but also enumerated were many rules that sought to protect Parliament from royal intervention. Because the incoming monarchs agreed, Parliament declared them king and queen of England. With the Bill of Rights, Parliament appropriated not only the authority to guarantee the rights of Englishmen, but also the capacity to choose monarchs and crown them. Thereafter, royal actions that contravened these rights would be not only unjust but also illegal.

Some legal experts reacted to Parliament's growing assertion of powers by reaffirming the centrality of judges. Adhering fully to the idea that common law was customary, one of the fictions they adopted was that legislation could not change the law. Statutory law passed by Parliament, as a result, could only "discover" rather than create the law. It declared what the law was; it did not make it. This fiction had important legal consequences. It implied that all legislative acts must be interpreted as pronouncements meant, not to change the law, but only to clarify it. Nonetheless, the growing powers of Parliament in the eighteenth and nineteenth centuries did eventually lead famous experts such as Dicey in his *Introduction to the Study of the Law of the Constitution* (1885) to the conclusion that Parliament was sovereign, having the right to make or unmake any law whatsoever, with no person or body having the right to set aside such norms.[7]

Another method to guarantee the centrality of judges was the idea of binding precedent. The notion that previous judicial decisions could either illustrate the meaning of the law or justify a future ruling was present in England as early as the thirteenth and fourteenth centuries and supported the reporting and studying of case law. Yet this practice was not mandatory, and judges could refuse to follow it. Over time, however, the tendency to cite past cases substantially grew. Boosted by the printing press, which allowed a greater dissemination of case law, an intensified involvement of judges in decision making, and a growing enrollment in the Inns of Court, this tendency led judges such as Edward Coke to make frequent use of precedent, even suggesting that they should have an authority of their own. Adhering to the idea that experts should trust their own art, in his opinion in the famous Calvin case,[8] Coke ruled that to determine what the law dictated, one had to observe examples, precedents, and judgments rendered in similar cases.

Nonetheless, it was not until the eighteenth century that binding precedent was introduced in both common-law and equity courts, compelling judges to follow the relevant decisions made in the past. A means to ensure that judges' identification of customary law would accumulate over time, mandatory precedent also changed the nature of judicial decision making. Rather than being ad hoc solutions, judicial decisions were now reconceptualized as constructing a long chain of rulings that, over many generations, declared and clarified the essence of common law. This transformation authorized our present-day conception of common law as a judge-made law, that is, a system whose principles can be deduced by studying cases.

Was England Exceptional?

The refashioning of local norms as customary law, the insistence that they included a constitutional pact, and the attempts to use both to limit royal authority were common to both England and the Continent. Also common was the understanding that customs could work both to confirm royal power (as in France) as much as to undermine it. Nonetheless, in the seventeenth century English legal experts began insisting that their system was radically different from (and superior to) all other European normative systems. This superiority was anchored in the claim that Europe allegedly followed Roman law *(ius commune)* whereas England had a genuine customary law of its own that reflected the spirit of its people.

This portrait omitted *ius commune* jurists' contributions to the creation and institutionalization of common law (see Chapter 6). It also ignored the role of university-trained professionals in the making of the English legal system. True, by the fourteenth century most common-law judges were no longer university graduates, yet university graduates continued to be admitted to the Inns and they were employed in the Chancery court, which dispensed equity, and in ecclesiastical tribunals. English humanists who applied philological and contextual analyses to the law were also profoundly influential. Indeed, jurists and ideas coming from the Continent were of such importance that much of the activity of sixteenth- and seventeenth-century actors described in this chapter can be interpreted as a response to this influence or at least as dialoguing with it. Sixteenth- and seventeenth-century English actors may have gradually perceived the English and Continental systems as distinct, but they were also aware of their constant proximity and their potential permeability.

Nonetheless, despite these striking similarities, and despite the continued use of French and Latin terms, expressions, and doctrines in England, during the early modern period the myth of English exceptionalism held strong. It survives to this day, notwithstanding scholarly research that insists on common roots and that suggests that if England took a different path, this happened mainly in the early modern, not medieval times, and was the result not so much of what English law actually was but of how it was reimagined.

9

From *Ius Gentium* to Natural Law

MAKING EUROPEAN LAW
UNIVERSAL I

DURING THE EARLY MODERN PERIOD, various European countries began engaging in overseas expansion. First among them was Portugal, whose sailors and merchants explored the western shores of Africa in the fourteenth century. By the mid-fifteenth century, the Portuguese had tapped into important trade networks in gold and slaves and instituted a profitable commercial exchange with local merchants. A short time later, in 1487, Bartolomé Dias rounded the Cape of Good Hope; in 1492 an expedition sponsored by Spain's Catholic Monarchs and led by Columbus reached the Caribbean; in 1497 Vasco de Gama landed in Calicut (India); and in 1500 Pedro Álvares Cabral reached present-day Brazil. These early expeditions were followed by subsequent voyages, eventually leading to the extension of European hegemony to parts of Africa, Asia, and the Americas and ushering in what we now identify as early modern colonialism.

These developments produced a huge variety of complex outcomes. They radically transformed some parts of Africa, Asia, and the Americas, but they also had enormous economic, political, and cultural consequences for Europe. In this chapter I examine how they shaped European law. I argue that the intense encounter with non-Europeans, as well as the need to settle rivalries among Europeans overseas, led to the renewed use of Roman law, spurred discussions regarding natural law, and made European law assume the trappings of universality.

The Antecedents: Roman and Medieval *Ius Gentium*

As explained in Chapter 1, ancient Roman law recognized the existence of norms that were common to all polities. These norms, reproduced in *ius gentium* (literally, the law of nations, peoples, gentiles, or tribes), were universally applicable because, rather than being dependent on place and time, they were said to be based on human reason and experience.

Romans appealed to *ius gentium* in their dealings with non-Roman citizens. Already in ancient times, identification between *ius gentium* and natural law was frequent. This identification was based on the assumption that what was common to all communities regardless of their concrete historical circumstances was also in some way innate to humans and therefore part of a natural law. Yet if, in theory, to decide what *ius gentium* included jurists would have to observe societies around them and, by comparing and contrasting their legal arrangements, arrive at a conclusion as to which norms were shared by all, in practice Roman praetors charged with implementing *ius gentium (praetor peregrinus)* did nothing of the sort. Instead they made assumptions regarding what was rational and what was reasonable, concluding that the rational and reasonable must be common to all polities.

Because by the first century BCE Roman jurists tended to consider their own legal system *(ius civile)* as embodying pure, atemporal, universal, and permanent reason, they began identifying *ius civile* with *ius gentium* and both with natural law. This move justified the imposition of Roman law on all citizens of the empire. After all, if *ius civile* was not based on the authority of a lawmaker or on the writings of a professional caste but instead was a rational, superior mode of conducting affairs, there was no reason it could not also be applied—indeed given as a privilege—to foreigners.

Assimilation of *ius gentium* with *ius civile* and both with natural law came under attack after the Roman Empire converted to Christianity, because the center of the Christian normative system was not reason, but a God who was both a creator and a lawgiver. This meant that natural law was now conceived as a divinely mandated order. A product of God and a part of Creation, this law was inscribed in the hearts of all men, and all men, whether Christians or not, could discover its principles by questioning their conscience.

Appearing as early as the first century BCE and enshrined in the writings of Saint Augustine (354–430), this vision of natural law was espoused by many medieval scholars. Christian thinkers such as Thomas Aquinas (1225–1274) argued that good and bad were not defined by human conventions, nor were they the arbitrary product of human reason. Instead, these distinctions were imprinted in man's heart by God so that man can understand divine mandates.

Although Christian natural law was by definition permanent, reasonable, and just, its powers derived not from its internal goodness but from the authority of its creator, God. Superior to all other normative orders, God's natural law could be used to criticize human institutions. Acting as a standard against which all legal systems could be measured, natural law could even justify opposing one's government—such disobedience being a religious and thus a sacred duty.

European Expansion: Iberian Beginnings

Although many European polities and intellectuals had to address the question of which law should apply overseas, the first country to face this dilemma was Spain. Its primacy in this regard was tied to the early development of settler colonialism, with Spaniards controlling large populations of non-Europeans. As a result of this domination, Spain's monarchs, officials, intellectuals, and subjects would ask by what right Spaniards extended their jurisdiction overseas, which norms should apply to this venture, and what they instructed.

These questions, which were asked almost as soon as Columbus returned from his first voyage, had important moral and political implications, but they also had significant legal dimensions. At stake was identifying rules that would determine how Spaniards would interact with both Europeans and non-Europeans overseas. Would European norms be extended across the oceans? Could they be applied to relations between Spaniards and natives? If they could not, which other norms could regulate these relations?

Initially Spaniards sought to justify their activities by obtaining a papal license, which was issued in 1493 in the form of a bull. Titled "Inter Caetera," it stated that the Catholic Monarchs of Spain had already engaged in the expansion of Christianity in Iberia, where they fought against the Muslims.[1] It suggested that they were now willing to do the same in the territories that had been discovered or that would be discovered across the seas. The 1493 bull concluded by giving Spaniards a monopoly that allowed only them to expand to these territories in order to propagate Christianity. The monopoly excluded other Europeans from doing the same, setting a meridian that was to divide Earth from pole to pole passing some 100 leagues from the Azores and Cape Verde Islands. Territories west of this meridian would be included in the monopoly, while territories to the east would be open to all.

As soon as it was proposed, this solution was criticized both inside and outside Spain. Spanish courtiers, intellectuals, jurists, and theologians argued against the implication that the pope had authority outside Latin Christendom and over territories and peoples who had never been under Roman occupation or were affected by the Church's missionary activities. Others disagreed with the assumption that papal authority extended not only to spiritual matters but also to secular issues such as jurisdiction over people and lands. A third group lamented that the bull potentially restricted Spanish privileges. Tying Spain's presence in the territories to the duty to convert, it limited Spaniards' activities to conversion, and according to some, if they ceased to pursue conversion, their rights would automatically expire.

Because the solution offered by the bull was not fully satisfactory, the following year the Spanish monarchs negotiated a bilateral treaty with Portugal, the only serious rival for expansion at that stage. This treaty (the Treaty of Tordesillas), signed in 1494 and confirmed by the pope in 1506, largely followed the arrangements included in the papal bull, but it moved the meridian dividing Earth from 100 to 370 leagues west of Cape Verde, potentially limiting territories under Spanish monopoly and giving Portugal a greater zone of expansion.

This answer also proved unsatisfactory. As a treaty between two European polities, there was no reason it would be observed by other Europeans. Furthermore, the treaty did not indicate what the relations between Europeans and natives would be, and it did not explain why a European accord would have validity over territories beyond the Continent.

Because of these misgivings, jurists suggested that the best way to regulate relations between Europeans and their overseas subjects would be by reference to the legalities of conquest. They appealed to the Roman law doctrine of "just war," which distinguished between wars that were justified (and were thus legal) and those that were not. This difference was important because, according to Roman law, only a justified war could legitimize sanctions against the vanquished such as appropriating their land, suppressing their rights and privileges, and even enslaving them.

According to early modern standards, to be justified a war had to be either in self-defense or against an enemy that was likely to attack. In the Middle Ages this theory was usually interpreted as legitimizing war against a familiar foe. It legalized, for example, many of the wars Christian Europeans launched against Muslims, because the latter were considered longtime rivals who were permanently hostile to Christians. Yet the employment of a just war against the indigenous peoples of newly "discovered" territories was plagued with difficulties. Aside from the issue, already raised, as to how a European-based law such as Roman law could be applied outside Europe to non-Europeans, critics also asked whether native reactions to European presence merited launching a just war. Natives were certainly not traditionally hostile to Christians, as the Muslims were, and it was hard to imagine how the invasion of their lands by Spaniards could be portrayed as a defensive rather than offensive attack.

To solve these issues and ensure that hostilities against natives could be portrayed as just, Spaniards devised a new legal ritual aimed at justifying their actions. Called "requirement" *(requerimiento),* it included a formula that was to be read to the indigenous people and, if necessary, translated to them before battle began. The formula included a brief summary of world history. It began with the creation of the universe, continued through Adam and Eve, the proliferation of men and their division into nations, the coming of Christ, the institution of the papacy, and the papal bull giving Spaniards the monopoly on converting natives. The requirement specified that to facilitate conversion, Spaniards also received the right to dominate lands and peoples. The requirement ended by explaining to natives their duty to obey, which included accepting with goodwill and without resistance their subjection to Spain. It also spelled out what would happen if they did not. If they "maliciously" refused what the bull mandated and the requirement specified, Spaniards would be authorized to enter their country forcibly, making war against them, subjecting their persons, and taking away their properties and liberty.

The requirement sought to transform Indian resistance to the invasion of their land into an act of legal disobedience that would validate the launching of a just war. Bartolomé de las Casas (1484–1566), a Dominican friar working in the Americas in the 1520s and 1530s, was said to have commented that when he heard about the requirement, he did not know whether to laugh or cry. But however absurd the document might have been, we have ample evidence that it was carried around by many conquistadors and indeed read to the indigenous peoples before hostilities began.

The Rebirth of *Ius Gentium*

While Spaniards' initial response to the legal aspects of colonialism was fairly restricted in scope and imagination, in the 1530s and 1540s new theories emerged. Attributed to a Dominican friar teaching at the University of Salamanca, these theories eventually revolutionized the way Europeans discussed their rights and obligations. The scholar, Francisco Vitoria (ca.1486– 1546), belonged to an intellectual movement we identify today as the "Second Scholastics" or "the School of Salamanca." This movement sought to give moral theology the status of an autonomous discipline, suggesting that the duty of theologians was to propose solutions to the most pressing political and moral questions of their time.

Vitoria's best-known essay was probably written in 1539. Formally seeking to answer the question of whether children of nonbelievers could be baptized against their parents' wishes, Vitoria set out to explore the legal order that underpinned Spain's presence in the Americas. He enumerated the seven traditional justifications that had been given for this presence and dismissed them all. He explained that the Spanish king (Emperor Charles V) was not lord of the entire world and therefore had no jurisdiction in the New World. He affirmed that the pope was not a universal lord nor did he have power in civil matters. A papal bull, as a result, could give Spaniards nothing. Vitoria agreed that, by law, discovery might be a good basis for the acquisition of rights, but he immediately explained that this could happen only when the land discovered was truly vacant, and the Americas were not. Native refusal to convert to Christianity and their mortal sins were two other reasons that contemporaries invoked to justify Spanish domination, which Vitoria also rejected as illegitimate. A voluntary choice exercised by natives who agreed to subject themselves to Spain would be legally sufficient, but there was no evidence that such a choice had been exercised in the Americas. The seventh explanation Vitoria explored was that God gave Spaniards the Americas as a special gift. One could not discuss such a hypothesis, Vitoria argued, because rather than based on law or reason it was anchored in faith. Either one believed it or one did not.

Having discarded all these traditional justifications for Spaniards' extending their jurisdiction to the Americas, Vitoria came up with a new proposition. Following the teaching of Thomas Aquinas he suggested that, in their condition as humans, both Spaniards and the native inhabitants of the New World formed legitimately organized societies and both were therefore under obedience to natural law. This natural law, which he also called the law of nations *(ius gentium)*, was universal. It could apply to all human communities whether their members knew about it or not, consented or not, inhabited Europe or not, were Christian or not.

Natural law, Vitoria affirmed, recognized several fundamental freedoms. Believing in the sociability of man, on the one hand, and as a Spaniard legally experiencing these freedoms, on the other, Vitoria argued that men enjoyed the freedom to communicate, travel, conduct commerce, and dwell wherever they wanted to. This freedom allowed Spaniards to arrive, settle, and trade in the Americas. It also sustained their liberty to tell the truth, which as far as Vitoria was concerned included above all the duty to preach the gospels and bring the message of the Christian God to natives. These were the freedoms Spaniards exercised, Vitoria concluded, when they sailed to the Americas, traded with natives, established fortified settlements, and endeavored to convert the local population. Because Spaniards were authorized by natural law to do all this, if the natives refused to allow it or reacted with violence, they contravened natural law and could be legitimately attacked. Vitoria also explained that natural law included other provisions authorizing Spaniards, for example, to protect Indian converts to Christianity, elect a Christian king to rule over them, defend natives against tyranny, and help their friends and allies.

In the long run Vitoria's analysis produced the same results as previous explanations, namely, it authorized Spaniards to wage just war against natives. Yet his approach was nevertheless revolutionary. It introduced the idea that a natural *ius gentium* regulated relations between Europeans and natives. It imposed a system of rights and duties that did not require intervention of a superior authority such as the pope or the emperor or agreement among interested parties. The law of nations that Vitoria subscribed to was derived directly from nature and applied automatically and equally to all peoples. It could be discovered by observing human societies, but (following Aristotle and Aquinas) it was above all inscribed in man's heart by his creator and it was part of the rational understanding with which God had endowed humans.

The Colonial *Ius Gentium*

The *ius gentium* that sixteenth-century Europeans imagined was not based on empirical research. Instead it was founded on deeply held beliefs regarding what was just and what was reasonable. Thus, although Vitoria insisted that the law of nations was created for the whole universe and was appropriate for all peoples, like Roman jurists did before him, he tended to consider the norms of his place and time the most logical and thus universal.[2] He arrived at such inferences even in extreme cases, in which the norms he defended were rarely followed even in Europe. One such example was Vitoria's insistence that natural law recognized the freedom of immigration. This freedom, which formed a basic right in Spain since as early as the fifteenth century, was a particular Spanish arrangement that almost no other European country followed.[3] Nevertheless, because it made perfect sense for Vitoria and because it formed part of his daily experience and suited his beliefs, he had no doubt about giving it an important place in the emerging law of nations he imagined.

Vitoria's ideas were essential in moving *ius gentium* further into the realm of natural law and in making both universal. Rather than local law being applied to foreigners as was the case in Rome, Vitoria imagined the law of nations as an instrument defining relations between polities and among their members. This new law of nations ruled among sovereign entities rather than individuals. A precursor of today's international law, it was mainly concerned with the activities of public powers, not private individuals. Its ultimate justification was that it expressed norms Europeans considered natural and thus universally valid. That is, instead of recognizing that these norms were anchored in tradition, place, religion, or system, these norms were decontextualized and made to appear absolute.

The path opened by Vitoria was soon trod by other intellectuals. Following Spanish lead, the Portuguese incorporated these discussions into their jurisprudence, and the Dutch and English followed suit. In England, Alberico Gentili (1552–1608) referred to the law of nations as natural law in his essays *On the Law of War* (1588–1589). In the Netherlands, Hugo Grotius (1583–1645) did the same to advocate the freedom of the seas (1609) and to study the laws of war and peace (1625). The British crown and British colonialists also espoused this new language to refer to their commitments to natives and in their relations with other European powers. As *ius gentium* penetrated England, eventually English legal experts recognized the law of nations as being part of common law.

The success of these new ideas was tied to the need to solve concrete questions, but it was also motivated by the search for norms that would be consensual among Europeans who were now bitterly confronted not only politically but also religiously. The breaking down of the Christian unity, the growing number of reformed denominations, and the wars that ensued encouraged the quest for a new normativity that could rule over relations not only between Europeans and natives but also among rival Europeans themselves.

By the end of this process, most Europeans agreed that law regulated relationships between them outside of Europe and with non-European natives. They also agreed that this law, which they identified either as the law of nations or as natural law (or both), included several unquestionable principles. Initially Europeans searched for these principles in Scripture, tradition, or Roman law, but eventually they came to justify them by reference to reason and reason alone. They concluded that, because they were reasonable, the rules they proposed were sufficiently self-evident that they no longer required external validation.

The Reign of Self-Evident Truth

The reign of self-evident truth that required no proof is usually said to have begun with Grotius. Grotius cited the work of previous authors, as well as many sacred and Roman texts, but he also appealed to commonsense conclusions based on a reasonable analysis of the situations he examined. These conclusions, he argued, were so natural that they could be understood by all, Europeans and non-Europeans, lawyers and nonlawyers alike. Rather than having been systemized from existing laws and regulations, Roman law included, they could be deduced by observing society and nature and employing reason. Rather than being complex, they would be simple and straightforward.

To explain how private property came to be, following the Bible, Grotius reasoned that God gave the world to mankind collectively, so that it can survive and reproduce. Yet because men began fighting, the need arose to divide this common inheritance among them. This had led to the emergence of private property and to the notion that what one has in his possession should remain his. Similarly, to argue for the freedom of the seas, Grotius first defined property as something that people could possess, and then he demonstrated that the sea, because it could not be taken over and occupied, could never be appropriated. The conclusion he reached was that Portuguese claims for monopoly over sea routes from Europe to Asia were absurd and that, as a result, the Dutch could establish their own trade in the region.

Grotius's wish to cite authorities and yet also move to logical, common-sense explanations that did not depend on these rules having been pronounced before in reputable sources, was probably tied to the conditions of the period. The Reformation and the proliferation of Protestant denominations forced Europeans to search for a common language that would no longer be based on religious precepts but instead would be organized around shared experiences. The absence of an overreaching authoritative voice within Europe, such as the popes and emperors once provided, diminished the feasibility of depending on sovereign will to resolve issues between different communities. European expansion further pushed scholars toward secularization because of the need to find a normative system that could be shared with non-Europeans and non-Christians. But if the Reformation, the affirmation of states, and the expansion were vital to these processes of reinvention of natural law, so was the so-called seventeenth-century scientific revolution, which led to the elaboration of new epistemologies suggesting that true knowledge could be acquired only by means of observation. Having first collected factual data, humans could then process it, striving to understand what it meant by employing reason.

The most extreme example of how this new method was to affect scholars, including jurists, was the work of the French philosopher René Descartes (1596–1650). In his *Meditations on First Philosophy* (1641), Descartes argued that to reach truly logical conclusions, man had to forget all that he knew. Adopting the policy of "systematic doubt," Descartes called upon contemporaries to examine even the most basic assumptions, including the postulation that they existed. According to Descartes, only by getting rid of the conventions that obscured human's ability to reason and by setting one's mind free would humans be able to guarantee that their knowledge and understanding of the world were truly based on facts and reason. On the basis of a very primary and verified truth—the truth of his own existence—Descartes would commence gradually rebuilding all other certainties.

Although Descartes described at length the effort humans would have to invest in overcoming their own prejudices, he was nevertheless convinced that if they domesticated their body and their senses, humans would be capable of true reason. This belief was shared by many of his contemporaries, who were convinced not only that pure reason existed but that it was shared by all humans. If exercised correctly, it would lead them all to the same conclusion.

By the late seventeenth century, scholars and jurists began applying this new epistemology to their analysis of society. Developing philosophies that we now identify as "Enlightened," many argued that, like humans, society needed to abandon its veneration of tradition and instead return to simplicity and nature, that is, to pure reason. Only after intellectuals understood what nature dictated would it be possible for jurists to translate these findings into a new, perfect normative order that would guarantee happiness.

Thus, if the search for order in overseas expansion was one motive to pursue self-evident truths, another was the aim to reform Europe itself. In order to accomplish this task, in the late seventeenth century political philosophers and jurists across the Continent set out to discover what nature dictated. They hypothesized about how humans behaved before tradition and history obscured their capacity to reason, and they attempted to reconstruct humans' primitive state before society was created. Fabricating in their minds abstract individuals who had no past, present, or cultural traits, these scholars imagined a natural man who was unchangeable, timeless, and universal. A presocial being, this man subsisted before family and society came into existence. Because he was reasonable, however, his decision to enter into social relations must be explained by reference to the advancement of his own goals and the satisfaction of his basic needs.

Most scholars went along with this exercise of imagining a remote, hypothetical, presocial past, but they differed as to what were the terms man agreed to when he entered society. According to Thomas Hobbes (1588–1679), because the presocial state featured a permanent situation of anarchy and war, when he entered society, man consented to surrender many of his natural liberties in exchange for safety. According to John Locke (1632–1704), because the presocial state was fairly comfortable and orderly, when entering society man agreed to very few concessions and preserved most of his natural rights intact. Locke believed, not that man entered society out of fear, as Hobbes suggested, but instead that he freely chose society with the aim of further safeguarding and developing his rights. As a result of this analysis, while for Hobbes the social contract included the duty to obey the state, for Locke it was a means to protect rights as well as defend individual self-interest.

These debates, extremely serious yet with a completely fictional basis, were mostly used by seventeenth- and eighteenth-century scholars to scrutinize their present-day society. Rather than being ideologically neutral, they were profoundly political; they either justified or questioned the emerging social, economic, and political structures. But regardless of the position they chose to take, early modern scholars no longer invoked the power of God or the mandates of tradition. Instead they referred to reason and reason alone. At the center of their narrative was man, whom they portrayed as an individual who acted out of self-interest. This individual was capable of making informed decisions, and his decisions ended up constituting the social order.

The Road to Revolution

The new natural law that resulted from these discussions was rational and individualistic. Departing from the assumption that man created society in a deliberate and reasonable attempt to advance his interests, this new law, most particularly as it developed in the eighteenth century, placed man and his needs at the center of the normative order. Not only was society the product of individuals and their decisions, but individuals were conceived as persons with the capacity to govern themselves and freely determine their future. Ruled by reason, they no longer needed to justify their activities by reference to external authorities. Instead, each individual was, in theory, authorized to employ his own reason to decide what was right and what wrong. The conclusion that no external input was needed to reach a correct inference, and none was required to legitimize what had transpired or would transpire, was clear, for example, in the claim that there were such things as "self-evident truths" or "indisputable principles."

Rational and individualistic, modern natural law was also radical. It allowed contemporaries to voice a series of vindications that were justified by reference to rights that were said to be natural and inalienable. Society, it was now argued, was instituted only to protect these rights, and its main task was to resolve conflicts between the concurring rights of its various members. Thereafter, the normative order would be seen as a system exclusively aimed at harmonizing the rights of different individuals, allowing their free exercise as long as it did not interfere with the rights of others. Together these messages placing reason, man, and rights at the center of the political and legal system produced an explosion. They eventually led to extreme turmoil that would find expression in the American and French Revolutions (described in Chapters 10 and 11) and would, according to many, introduce a brave, new world.

Colonial debates, which began in Spain but then engulfed many other European countries, whether or not they were directly involved in expansion, did not only affect overseas possessions nor was their influence restricted to their consequences on indigenous peoples. Instead, discussions regarding the rights of Europeans across the seas and vis-à-vis non-European natives greatly altered Europe and its law. Pushing Roman and medieval *ius gentium* into the realm of natural law and making both universal, these discussions informed the hypothesis, later accepted as fact, that some things were natural because they were reasonable, at least in the eyes of those proposing them.

PART FIVE

Modernity

10

North American Developments

IN 1776 THIRTEEN British colonies in North America declared their independence and proceeded to form new republican governments by adopting constitutions that replaced the existing colonial regime. In 1787 representatives of these newly founded states proposed a federal constitution, in which the basic structures of their common government were detailed. In 1789 twelve amendments to the federal constitution were proposed. Of these, the ten ratified by a sufficient number of states became known as the Bill of Rights (1791).

Ever since these developments took place, historians have asked how they could be explained. They surveyed the social, cultural, economic, intellectual, and political circumstances that had allowed them to transpire, and they examined their consequences. Most stressed the importance of a constitutional disagreement that distanced policymakers in Britain from the colonies. According to this interpretation, at the center of the debate was the question of whether Parliament represented the colonies and whether, therefore, its approval of taxation was sufficient to apply new duties on colonial subjects. Also debated was the status of colonial assemblies and colonial governors and their authority to regulate local life. Colonial subjects, believing that the behavior of the king and Parliament violated their ancient customs and liberties, determined that this violation authorized them to rebel.

Having reached this conclusion, the colonists moved to constitute themselves as autonomous polities by declaring their independence and appointing constituent assemblies to draw up new pacts between themselves and their government. How they proceeded and what it meant for the development of European law are the subjects of this chapter, in which I ask which legal antecedents authorized these developments and how what transpired affected European law.

The Foundational Documents

The Declaration of Independence announced in 1776 the Thirteen Colonies' right to dissolve the political ties that connected them to Britain. To justify this measure, the declaration included a brief survey of how human societies came into being. This narrative stated that all men were created equal and had certain inalienable rights, among them the right to life, liberty, and the pursuit of happiness. Governments originated in the consent of those ruled, and their work was geared toward the protection of these rights. If governments failed to accomplish this task, those who gave their accord could alter or end their agreement, instituting a new government according to the design that was most likely to ensure their safety and happiness. The declaration also enumerated the "injuries and usurpations" inflicted by the king, showing that Britain had violated the compact that bound the colonies to the homeland. The declaration ended with the assertion that those acting did so in the name and the authority of the "good people of these colonies."

Following the declaration (though in some exceptional cases even before it), the various colonies drew up constitutions. Some did so of their own initiative; others responded to the call of the Continental Congress (the assembly of delegates representing the Thirteen Colonies) that instructed local assemblies to adopt written constitutions in which they would declare their colony free and independent. This was regarded as a necessary preliminary step before the colonies could associate with one another. Most state constitutions reproduced existing political arrangements. Redescribing traditional structures by using a new, enlightened vocabulary, these constitutions of course eliminated references to the king and dependency on England, but many conserved much of the previous local legal and political system that, according to contemporary perceptions, already functioned well. Eight states added to their constitutions a declaration of principles.[1] These declarations, usually identified as bills of rights, listed both universal principles and specific arrangements that originated in common law. According to those who advocated their elaboration, such bills were necessary because "the people" invested in their new governments all the powers they did not reserve for themselves. It was thus essential that checks on government would be made explicit.

After a prolonged and heated debate, representatives of the newly founded states adopted a Constitution that defined common institutions and set rules regarding relations between the states. Drafted in 1787, the Constitution instituted a federal structure with an executive branch (president), a bicameral legislative branch (Congress), and a judiciary. In the name of "we, the people of the United States," it mandated that the legislature would be made of a Senate and a House of Representatives, whose members would receive salaries and enjoy certain immunities. The executive power was given to a president, whose powers were detailed. The Constitution also instituted a Supreme Court with remunerated judges.

The first ten amendments to the federal Constitution (the Bill of Rights) listed the protected rights that the government could not violate. These included freedom of religion, speech, assembly, and petition, the right to form militias and bear and keep arms, the requirement that the government secure consent for the lodging of soldiers, security against unreasonable searches and seizures, several protections in the field of criminal law (no indictment without grand jury, no double jeopardy, no self-incrimination, guarantee of due process, no cruel and unusual punishments), and the right to trial by jury in both criminal and civil cases. The Bill of Rights also contained two amendments that addressed general principles. The first stated that the rights included in the bill were not exclusive and that other rights could be retained by the people even though they were not enumerated (Ninth Amendment). The second stated that powers not specifically delegated to the United States or explicitly prohibited to the individual states were reserved for the states or "the people."

The Creation of New Polities

Many of the arrangements included in the Declaration of Independence, in state constitutions and the federal Constitution, and the various bills of rights, were informed by English legal and political traditions, but others were completely new. The separation of powers, for example, had been proposed by many authors—perhaps most famously by Montesquieu (1689–1755) in his *The Spirit of the Laws* (1748)—but this was its first formal implementation. The federal Constitution also instituted a new type of polity that featured a division of labor between federal and state governments and made the citizens of each state entitled to treatment as citizens in all other states.

Although these innovations were important, what was particularly revolutionary was not the constitutions' contents but the transformation of law itself. As narrated in Chapter 8, the English conceived of their constitution as ancient. According to the narrative that emerged in the seventeenth century, it depended on a pact that was medieval in origin. Having survived numerous confirmations, this pact was part of a customary law that was said to be both ancient and oral. A few emblematic documents such as the Magna Carta or the (English) Bill of Rights of 1689 confirmed the existence of this pact, but these documents did not create it, they only reproduced parts of it in written form. The English constitution was extremely casuistic. Rather than including an enumeration of principles, or a global vision of what the social order should be, it contained a wide array of particular, ad hoc arrangements.

Under the English system, furthermore, individual rights were protected by the courts, which provided remedies against their infringement, but there were no legal checks on Parliament. Parliament was said to be sovereign and, in theory, could pass legislation that infringed even the most basic rights. The expectation was that this would not happen because the House of Commons represented the people and was to guarantee their rights. A system of checks and balances was also supposed to ensure that Parliament (both the House of Commons and the House of Lords) would behave, but there was nothing built into the English constitutional system other than self-restraint (or the upcoming elections) to ensure that rights would be respected.

The Thirteen Colonies adopted a radically different constitutional arrangement. Although sharing the belief in an ancient political pact that guaranteed their rights, they searched for a distinct solution. Mixing customary arrangements with innovations that were justified by reason, they proceeded to adopt a series of elements that would constitute a new pact (Constitution) between them and their government. In other words, they asserted their absolute power to do and undo society and its laws.

Alleging continuity with the English tradition—in their foundational documents colonists accused the English monarch of breaking the pact that they wished to preserve—in practice these colonists turned the English tradition upside down. They made several important structural innovations. First, they began by affirming in the Declaration of Independence their right to constitute a new polity that would be based on a new social pact. They then defined the new pact by elaborating a Constitution. Although the Constitution contained some familiar elements, it no longer represented a customary agreement that had evolved historically. Instead, it included a program for government that was designed and planned according to what contemporaries trusted would be most efficient. Including general principles rather than a casuistic list of elements, this new pact was meant to be comprehensive and enumerated all the most important legal arrangements. Rather than trusting tradition, it represented a profound belief in human reason and a faith in human capacity to rethink the social order in ways that would improve the lot of humankind.

Second, contemporaries stated that the steps they took required no justification other than the suffering they had endured. There was no need for old documents, laws, doctrines, or judicial opinions that would prove their preexistence or assent to their worth. Instead, the measures taken were supported only by "self-evident" truths.[2] The drafters of the Declaration of Independence and of the state and federal constitutions appealed to the "Supreme Judge of the world" and affirmed the "rectitude of their intentions" to support their claims that their vision was correct. There was no room for questioning. The Laws of Nature entitled them, they claimed, to create their own polity and adopt for its management the rules that best fit their interests. Identifying their traditional and customary rights also as natural rights and acting in the name of the people, they sought to "form a more perfect union, establish justice, insure domestic tranquility, provide for the common defense, promote the general welfare, and secure the blessings of liberty" for themselves and their posterity.[3] Nothing else needed saying.

The third innovation introduced during this period was the adoption of writing. Representatives of the new states prepared foundational documents that drew up the rules for the new polities and listed their authority and powers as well as the rights that should guide or limit their activities. This move—the writing down—was also revolutionary. The ancient English constitution was said to be oral. It was dispersed in many different sources, some documentary, but most not. As for natural law, there was no officially sanctioned recompilation of what it included, nor was it ever restated in a legislative act. By the 1770s, philosophers, theologians, politicians, lawyers, and jurists of course were writing extensively on what natural law was and what it included, but none of these writings was prescriptive.

Fourth, the rights Americans proclaimed were also new; they were no longer privileges or liberties granted by a monarch. Instead they were something that each person owned by birthright and because nature so dictated. A mix and match of traditional common-law entitlements and abstract principles based on natural law, the Declarations of Rights (1776) of Virginia and Pennsylvania, for example, stated that these rights were to guide (rather than be the result of) the formation of new structures. Worded sometimes as reflecting truth ("all men are born equally free and independent") but sometimes as conveying an aspiration ("elections ought to be free"), the two declarations asserted that men have certain inherent natural rights of which they cannot be deprived, such as life, liberty, property, happiness, and safety; that all power is vested in the people and that government is or ought to be instituted for the common benefit, protection, and security of the people, nation, or community and must adhere to justice, moderation, temperance, frugality, and virtue. Both declarations also instituted a certain freedom of worship and expression and upheld the right to fair trial.

Yet the task of reproducing not only traditional rights but also natural law and self-evident principles in writing and then transforming them into a legally binding document proved extremely dangerous. This was particularly evident with regards to the Bill of Rights. Originally meant to serve as a statement of principles, mostly expressing a set of standards against which to measure the legitimacy of government and with which to educate citizens and remind them of what needed protection, it took a while before the bill was understood to convey legal prescriptions. Applied in the nineteenth century to the federal government and only after World War II to state governments, many questions had to be answered. Was the enumeration of rights a recognition that those rights already (naturally) existed, or did it transform those rights into legally binding commitments? And what happened to rights that were not included in the list? Did they cease to exist, or was their force the same as always, despite their omission from this foundational document? If nothing changed because of the writing down (because natural rights depended on a higher external norm that predated the Bill of Rights and existed independently of it), what was the purpose of the Bill of Rights? If the Bill of Rights did make a difference, how could the natural rights, which were not enumerated, not suffer from their exclusion? And what about rights that did not yet exist but might come into being in the future?

Although the Ninth Amendment referred to this question by stating that the enumeration was not meant to deny the existence of additional, unlisted, fundamental rights, lawyers and scholars have since asked what to do with this amendment.[4] Was it proof that the writing down of rights was only a means to facilitate their defense in a post-independence period, or was the inclusion of certain rights but not others an indication that they were of a greater importance? Could the legislature, the executive, and the judiciary add rights to the list by using this amendment? Must these additional rights be part of a recognized tradition of natural rights, or could they be completely new?

Because of this complexity, U.S. courts have almost universally avoided making use of the Ninth Amendment. Instead they tend to justify the recognition of new rights by reading them into existing clauses. They did this, for example, with the right to privacy. Starting in the 1920s, the U.S. Supreme Court began inferring this right from several other amendments such as the First Amendment, which prohibits laws related to religious matters and guarantees freedom of speech (this was comprehended as including the privacy of belief), or the Fourth Amendment, which protects the "freedom from unreasonable searches and seizures" (interpreted as guarding the privacy of the person, his possessions, and household). They also searched to ground the right to privacy in the Fourteenth Amendment (added 1868) in its "liberty clause," which forbade states to deny any person the right to life, liberty, or property.

The fifth and perhaps most important innovation introduced by the representatives of the Thirteen Colonies / States was the determination that the new constitutional arrangements belonged to a higher normative order above and beyond ordinary laws. According to this vision, they not only represented a framework for governance, they also limited the power of lawmaking. Because the Constitution was now part of a new, superior sphere of legality, no law or governmental action could contravene it. Contrary to England, where the ancient constitution was a part of common law invoked mainly to place checks on the king, in America the Constitution would be the highest form of law, higher than all other normative sources, and it would also seek to limit the discretion of Congress. Whereas in England the Parliament and the king were said to be sovereign, in America, the Congress and the executive were not sovereign because they were limited by what the Constitution dictated. The aim was not only to protect "the people" against government (as in England), but also to protect them against the decisions of majorities exercising their otherwise legitimate power to legislate at the state and federal levels.

The Thirteen Colonies' claim to a right to constitute a new polity based on a pact that was both traditional and new, the pretense that this right for self-determination needed no justification, and the writing down of foundational documents with a higher normative value than other laws were all acts that, although innovative, could be explained by observing who the former colonists were or wanted to be. These acts also depended on the beliefs propagated by intellectuals; they were based on the drafters' familiarity with the law; and they were the result of the colonial experience.

English Antecedents

To explain why the colonists chose to rebel and how they framed their new government, most historians point to the great affinity between developments in seventeenth-century England and the eighteenth-century colonies. Facing a legitimacy crisis and royal absolutism, seventeenth-century English opponents proceeded to undertake their own revolution. During this revolution they stated that, from time immemorial, England had an ancient constitution that defined a pact of protection and obedience between the monarch and his vassals. This constitution placed checks on the king while also guaranteeing the rights of his subjects. Seventeenth-century English actors found written proof of this compact in the Magna Carta and other enactments. The most noteworthy elements of this ancient constitution were the rights to no taxation without representation, due process, and trial by jury.

Developments in the colonies followed a similar course. A legitimacy crisis backed by claims that Parliament and monarch did not have the powers they pretended to have led colonists to vindicate their ancient rights. Allegedly in order to protect these rights, they broke ties with Britain and instituted a government that would be limited by a constitution. The constitutional arrangements they adopted were different, and so were the tools designed to protect them, yet the method was similar, because in both places the opposition adopted the claim that the king could not rule by fiat or prerogative but must obtain consent to his laws, which must obey fundamental rules.

Most historians judged this close affiliation between events in England and events in the colonies as natural, even self-explanatory, because it was normal that colonies inhabited by British migrants and ruled by the British would use a common-law framework both to rebel against the old and to construct a new polity. But these conclusions regarding the naturalness of the relations between English and colonial developments included several assumptions whose veracity was not evident. Foremost among them was the conviction that the legal system operating in colonial North America was common law. This conviction, which is often referred to as the "transfer theory" (common law having allegedly been transferred from England to the Americas), was once the consensual view, but it has been widely criticized in recent years.

Historians who question the "transfer theory" point to several reasons common law could not have been the legal system operating in the colonies. They explain that common law consisted of a system of adjudication that depended on the existence of royal courts (see Chapter 6). As a result, where such courts were absent, as in the colonies, where only local (customary) courts existed, common law could not have been practiced. This opinion reproduces the conclusions of a series of early modern thinkers, among them Edward Coke, the great reformer of common law. In 1628 Coke asserted that common law "meddled with nothing that was done beyond the sea." Specifically referring to the ancient constitution, Coke determined that it operated only in England. In the mid-eighteenth century, William Blackstone, author of the popular *Commentaries on the Laws of England* and a celebrated lawyer and professor of law, also agreed that common law had no authority in the colonies.[5] According to his argument, if colonial legal systems were somewhat reminiscent of this law, this similarity was not proof of automatic application of English law in the Americas. Instead, it was the result of colonists' deliberately copying some parts (but not others) of common law.

The reason both Coke and Blackstone could disagree with the transfer theory was that both believed that common law did not consist of rules and principles that any court could apply. Rather than a substantive law that existed everywhere in England (as many erroneously tend to view it today), common law for them was the sum total of very specific procedures that only certain royal courts (common-law courts) could apply. Yet, though denying that common law was transferred in bulk to the colonies, Coke nevertheless determined that the ancient pact (the constitution) that established mutual obligations between the monarch and his natural subjects persisted even when these subjects migrated to other royal domains. As with the natives of Scotland in England (see Chapter 6), the English who migrated to the colonies did not sever their ties with the king, and neither could the king break his obligation to respect their fundamental rights. Thus, although neither common law nor the ancient constitution crossed the Atlantic, English monarchs were still obliged to respect the core liberties of their subjects abroad, mainly property rights and their consent for taxation.

This interpretation was validated by colonial charters and letters patent that usually guaranteed colonists the liberties, franchises, immunities, and privileges of English subjects.[6] But what eventually consolidated the rights of Englishmen in the colonies was not what the king promised (or was forced to accept) but the way in which common law itself had evolved. Reimagined in the seventeenth century as the only law of importance ever in existence in England, and comprehended no longer as the product of royal courts (as it really was) but instead as a customary law that was the property of all Englishmen (see Chapter 8), in its new trappings common law could easily be implemented overseas. With common law now representing a set of principles, that is, a substantive law and a repository of rights, it could be applied by local colonial courts (though they were not royal common-law courts) and be claimed by the subjects living in the Americas.

As a result of these developments, paradoxically, over time colonial law gradually converged with rather than diverged from that of England. These tendencies were also enhanced by the growing presence of the state and the greater role of colonial merchants and merchandise in imperial markets. This portrait—which suggested that the colonies gradually "Anglicized"— implies that Americans were never as English as in the decades immediately preceding their independence. Thus, if the transfer theory could be challenged for the seventeenth and early eighteenth centuries, it is nevertheless possible that by the end of the colonial era common law was indeed widely present in the Americas.

But even if so, which common law? The colonies were a loose association of autonomous bodies, each having a somewhat distinct legal regime. Massachusetts in particular had a system that was so divergent from England's that it is questionable whether it was part of common law at all. This difference was not considered problematic as long as colonial legal arrangements were not "repugnant" (that is, directly contradictory) to English law. The principle of repugnancy allowed constant debates between authorities in Europe and in the Americas regarding which differences between England and the colonies could be tolerated and which not. It also enabled disagreement as to which part of English law applied overseas and to what extent.

Adding to this complexity was the existence in England of a great diversity of laws and systems, with common law cohabiting with several hundred local, feudal, and ecclesiastical courts, each implementing their own normative order. Given this background, there was no reason to believe that multinormativity was not reproduced in the colonies. And if most individuals in England had hardly any contact with royal courts, as many historians now argue, neither is there reason to assume that the Englishmen who crossed the Atlantic were any different. Having mostly experienced local or feudal law in England, these immigrants-made-colonists must have brought with them familiarity with these systems rather than with common law.

The transfer theory was also challenged by historians who stressed that many migrants to the colonies were not English. Either excluded from the privileges of Englishmen (as were the Germans and the Dutch) or simply unfamiliar with it (as were the Scots), these migrants brought with them their own legal visions, whose influence on local law has not yet been sufficiently studied. Equally neglected was the question of how the presence of Africans (free or enslaved) and native Americans might have influenced legal developments. Common law, in short, might have been present in the colonies by the end of the colonial period, but so were a great many other norms and systems. Did they not make a difference?

As a result of these discussions it is possible that even if common law had been introduced to the colonies at some stage, it certainly was not the only legal system operating there, nor was it even the most important. But it is nonetheless possible that growing demand for rights in the late eighteenth century led common law (which authorized such demands) to prominence. This perhaps explains why at the time of independence the leading voices in the colonies appealed to common law. They debated their options by analogy to England, and they constructed their new polity by reference to English traditions. Most of them even argued that they were compelled to rebel because they were more faithful to common law than were Parliament and monarch, whom they now accused of violating the customary arrangements. Yet, there was nothing automatic or natural about their reliance on common law. It was instead the result of a long process, which also involved many strategic decisions.

Enlightenment Roots

The Enlightenment was an intellectual movement that took hold in various parts of Europe in the eighteenth century. As described in Chapter 9, in its core was a firm belief in rationality as well as in human capacity to reform the legal order. Following in the footsteps of earlier generations, enlightened thinkers concurred that society came into being after individuals living in a state of nature negotiated a "social pact." These negotiations involved reasonable individuals who were moved by the wish to improve their conditions. They therefore agreed to certain stipulations that exchanged benefits with restrictions and duties. Because these individuals were capable of understanding how society functioned, they could plan their activities. By employing reason, they could discover the laws of nature and apply them to their institutions and laws. The Enlightenment, in other words, affirmed human agency and insisted that humans were rational beings who were conscious of their rights (and duties) and were willing to limit them only for a very important and worthwhile cause.

Through debates as to which system would lead to the greatest happiness, the Enlightenment sought to liberate men from relying on ancient traditions and authorities. As Immanuel Kant beautifully put it in 1784, the Enlightenment was to mark the end of men's dependence on knowledge obtained by others and designate the move to think for oneself, relying only on one's own ability.[7]

Reverberating throughout Europe, these proposals found a warm reception on both sides of the Atlantic. In Europe they eventually produced what we now identify as the French Revolution. In Anglo-America they led to the colonists' decision to part from their motherland as well as design new structures of government that would protect their rights more efficiently. Appealing to such principles first in the Declaration of Independence, which included a summary of enlightened theories, it was in the federal Constitution of 1787 that the representatives of the new independent states spelled out their program. This program, they declared, was not mandated from above or dependent on tradition but instead came from a rational analysis done by "we, the people."

The Enlightenment allowed late eighteenth-century actors to believe that they had the power to remake society by following both their experience and their reason. It also endowed them with the conviction that these measures (which, in reality, were extremely revolutionary) required no justification. Presenting them as the reasoned outcome of a law of nature, late eighteenth-century actors declared them to be self-evident truths. Their only justification was the fictitious tale, philosophical rather than historical, about how societies came to be, which was conveniently reproduced in the Declaration of Independence.

These convictions, enumerated in the foundational documents of the United States, were pan-European rather than particularly English or American, and they would be again invoked during the French Revolution (1789–1799), producing even more dazzling effects. The affinity between developments in the Thirteen Colonies and what was to happen in France a few years later led many historians to ask who affected whom and to what degree. Regardless of questions of genealogy, which are often impossible to answer with certainty, it is nevertheless clear that despite differences in legal traditions and local contexts, and despite producing a somewhat divergent impact, both the Americans and the French ended up with written constitutions that upheld a strict separation of powers and declared the existence of a similar list of inalienable rights that needed no proof because they were self-evident. Perhaps more than anything else, this similarity suggests that late eighteenth-century American developments should not be considered from a local or even an English perspective. Instead they should be explained also by observing what transpired elsewhere. For the same reason, although what happened in the Thirteen Colonies took place in the Americas, it formed part of a European-wide movement and participated in, as well as precipitated, the development of European law.

The Law of Nations Turned Natural Law

The framers of the Declaration of Independence and the Constitution directly appealed to the law of nature. Part and parcel of the Enlightenment's philosophical toolbox and omnipresent in the thinking of English scholars (although less so in the work of lawyers), most particularly in the eighteenth century, the law of nature had a long history that began with *ius gentium* (ancient Roman law applied to foreigners), moved through divinely mandated law (in the Middle Ages), and in the late sixteenth and seventeenth centuries was explained by reference to experience and reason. During the early modern period, natural law was a repository of norms that governed relations among Europeans as well as between them and non-Europeans. Initially used to justify European actions overseas, it was also a powerful tool with which to criticize existing structures and laws—casting them as being unnatural would imply that they needed modification, even abrogation.

Typical of such perceptions was Emer de Vattel's *Droit des gens* (1758), in which Vattel suggested that nations are political bodies or societies of men united to procure advantage and security. This association required a constitution—a fundamental regulation determining the manner in which public authority must be exercised.

The representatives of the Thirteen Colonies-made-states made extensive use of such theories. These theories allowed them to explain the breakup with Britain (because what the king did was unnatural) and they justified the constitution of a new polity (a development authorized by the law of nations as well as by natural law). Yet natural law not only sanctioned the assumption of sovereignty, it also allowed contemporary actors to confirm that, as representatives of a legitimate polity, they could contract with other powers that should recognize them as equals.

According to some scholars, this might have been the original aim of the Declaration of Independence, which was not necessarily directed at the home audience, or even at Britain, but instead at the "international community" (to use an anachronism). The declaration began by confessing this point, namely, the need to appeal to the "opinion of mankind," explaining why the colonies proceeded in the way they had. It ended affirming that the colonies were now ' "free and independent states" that could, as sovereign bodies, "levy war, conclude peace, contract alliances, [and] establish commerce." In this way the former colonists sought to transform what was essentially a local insurrection, perhaps a civil war between them and their government, into an international conflict between two sovereign bodies. Precisely to this end, the Declaration of Independence accused King George III not only of acting unjustly against his subjects (violating their ancient customs and liberties), and of acting unnaturally (violating natural law), but also of violating the laws of war and the customs of commerce, which governed relations between polities.

Federal and state constitutions also sought to convince foreign powers to acknowledge the new states as well as their association with one another. These constitutions not only wished to give legitimacy to the new polities, they also offered a model that, based on an ideology that was transnational rather than local, would demonstrate how contemporary theories could be implemented. They allowed for a European-wide discussion regarding how to perfect society and its institutions, and were considered by many a test case for what could or should be done. Centering not on its antimonarchical or anticolonial aspects but instead on the structures of government and the rights of man, the American example could thereafter be universalized.

The Colonial Background

The nature of the confrontation between colonists and the British government also influenced the legal shape the new country would acquire. Complaints against Parliament's assertion of sovereignty led colonists to search for a mechanism that would limit the powers of representative assemblies. If the move to restrict Parliament by enacting a constitution was understandable, so was the wish for a written document that would transform what otherwise belonged to an oral customary law (in England) into a formal legal arrangement (in the United States). The writing down promised greater transparency and clarity, but it was also part of the colonial tradition, which relied greatly on written material, with charters enumerating the rights of subjects and many laws detailing what the normative order was like. By the late eighteenth century, colonial charters were already seen as a sort of constitution (a legislative governmental framework) that could be used as a defensive mechanism against the misuse of power. They were also a means to recognize rights, because they embodied a sort of covenant between colonists and the king.

The foundational documents of the Unites States reflected these particular conjunctures, needs, and traditions. The Bill of Rights was especially indicative of this dependence; the topics it enumerated were perhaps objectively important, and were definitely part of the English tradition, but their inclusion in the Bill was directly related to the events that took place before and during the War of Independence. Taxation without representation was obviously one such case, but colonists and metropolitan authorities also debated other issues, such as the quartering of troops, the right to have local militias, and the promise of due process in local courts with juries and independent judiciary, all of which made their way into the Bill of Rights while other, not less important ones, did not.

The Legal Significance of These Developments

The Declaration of Independence, the federal and state constitutions, and the bills of rights ushered in a new age in legal and political history. Since their promulgation at the end of the eighteenth century, numerous other countries proceeded to declare their independence by claiming the right to constitute new polities after registering complaints against their former rulers.

Equally popular was the adoption of constitutions that were not dramatically different from the American one. These usually expounded a scheme of government that, although often distinct from the one espoused by the former Thirteen Colonies, nevertheless included the separation of powers as well as, more recently, judicial review. These constitutions were understood to embody a superior level of normativity that other laws or governmental action could not violate.

Although this American contribution to European law was not completely autochthonous—after all, it was based on English legal traditions, European debates on natural law and the law of nations, and Enlightenment philosophy—it is nevertheless clear that the representatives of the Thirteen Colonies were the first to convert these ideals into formally sanctioned legal structures. They were also the first to decide that the most basic elements of collective life (the structures of government) would be decided by votes in assemblies that allegedly reflected and refined the desires of "the people." The constitutions they imagined were the product of both tradition and reason, but their ultimate goal was to ensure the happiness of all.

These developments set an example that others could emulate. The list of countries that were directly or indirectly affected by them, that proceeded to declare their independence or adopt constitutions, was massive. Among them (the list is not exhaustive and contains anachronistic names) were Belgium, Haiti, most former Spanish colonies in the Americas (Gran Colombia, Venezuela, Argentina, Chile, Costa Rica, El Salvador, Guatemala, Honduras, Mexico, Nicaragua, Peru, Bolivia, Uruguay, Ecuador, Colombia, Paraguay, and the Dominican Republic), Liberia, Hungary, New Zealand, Germany, Italy, Japan, the former Czechoslovakia, and the former Rhodesia.

By the end of this process, American revolutionaries' powerful message regarding their rights indeed became the self-evident truth they had prematurely imagined. This truth—that communities have the right of self-determination, that they can construct new polities, modify the conditions of the social pact, design an effective government, institute a constitution that would limit the actions of the legislative and the executive, and proceed to identify and defend their rights—are presently considered so consensual that they no longer require justification.

11

The French Revolution

On July 14, 1789, an angry mob stormed the Bastille, a fortress on the eastern side of Paris, in an episode that came to mark the beginning of the French Revolution. Since then many scholars have attempted to decipher how the Revolution came about and what its short- and long-term consequences were. They have described how the king was forced to relinquish much of his control, how peasants began attacking seigneurial properties, how new constitutional arrangements were developed, and how King Louis XVI was sentenced and executed. They have narrated how the Revolution grew more radical and more violent over time and how those who resisted it were persecuted. Symbolized by the invention of the guillotine, persecution led to the execution of many, most particularly in a stormy era identified as "the Terror." After several constitutions and a period that featured extensive violence and chaos, in 1799 Napoleon Bonaparte ascended to power. Some scholars saw the coming of Napoleon as signaling the end of the Revolution. Others saw it as leading to the spread of the Revolution's main principles throughout Europe.

In what follows, I concentrate on the legal significance of what transpired. I argue that the French Revolution featured a radical transformation, perhaps the most radical transformation that European law has ever experienced. Turning existing traditions upside down or inside out—contrary to what happened in the Thirteen Colonies, where most actors appealed to natural law yet also wished to continue upholding many traditions—the French declared the need for a complete overhaul of the legal and political system.

This would include not only constitutional changes (as in the Thirteen Colonies, where pre-independent law often continued intact despite the political upheaval) but a modification of the entire legal system. Discarding customs and existing structures, the declared aim was to create a new order, where norms would no longer be inherited from the past. Instead they would herald a future in which all decisions regarding both public and private law would be mandated by natural law and reason, and guided by the will of the nation. This vision, which was sometimes more radical than the actual legal changes, transformed the French Revolution into an earthquake that allowed for the emergence of law as we know it today.

The Making of a Revolution

These radical political and legal transformations began in 1789, when members of the Estates General (the Parliament) declared their meeting a National Assembly. This declaration implied that instead of a body divided by estates (nobility, clergy, and commoners) and representing (in the case of commoners) specific regional interests, as had been the case, the assembly would now have only one chamber, which would represent all estates and regions. It would speak on behalf of the nation, now conceived not as a body made of corporations and orders as it had been but as a society of citizens.

Following this declaration, the members of the Assembly announced that they had powers to modify existing political and legal structures. They proceeded to abolish the feudal system and many of the privileges of the Church, such as the right to collect tithes. They eliminated the sale of judicial and municipal offices, declaring that all public functions were open to all candidates according to merit. They also ended fiscal privileges that had spared nobles and the clergy from important tax payments. In a series of decrees (known as the "August decrees"), the members of the Assembly also declared that, because the union of all Frenchmen was more advantageous than the particular privileges that some French provinces enjoyed, all provincial, district, local, and urban legal particularities would cease to exist and a single law would instead apply all over France.

The Assembly then moved to adopt the "Declaration of the Rights of Man and the Citizen" (1789). This declaration proclaimed the existence of inalienable rights, including equality, liberty, property, security against oppression, presumption of innocence, no taxation without parliamentary consent, and freedom of speech and the press. It listed a series of constitutional elements, including the assertions that sovereignty resided in the nation, legislation expressed the general will, and the armed forces were to protect the common good rather than the king. The declaration also established as a general principle that what was not prohibited by legislation was allowed and that no one could be constrained from doing anything unless legislation so mandated.

These legal arrangements were entirely new, yet the declaration presented them as requiring no explanation or justification other than that they were "natural, inalienable and sacred . . . simple and incontestable principles," which the representatives of the French people "set forth in a solemn declaration . . . under the auspices of the Supreme Being."[1] Like the representatives of the Thirteen Colonies, the authors of the Declaration of Rights appealed to self-evident truths, suggesting that the changes they introduced were in reality a restoration. According to the preamble to the declaration, it was precisely the ignorance, neglect, or contempt for these self-evident truths that had led to the public calamities and corruption the members of the Assembly sought to correct.

In 1790 the National Assembly abolished all ecclesiastical taxes, confiscated Church property, and forced the clergy to become state employees. The assembly then proceeded in a very short time span to adopt several constitutions. In what was to become an extremely volatile period of political experimentation, with one constitution replacing another and each substantially modifying the structures of government, different revolutionary groups and individuals sought to identify the structures that would best fit their image of an ideal society.

In 1791 the National Assembly voted on the first new constitution, which included many of the initial foundational changes. Its preamble stated that the aim of the document was to abolish irrevocably institutions that undermined the liberty and equality of man. In the future there would be no distinctions based on birth and no privileges other than the ones bestowed on all Frenchmen. Labor would be liberated too—instead of being limited to guild members, all employment would be made available without distinction other than virtue and talent. The aim was to guarantee the natural and civic rights of all Frenchmen, including the right to hold jobs, a fair distribution of taxation according to financial ability, equal punishment for equal crimes, freedom of movement and protection from arrest, freedom of speech and press, freedom of assembly, and freedom to address the authorities. The 1791 constitution protected the inviolability of property, stating that no one could limit this right unless public security or the rights of third parties were in jeopardy. It declared France a single indivisible polity and announced that sovereignty, which was inalienable, resided in the nation. Ensuring the separation of powers, the constitution instituted an executive (exercised by the king), a legislative branch (composed of deputies elected by the people,) and a judiciary (also elected). French citizens were divided into active citizens who could vote because they were males over 25 years old and paid a certain amount of taxes and passive citizens who could not vote.

In yet another radical transformation, in 1792 France was reconstituted as a republic, whose assembly was to be elected by universal male suffrage. In 1793 Louis XVI was executed and a new constitution was adopted. According to this constitution, the National Assembly would be elected by all male citizens and was to suggest laws that regional "primary assemblies" would have to ratify. The National Assembly would appoint the executive from lists of candidates proposed by these primary assemblies. Debates in the National Assembly would be open to the public and would be decided by the majority of members present. The 1793 constitution ended with several clauses enumerating the main rights of Frenchmen, including equality, liberty, security, property, free exercise of religion, the right to education and public assistance, freedom of the press, and the right to hold popular assemblies as well as enjoy all the other rights of man. The constitution also guaranteed "respect" for "loyalty, courage, age, filial love, misfortune, and all other virtues."

Radical in its conception of popular sovereignty, the 1793 constitution was ratified by popular referendum, yet its implementation was delayed and then set aside indefinitely until peace would be achieved. In 1795 yet another constitution was adopted. It sought to grant greater power to a five-person executive called the Directorate as well as obtain control over the political process while augmenting the protection of private property and the inviolability of private residences, which could not be entered or searched without an appropriate warrant. The 1795 constitution also forbade the formation of corporations and associations that were contrary to public order, and the creation of societies concerned with political questions. Political rights, it stated, should be exercised only in primary and communal assemblies subject to the law. Any other unauthorized gathering would be considered an attack on the constitution and would immediately be dispersed. To usher in this new age, the constitution proposed that "the French era" date from September 22, 1792, the day of the establishment of the Republic. According to this new calendar, the 1795 constitution was therefore enacted in year III.

A New Vision of the Law

Chaotic, piecemeal, and sometimes contradictory, these new legal arrangements were often the result of compromise. They were adopted following long debates between individuals and groups who often took to violence in order to guarantee the submission (or elimination) of their opponents. Although the solutions proposed could vary dramatically, the results obtained were often less coherent than what was intended, and actual implementation left much to desire, it is nevertheless clear that many of the changes proposed in France in the late 1780s and early 1790s were truly radical. Beyond the particularities of laws and constitutions, and despite the vicious power struggle among factions, these developments all contributed to the reformulation of what law was, where it came from, and what it was based upon.

Paradoxically, this new conceptualization of law was fairly consensual among rival factions. Evident, for example, in the Declaration of the Rights of Man and Citizen, it stipulated that (1) sovereignty resided in the nation, which expressed its general will by creating laws; (2) anything not prohibited by legislation was allowed; and (3) no one could be constrained from doing anything unless the law so prescribed.

Together, these revolutionary measures implied that legislation, guided only by the will of the people, was now the only legitimate normative source. No longer could individuals and communities appeal to customs, doctrine, religious and moral duties, or even jurisprudence. Instead, either the legislation sanctioned a certain arrangement, making it legal, or it did not, in which case this arrangement did not exist. The legal order was now a clean slate upon which it was possible to draw whatever one wanted as long as it was reasonable, did not contradict natural law (whose meaning and extension could, of course, be a matter of debate), and obeyed the general will.[2] Thereafter, all laws in both the private and the public realm (to use an anachronism) would become the product of willful and deliberate human activity and would be enacted, not spontaneously within the community (as customs were said to have been promulgated), but following reasonable discussion and debate. Laws would no longer be mandated by tradition, professional advice, or judicial activity, but would be adopted as the need arose by new actors we would come to identify as "politicians." Because proposed by reasonable nonprofessionals elected by the citizens, these laws would be so simple and so straightforward that their contents could be summarized in a textbook that every citizen could comprehend and every family could own. This simplicity would justify eliminating the mediation of professionals. There would be no longer a need for judges and lawyers trained in law. Instead, the exercise of much of their former activities would be delegated to reasonable men, who would require no special preparation and would have no monopoly over their office. For the same reason, most of the litigation could be redirected from formal courts to informal arbitration focusing on reconciliation.

This new vision radically departed from previous arrangements. While Old Regime law included a multiplicity of sources (customs, doctrine, juris-prudence, divine mandate, and legislation), the new law ushered in by the French Revolution validated only legislation, theoretically tossing out all other normative sources. Whereas in the Old Regime law was the mono-poly of jurists, who were charged with both identifying and applying it, under the new system it could be made, implemented, and understood by any rea-sonable person. While in the Old Regime the main task of jurists and judges was to discover and apply a preexisting law that was anchored in the way things always were or ought to be (customs) or by reference to accumu-lated professional know-how *(ius commune)*, or divine will (canon law), the measures adopted during the French Revolution enabled, even advocated, legal creation. The aim of the legal order would no longer be to safeguard the status quo but instead to change and improve society. Paradoxically, these revolutionary measures were advocated by jurists turned deputies who, po-sitioning themselves as technical experts rather than as politicians, success-fully pursued a program that could potentially eliminate their monopoly as a group.

If the nature of the law itself changed, so did the community to which it would be applied. During the Old Regime, there was a pan-European legal order in which an overreaching system *(ius commune)* coincided with ex-tremely localized legal arrangements *(ius proprium, now also identified as* customary law). The new French system now imagined instituting a national law—there would be only one law in France, and this law would apply to all Frenchmen equally. No longer would it be the case, as Voltaire (1694–1778) had once argued, that when traveling through France, one changed laws more often than horses.[3]

The normative order that emerged from the French Revolution therefore established that laws would be made by the elected representatives of the nation. Guided by reason and based on the assumption that contemporaries could—indeed, on occasions must—intervene in the legal order, legislation would seek to improve or even redesign society. It would apply only within the territory of the state but it would apply to all citizens equally. All these traits, which describe our present-day understanding of what law is, were perhaps not born with, but certainly for the first time were legally instituted with, the French Revolution.

Beyond its enormous contribution to the redefinition of the normative order, the French Revolution also pioneered three other changes that were fundamental to the emergence of legal modernity. The first was the unification of the legal subject, allowing us to imagine identical individuals who all carried the same rights and duties. The second was the unification of various rights over things into "property rights" the way we know them today. The third was the unification of power and the creation of an undivided sovereignty.

The Unification of the Legal Subject

Breaking away from the preexisting axiom that men were dissimilar because distinguished by birth, occupation, residence, or religion, the various enactments made during the French Revolution declared all men equal. In practice, this meant the abandonment of an old system that bestowed rights and privileges to individuals according to who they were, replacing it with a new regime that no longer acknowledged the appropriateness of distinctions in estate, profession, or place of residence, declaring these either abolished or irrelevant. The promise of equality, however, was not complete. Some distinctions survived. Among them were differentiations based on gender, wealth, civic state (slavery or freedom), and, to some degree, religion.

The move to abolish distinctions in estate, profession, and place of residence required imagining a new type of person, an abstract individual who, regardless of his or her distinct history and traits and despite having obvious particularities, would be considered identical to all others. This new individual would be decontextualized by way of a legal fiction that, in the name of equality, would ignore all factors that made him or her particular or would classify them as inconsequential.

If ignoring differences was one requirement, the need to piece together a new legal subject was another. What this entailed can be best explained by using an example. Under the Old Regime, a nobleman who resided in a city and was employed in the military held various legal personalities. As a noblemen, he enjoyed one legal regime, as a resident of a city, another and, as a military man, yet a third. Each legal regime implied a different set of privileges and duties. This diversity in law was maintained through the existence of various jurisdictions. The nobles had their own authorities and tribunals in which they adjudicated conflicts, and so did the city and the military. These authorities and courts were responsible for enforcing the particular regime that applied to the members of the group, one that sometimes was bothersome but on most accounts was considered advantageous.

Wearing multiple hats—as in Gilbert and Sullivan's *The Mikado,* where Pooh-Bah was the first lord of the treasury, lord chief justice, commander in chief, lord high admiral, master of the buckhounds, groom of the backstairs, archbishop, and lord mayor—our nobleman could alternatively invoke his different legal personalities, but he could not combine their elements. Either he was treated as a nobleman and received the rights that applied to nobles and carried the duties of his estate, or he enjoyed the privileges of his city and was under the protection of its authorities, or he appealed to the military jurisdiction. Under the Old Regime this multiplicity represented reality, not a comic or absurd situation.

The nearest example for such a situation today would be when the same physical person (an individual) acts for a company (his or her first legal personality) or for him / herself as a private individual (his or her second legal personality). If he / she is a trustee, he / she may have a third legal personality when acting for the person or company, for which he / she is a trustee. But what this person cannot do even today is combine his or her rights as president of the company with his or her rights as a trustee or as a private individual. As far as the law is concerned, although we all know that the very same physical individual fulfills all these roles, he or she embodies three diverse legal personalities, and each action is ascribed to only one of his or her personalities, as if the others did not exist.

Although some measure of multiplicity persists today, what was different before the French Revolution was that, legally, there was no single legal personality to match the private actions of individuals. In their private lives, that is, not only when they acted for a corporation, as would be the case today, most individuals embodied a multiplicity of persons: a nobleman, a resident of a city, and a military man, to return to the previous example. To create a single legal subject out of these various fragments required not only imagining that different individuals were essentially the same (and thus equal) but also devising a system that would combine their various personalities into one. Destroying the existing orders and jurisdictions and dissecting them into individual rights and duties (the right to own property, the right to work, the right to reside in the city, the duty to pay taxes), revolutionary enactments then proceeded to imagine an abstract individual and attach to him / her all the traits worth protecting.

The Unification of Property

If the unification of the legal person was one project, the unification of property was another. Under the Old Regime, most rights we now identify as property rights did not belong to a single individual but instead were distributed among many. With regard to land rights, jurists distinguished, for example, "direct dominion" *(dominum directum)*, which included the right to direct what would happen on the land, collect dues, and exercise authority, from "useful dominion" *(dominium utile)*, which included the right to use the land and, mostly, keep the income it generated. Jurists also recognized an abstract right that all monarchs had over all lands in France, a series of communal rights that entitled members of the community or all Frenchmen to use the land for certain ends, such as pasture or gleaning. The Church also had rights to certain fees on the land, which were considered real rather than personal obligations, and most lands were also under additional impositions, monopolies, and servitudes. The hierarchy among these rights was not always clear, leading to conflicts. Meanwhile, the fragmentary nature of land rights led to a certain fossilization, making it difficult to sell or buy land. Added to this complexity were multiple legal impositions that instructed how the land could be used, what could be planted, what could be cleared, and when cultivation was allowed. Land rights were also subject to local codes that varied from place to place, region to region, and depending on the type of land and how it was acquired.

One of the first goals of revolutionary legislation was to change this situation, which many perceived as both chaotic and extremely prejudicial. Lawmakers wished to distinguish between jurisdiction and property, that is, the right to exercise power (such as the powers of lords in their seigniorial domain) and the right to own land. They also hoped to reform the land market and transform peasants into small proprietors, improve the state of agriculture, protect property against abuse, and appeal to principles of reason and simplicity.

Embracing the idea that property rights should be as complete and free as possible, French revolutionary legislation imagined a new, modern property that would include all the entitlements previously divided among many individuals. Thereafter there would be a sole owner with the right to direct, use, and collect income. This owner would be free of state regulation and of impositions by third parties, and his rights would not be limited unless considerations of public utility and the rights of others justified it. Property, as the Declaration of the Rights of Man and Citizen proclaimed in article 14, would be "natural and imprescriptible" as well as "sacred and inviolable." Or, as the French civil code of 1804 would eventually determine, property would become "the right to enjoy and to dispose of things in the most absolute manner provided that one does not make use of them in a manner prohibited by laws or regulations."[4]

Unification of Power and Indivisible Sovereignty

No less important was revolutionary trust to unify into one and indivisible sovereignty all pubic power, which in the Old Regime was distributed among many individuals, officials, and entities. This unification was already proposed by Jean Bodin (1530–1596). Responding to the chaos provoked by the Wars of Religion (1562–1598) between Catholics and Protestants, Bodin advanced the theory that society needed to have a government that would display supreme command over all citizens. Rather than public power being divided among many individuals (the king, seigniorial lords, the Church, guilds, and so forth), there would be one person (the king) who would accumulate all powers and would be placed in a position of clear superiority to all other jurisdictions. He would be able to declare war and peace, hear appeals in the last instance, nominate and remove officers, and impose and collect taxes, but most importantly he would have the absolute power to make and change the law without needing to obtain the consent of others. Unlimited in his actions and free of constraints other than divine and natural law (including the Law of Nations), sovereignty, Bodin argued, was a necessary condition for the survival of all polities.

Although they were relatively novel, even scandalous, when proposed, Bodin's theories, which were also discussed by Grotius, Hobbes, Locke, and Pufendorf, to mention just a few examples, were brought into fruition by the French Revolution. One of the first moves of revolutionary legislation was to insist on creating a sovereignty that would be indivisible. Gradually eliminating the powers possessed by officeholders who purchased their offices, by lords, and by the Church, it collected these pieces of jurisdiction together to create a new type of public authority that would be charged with all public power and would be placed hierarchically at the top. The constitution of 1791 pointed to this by asserting that "sovereignty is one, indivisible, unalienable and imprescriptible."[5]

As with developments in the Thirteen Colonies, many of these ideas were not French in origin nor did they find receptive audiences only in that country. However, the particular preconditions in France and the way the Revolution developed made arguments and goals that were also present elsewhere exceptionally powerful there. To understand why this was the case, it is essential to trace the effects of Enlightenment philosophy, the propensity of French monarchs to claim and use legislative power, and the way the confrontation with the king took shape.

The Enlightenment

The intellectual movement known as the Enlightenment took hold in various parts of Europe in the late seventeenth and the eighteenth century. Believing that society is ruled by natural laws, late seventeenth-century thinkers suggested that society was instituted by rational individuals who chose to live together in an organized structure. These individuals bargained with one another, consenting to cede certain things in exchange for receiving others. Although these thinkers disagreed on what the conditions for the formation of society were, they nevertheless conceded that societies were consciously and purposely created by man and that, as a result, they were regulated by a foundational social pact. The implication was that certain norms embedded in this primordial pact could not be modified without refounding society.

By the eighteenth century, alongside these convictions came the belief that human society could improve if its organization and laws were more attuned to nature. Thereafter, methods of inquiry applied to the hard sciences could also serve to explain society. Like nature (and in its condition as part of nature), society was subject to regular and uniform laws, which men could understand by employing reason. Discovering these laws was essential because this knowledge allowed men to plan their activities and their societies by forming appropriate institutions and devising rules to lead them to greater happiness. And if men created the foundational social pact, they also could change it by reaching a new agreement if circumstances so required. By the eighteenth century, in other words, the original pact no longer simply restrained what people and governments could or could not do; it could also become an instrument of change. Thereafter, people living together in a polity were seen as having the power to make and unmake their association, as well as modify the terms of their agreements.

Radical strains within enlightened thought suggested that the existing social pact restricted rather than advanced human happiness. To redo society, what was needed was a profound change, not cosmetic innovations. To imagine a better future, it was necessary to destroy the past. The best known among proponents of such radical moves was Jean-Jacques Rousseau (1712–1778). In his *Social Contract* (1762) Rousseau concluded that society corrupted rather than improved man, and he advocated its refoundation on the basis of a better agreement. The new social contract he proposed would not subject man to state, king, or government, as the present one did, but instead would subject man only to the community of which he was a member. According to Rousseau, this structure would ensure that all men would be both equal and sovereign, and it would guarantee true happiness.

These visions, which embodied enlightened beliefs, might have also been influenced by the constitutions and bills of rights that the representatives of the rebellious Thirteen Colonies adopted in the 1770s and 1780s. These documents—which some have described as a portfolio deliberately prepared, copied, and translated in order to legitimize the uprising and rally international support—were widely available in France. They were read and discussed by crown officials and intellectuals, some of whom came to believe that the events taking place in North America were the beginning of a transformation that would spread across the civilized world. This transformation, they hoped, would usher humanity into a new century, in which the experience of the Thirteen Colonies would serve as the experimental grounds.

Although revolutionary and groundbreaking, many of the beliefs advanced by the Enlightenment of course had deeper roots. They were based on seventeenth-century debates regarding the social contract, and they relied on juridical discussions concerning sovereignty and property, to mention just two examples. Jurists and intellectuals who pursued them were well versed in past traditions and often acted not only against these traditions but also in continuity with them. Their debates were geared toward learning what needed changing and what could remain intact, what could be modified and, often, how.

Local Conditions I: Legislation

As we have seen, during the fifteenth, sixteenth, and seventeenth centuries, French monarchs gradually assumed the power to legislate. Under the guise of continuity and pretending their intervention was a sign of respect toward traditional rights, monarchs encouraged, sometimes even forced, campaigns to write down the customary law of the various French regions. During these campaigns, royal jurists selected which customs would be written down and which forgotten. They also chose how customs would be worded, and which customs, originally restricted in their geographical scope, would be applied throughout the realm. As a result, by the seventeenth century the customary law of France had profoundly mutated. Rather than relying on ancient practices or negotiated solutions as was originally the case, it was made into a royally sanctioned written law that recorded only certain customs in particular ways.

While, formally, the writing down of customs did not change the norms but only clarified and recorded them, beginning in the mid-sixteenth century French kings began intensifying their intervention in the legal order. New royal enactments modifying existing jurisdictions, affecting procedural law, and redefining many institutions worked to change the French legal system. Particularly famous in this regard were the mid-seventeenth-century reforms undertaken under Louis XIV. During his reign, committees of jurists drew up general ordinances that refashioned civil and criminal procedure and regulated many other aspects of commercial life and navigation. Louis XIV also introduced the study of French law into local universities and encouraged jurists to write textbooks. Royal legislative efforts continued into the eighteenth century and were particularly clear in areas of private law such as donations and inheritance.

According to royal jurists, these interventions were necessary because French law was far too chaotic, far too difficult, and far too impractical. It required systematization, as well as scrutiny as to which remnants of the past were suitable for present conditions and which not. Despite the immensity of these measures, however, royal jurists did not pretend to overhaul the system; instead they viewed their work as intervening and changing what was necessary to modify according to contemporary criteria of what was just and what efficient.

This goal, which was juridically and politically motivated, was also supported by emerging philosophies. Bodin (1530–1596) and those following him suggested that public power had to be concentrated in one person (the king), who should exercise his faculties by making laws. For Bodin as for many of his contemporaries, law continued to be justified by a theologically based truth *(veritas)*, but it was now in the hands of monarchs and depended on their will *(voluntas)*. If sovereignty was one element in the puzzle, another was theories of "reason of state" that demanded that rulers actively intervene to ensure the well-being of their kingdoms even at the expense of taking measures that otherwise would be immoral or illegal. The greater good, in short, justified contravening the ordinary way of doing things. Thereafter, royal intervention in the normative order became an obligation rather than a privilege.

By the eighteenth century, this intervention was almost routine. If it provoked opposition, it also became a habit, instilling the idea that legislation was an effective way to transform reality. As a result of these developments, by the late eighteenth century France had a legal system that gave legislation a relatively central role. The country also had a strong political tradition that justified sovereignty (understood, paradoxically, as the power to act outside the law, among other things, by creating new norms) and theories that demanded that government not only guarantee the status quo but proceed to ensure greater happiness.

Local Conditions II: The Role of French *Parlements*

While royal practice and enlightened ideas furnished contemporaries with new ways of conceiving the legal order, just as important were the particular circumstances in France on the eve of the Revolution. As we have seen, the centuries that predated the Revolution witnessed growing royal activism, mainly expressed through intervention in the legal order. Resistance to these tendencies, which were interpreted as attempts by the kings to institute themselves as absolute monarchs, was mostly channeled through the work of French *parlements*. These were not political assemblies as the English translation (Parliament) would indicate. Instead, they were royal courts that represented the king locally. As overseers of law in Paris (the *Parlement* of Paris) and the provinces (provincial *parlements*), these courts received all royal orders (ordinances, royal letters, edicts, treaties, and the like) for their area and registered them on their rolls before the orders were published and obeyed.

Although initially this was a relatively innocent formal bureaucratic practice that informed judges of what the king instructed, during the early modern period the *parlements* began using registration to place checks on royal will. Their magistrates argued that they had the right to remonstrate against decrees and could refuse registration until they were heard or the necessary amendments were made. Although in theory decrees were valid whether the *parlement* registered them or not, French jurists often considered registration a de facto ratification.

The most common pretext to complain and delay the registration of royal decrees was that they violated royal legislation or provincial norms that were deemed fundamental. The *parlements*, it was argued, were guardians of the law and it was their duty to remind the king of his obligation not to violate the established legal principles and the fundamental laws. Responding to such protests, most kings ordered the *parlements* to register the decrees and threatened magistrates with punishment. By the sixteenth century, French monarchs also replied by personally attending the meeting of the *parlement,* a ceremony *(lit de justice)* that commanded respect and obedience in ways that written orders did not.

Although the relations between the *parlements* and the French monarchs changed over time, on the eve of the French Revolution the magistrates of the various *parlements* and the royal administration were locked in a power struggle. The king, acting as an absolute sovereign, attempted to levy new taxes and change state structures, and the *parlements* responded that he must obey the fundamental laws of the country, which the magistrates claimed to defend. As in seventeenth-century England, eighteenth-century French magistrates asserted that France had basic legal arrangements that functioned as a constitution that the monarch could not alter. Particularly adamant regarding this point were the magistrates of the *Parlement* of Paris, which in 1753 declared that there was a contract between the king and his subjects according to which if the subjects obeyed the king, he had to obey the law.

The struggle over registration of royal decrees by the *parlements* allowed some members of the French elite to resist the expansion of royal prerogatives under the guise of obedience to the normative order and defense of traditional liberties. Particularly active in the 1770s and 1780s, the Parisian *Parlement* insisted that royal actions could not contravene not only the fundamental laws of the kingdom but also the "rights of the nation," which the *Parlement* was charged with protecting. The radicalization of the conflict led the monarch to reform the *parlements* (in 1771) and abolish them (in 1788).

The role that *parlements* appropriated in the name of the provinces and the nation was clearly summarized on May 3, 1788, one year before the Revolution began. In The Declaration of Fundamental Laws, the magistrates of the Paris *Parlement* expressed their conviction that France had a customary ancient constitution that the king must uphold. According to their understanding, the most fundamental norms included in that constitution were succession to the crown by a male heir according to primogeniture, the right of the nation to grant taxation freely as decided by its representatives in the Estates General (that is, no taxation without parliamentary consent), obedience to the customs and rights of the provinces, the irrevocability of magistrates (who were not nominated by the king but instead purchased or inherited their offices), and magistrates' right to verify the king's legislative acts and register them only if they conformed to the "basic laws of the province" and the "fundamental laws of the state." Also enumerated in the 1788 declaration were the rights of citizens to be summoned only before their "natural judges" and to see a magistrate immediately after their arrest (a right somewhat akin to *habeas corpus*).

The *parlements* were extremely successful at curbing royal power, yet by the time the Revolution took place they were greatly discredited. Identified as bastions of provincialism and manned by jurists many of whom were noblemen who had purchased or inherited their offices, the *parlements* were criticized and ridiculed rather than admired. The *Parlement* of Paris was particularly censured for taking what was considered a conservative stand in favor of continuity, as embodied, for example, in its demand to call for a meeting of the Estates General in its old form, which gave the clergy and nobility (most *parlement* members belonging to the nobility) an advantage over the commoners (the Third Estate). The *Parlement,* in short, was no longer considered a channel for advancing demands but instead was seen as a petty institution that mostly protected the interests of its members.

Although *parlements* were eventually seen as undesirable, the lesson they taught remained intact. Law was (or could be) a formidable tool to limit the pretensions to absolutism. Following this lesson, the various revolutionary factions and individuals who searched for a new social pact sought to identify legal mechanisms that would curb executive claims to powers. They did so by instituting a National Assembly with legislative powers, elected by the people and for the people. Paradoxically, another important lesson they learned was the failure of the monarchy to win its battle against the *parlements.* Judges, contemporaries understood, had tremendous powers to limit what governments could do. As a result, they must be deprived of any lawmaking capacities and transformed into passive implementers of laws decided upon and perhaps even interpreted elsewhere. On both accounts, these lessons indicated the need to clearly separate the powers of the executive, the legislative, and the judiciary.

First Dilemma: A National System for a Universal Audience?

The revolutionary measures taken in France in the late 1780s and in the 1790s were on some levels profoundly contradictory. Seeking to empower the nation and affirm its sovereignty as well as its ability to modify the legal order, they also appealed to a larger community, including all humans, and to a natural law that was said to be universal. Thus, although the law created by the general will of the National Assembly was to apply only within France, it was nevertheless theoretically based on principles such as reason that were common to all humanity.

The emergence of a specifically national law marked the end of a unified European legal system, indeed the end of a *ius commune* that applied throughout the Continent. Instead of the old commonality based on tradition, experience, and Christianity, what was now proposed was a new commonality anchored in reason and natural law. This move was made possible by the belief that, rather than being dependent on cultural assumptions, as it is currently viewed, human reason was one and the same everywhere, always. This implied that, although it was nationally created and nationally bound, because it was inspired by reason and reason alone the law enacted

by the general will of the French could potentially be valid for other countries and constituencies. Not only could this law be exported, it must be,
because human happiness depended on the expansion of reason and on all
societies obeying it.

The universality of this message would eventually justify the revolutionary
wars as well as Napoleon's efforts to implement at least some of the revolutionary legislation across Europe, but it was present even in the early years.
Typical in this regard was the 1789 adoption of the Declaration of the Rights
of Man and Citizen. Protecting citizens, that is, members of the French
political community, but also man in general, the declaration created an
instrument that would be relevant both to "we the people" (as the representatives of the Thirteen Colonies had done) and humanity at large. It enumerated rights that were general and forward-looking, including the right to
freedom and equality, liberty, property, security, and resistance to oppression. Also listed were some of the structures of good government, which
were to guarantee those rights everywhere.

As happened with the U.S. Bill of Rights, much of what was enumerated
in the French declaration was a direct result of the political confrontations
that unfolded in the 1770s, 1780s, and 1790s. The declaration focused on affirming the equality of all men, which for French contemporaries implied
the end of the particular privileges of the nobility and the clergy. Also central to the declaration was protection against a royal government that, according to contemporary allegations, pretended to be sovereign when it was
not, arrested people without cause, assumed the culpability of enemies, and
constantly changed the punishments that could be inflicted. Safeguarding
freedom of speech, ensuring that the armed forces would be used only to
protect rather than to attack the common good, the demand that all taxation be authorized by consent, and guaranteeing judicial freedom were all
also important.

Although explained by the particularities of the moment, the French declaration pretended to announce principles that were general and timeless,
that is, ahistorical and unchangeable. To ensure its global applicability, the
language used was extremely abstract. It decontextualized rights and disconnected them from the particularities of place, time, or legal tradition. The first
article of the declaration, for example, stipulated that man is born free and
should remain free. The second stated that the aim of every political association is the maintenance of the natural rights of man, mainly liberty, property,
security, and resistance to oppression. The fourth determined that liberty

consists of being able to do anything that does not harm others. Subsequent articles declared that laws could forbid only those actions that are harmful to society and that there is a presumption of innocence.

This abstract language reflected the belief that the rights enumerated were indeed common to all men and all societies whatever their particular nature might be, but it was also a useful tool. The more abstract a description, the more potentially inclusive and the more open to a variety of interpretations it was. Returning to the first article, which stated that all men were born free, this abstract language acted as a safety valve of sorts. It allowed experts writing then and since to ask what was included in the category "men." Did it, for example, include women? Did it include children? Were all men included or only those who were reasonable (however reason was defined)? Were slaves included? Each author and period gave these questions a distinct solution. In the long run, this abstract language facilitated the adaptation of this declaration to the requirements of a constantly changing society, in which it was easier to achieve agreement on principles than on what they meant and how they were to be implemented.

Second Dilemma: The Status of Natural Law

If law was created by the representatives of the sovereign people and it was nationally bound, and what was not prohibited expressively by law was allowed, how could natural law, in which revolutionaries also believed, dictate anything? Or, inversely, how could the National Assembly be truly sovereign if its legislative activities were to be limited by natural law, as the Declaration of the Rights of Man and Citizen, for example, proclaimed?

To solve these dilemmas, eighteenth-century French lawmakers sought to reproduce in legislative acts what they considered to be the main mandates of natural law. The Declaration of the Rights of Man and Citizen was one such act. It included both a recognition of preexisting norms as well as the intent to give these norms a new character by recreating them legally through their formal adoption by the National Assembly. These two complimentary dimensions explained why the declaration both affirmed the superiority of the "natural, inalienable and sacred rights of man" and enumerated them. The aim was not only to remind the audience what they were. Instead, by identifying rights in legislation, the French sought to give these rights normative value in a system that recognized no other legal source but legislation.

However, this procedure offered an imperfect solution to the question of how to safeguard natural rights. The declaration might have transformed these rights into valid norms, but it was not powerful enough to restrict or limit the sovereignty of the National Assembly, which could still legislate in ways that would contravene these rights. To ensure the protection of rights, legislative and constitutional texts appealed above all to legislators' conscience. The 1791 constitution entrusted guardianship of rights to the "fidelity" of the legislative body, the king, and the judges, and to the "vigilance" of fathers, wives and mothers, young citizens, and all Frenchmen. The 1793 constitution mandated that lists of rights would be reproduced on large tablets placed in the halls of the legislative body and in public places. In 1795, guardianship of the constitution and rights was again "entrusted" to the fidelity of the legislature, the executive, administrators, judges, fathers, wives, mothers, young citizens, and all Frenchman.[6]

A Revolutionary Moment?

In England, the Thirteen Colonies, and France, resistance to monarchy led to the invocation of an ancient constitution that the monarch was accused of betraying, and the subsequent affirmation of parliamentary powers. In all three places, contemporaries claimed to be acting as guardians of both law and rights. Yet what this law was, and where these rights were located, was distinct in each case. Rights went from being traditional privileges that were owned by community members because the king so promised (England), to rational entitlements that should pertain to members but also all humans according to the law of nature (the Thirteen Colonies and France). Law also changed in the process as it passed from customary and inheritable arrangements (England and the Thirteen Colonies) to new solutions that, seeking to guarantee the greatest happiness possible, were theoretically based on investigating both nature and society and concluding what was reasonable and what just (France and to a lesser degree the Thirteen Colonies).

Regardless of these differences, what was most striking about the revolutions that swept England, the Thirteen Colonies, and France was not only what they achieved but the diverse attitudes that accompanied them. Despite the enormity of what was proposed, seventeenth-century English actors chose to present their revolution as a continuity. The representatives of the Thirteen Colonies, who also innovated, insisted on the superiority of their particular traditions, which they sought to uphold, while also invoking the dictates of natural law as if both things were one and the same. Disregarding all continuities between past and present (even when they were noticeable), most French actors stated that they favored a radical break.

Despite these images, events in England and the Thirteen Colonies were clearly revolutionary, and in France the aspiration to refound the social pact and begin a new age was not always obtained. Some measures, such as the institution of a legislative assembly or the adoption of trial by jury, were truly revolutionary, yet others were much less radical or were only partially implemented. The desire to do away with all the privileges of the nobility and with all professional guilds, to mention just two cases, did not fully prosper, as some nobles continued to receive payments due to privileges that were feudal in origin, and some guilds maintained their professional monopolies. Partly due to the need for political compromise, partly because returning to a blank slate was impossible, as happened in the English and the American revolutions, the French Revolution also allowed for both continuity and change.

Although a complete overhaul of the system was never achieved in France, the legal transformations resulting from the French Revolution were nevertheless dramatic. While in England a royal system of courts was refashioned as the customary law of the land, and in the Thirteen Colonies constitutional structures were radically affected even if law itself was not, in France a legal system based on *ius commune,* customs, and royal legislation came to rely mostly on legislation by the National Assembly. Also in France, a normative universe dedicated to preserving the status quo was redesigned intentionally to introduce change.

As a result of these innovations, and independently of where we live, most of us are to some degree or another heirs to the French Revolution. Developments in the Thirteen Colonies allowed people to imagine the right to constitute polities and decide on their structure, and they envisioned constitutions as superior laws that limited the sovereignty of Parliament. Meanwhile, developments in France led to the formation of a new type of legal system, based on the power of legislation created in a representative assembly by the will of the people and guided by reason. This system, which produced what most of us today identify as "law," was nationally bound and was designed to introduce change.

PART SIX

The Nineteenth Century

12

Codifying the Laws of Europe

MAKING EUROPEAN LAW
UNIVERSAL II

IN THE NINETEENTH CENTURY most European countries experienced codification fever. Starting with France and concluding with Germany, by the end of the century the laws of most European polities, England being the exception, were to some degree codified. Following the French Revolution, the central role assigned to legislation enabled jurists and politicians across Europe to substantially modify the normative order by enacting codes designed to replace most or all other legal arrangements. During this period, two basic models for codification emerged, the first originating in France and the other in Germany. The French code appealed to reason and searched for simplicity; the German code invoked tradition and was highly technical. Despite their differences the codes were also very similar, and both were imitated around the globe, driving yet another universalization of European law.

Nineteenth-Century France—From Revolution Within to War Abroad

The French Revolution introduced a new understanding of what law was and where it came from. According to this understanding, legislation was the only legitimate normative source, and it was to originate in the decisions of a sovereign National Assembly. Its aim was to create a new, improved society by inventing new, improved laws based on reason and will. Other, no less important aims were the creation of a single national law out of the multiplicity of local arrangements, and a new universality based on reason and rights rather than on tradition and Christianity.

The French Revolution met with extreme hostility both inside and outside France, which led to radicalization and chaos. From 1792 to 1802 in a series of wars, various coalitions that included in different configurations Prussia, Austria, Russia, Britain, Spain, Portugal, Sweden, the Netherlands, several Italian and German polities (to use an anachronism), and the Ottoman Empire confronted the new French revolutionary government. It was during this period that Napoleon Bonaparte, a highly successful military commander, emerged as a leader, becoming consul in 1799, consul for life in 1802, and emperor in 1804.

Napoleon strove to restore order inside France but he also took it upon himself to win over France's enemies and spread the tenets of the French Revolution beyond French borders. Until his unsuccessful invasion of Russia (1812) Napoleon seemed invincible, but it was not until 1815 that he was finally defeated.

Initial French success resulted in important legal changes involving the preparation and subsequent diffusion in Europe of legal codes that were said to embody the spirit of the French Revolution as well as reproduce some of its tenets. These codes were first applied in France, but soon after they were also implemented in territories under French occupation or influence, and eventually they were used or copied around the globe.

Napoleonic Codification

From as early as 1790, French jurists suggested that because revolutionary law was theoretically based on reason, it could be easily systematized, allowing for the creation of a single yet holistic legal text that, applied all over France, would guarantee the reign of liberty, equality, and fraternity. The ideal text would be clear, concise, and accessible, its comprehension requiring no expert knowledge or preparation. It would consist of a guidebook that would be kept in every household to be used by rational individuals to plan their activities. The text would also educate citizens as to their rights and duties.

The hope was to create a code that would be substantially different from previous codes that were elaborated in Europe in the late eighteenth century, such as the Feudal Code of Venice (1780), the Leopoldine Code of Tuscany

(1786), the various codes elaborated in Austria, and the General Code for the Prussian States promulgated 1794. While previous codes aimed to compile, simplify, and systemize existing norms, the new code proposed by French jurists was meant to innovate. It was to introduce a new, complete, and definitive legal order that would replace all that existed before and that would be based not on tradition but on the will of the people, as well as on reason.

Various commissions were appointed to elaborate drafts of such a text, yet the projects they authored were rejected by the National Assembly, mostly on the grounds that they were either too long and complicated, insufficiently conceptualized, and overly anchored in past traditions or, on the contrary, excessively short and vague. It was only after Napoleon ascended to power that members of a new commission proposed a text that a legislative body controlled by Napoleon promulgated in 1804 as *Le code civil des français*, better known as the *Code Napoléon*. The text covered private law and included 2,281 articles dealing with the law of persons and property.

The Napoleonic Code was not all that it was supposed to be. Although containing some of the most important innovations introduced by revolutionary legislation, such as equality before the law, protection of private property, secularization of marriage, legalization of divorce, and freedom of religion, the code also closely adhered to Old Regime structures in many other domains. With a mixture of Roman, customary, and revolutionary law, rather than departing from a clean slate, which was the stated intention, in practice it was an amalgam of both old and new.

If the code contained many Old Regime norms, it also was not as easy to read and understand as expected. In order to reproduce all of private law in a short text, the commission elaborating the code made use of general principles and often adopted extremely abstract language, which diminished intelligibility and precision. The hope that the code would eliminate dependency on lawyers and legally trained judges was thus frustrated. Instead, even after the promulgation of the code, law continued to be the exclusive domain of experts who were familiar with legal texts and cognizant of their possible meanings.

Jean-Étienne Portalis (1746–1807), a member of the drafting committee, was aware of these shortcomings, as were other contemporary jurists and subsequent historians. He seemed convinced that however much one would try, it would be impossible to produce a code that would cover everything and require no interpretation; neither would it be possible to reproduce the complexities of law in a short and simple text. What was possible, instead, was to state the law as a coherent set of principles that could be comprehended (and extended, when needed) by employing reason.

Despite these shortcomings, the Napoleonic Code was nevertheless perfectly positioned to produce a legal revolution. The law promulgating the code instructed as much, ordering that after its enactment all Roman law doctrines, general ordinances, local customs, statutes, and regulations would cease to apply in those matters covered by the code. In line with revolutionary legislation, the law also instructed that the code would be applicable throughout French territory and enforced on all those residing there, regardless of who they were.

Other drastic measures were hidden in articles 4 and 5. Article 4 determined that a judge who refused to adjudicate a case, alleging silence, obscurity, or insufficiency of the law, would be deemed guilty of denying justice. Article 5 instructed that judges were forbidden to issue general pronouncements that might be perceived as legislative. Together these measures sought to guarantee the supremacy of the code. They determined that, by definition, it was complete and conclusive, containing all answers to all possible questions. After its enactment there would be no legal void *(lacuna)* because the code admitted none. This was why judges could not legitimately conclude that the code was silent, nor could they create new solutions by way of general pronouncements. Article 5, which prohibited such creation, also sought to protect the separation of powers by prohibiting judges from engaging in the making of rules.

From One Code to Many

Following the enactment of the Civil Code, other codes made their appearance. The Code of Civil Procedure (enacted in 1806) dealt with process before the courts as well as the execution of court orders. The Code of Commerce that came into being the following year (1807) covered commerce in general, as well as maritime law, bankruptcy, and mercantile jurisdiction. The Code of Criminal Procedure (enacted in 1808) and the Criminal Code (1810) came next.[1]

These codes reproduced many of the advantages and shortcomings of the Civil Code. Although they were meant to change everything, they both enshrined the basic principles of the French Revolution as well as allowed continuity. Their main contribution was not the adoption of new solutions (which often they did not) but the refashioning of the law itself. Converting traditional, customary, royal, or Roman law arrangements into legislative enactments, the codes also accentuated the division of law into branches such as private law, commercial law, and criminal law. Their clear separation of substantive law (as in the civil and criminal codes, which defined what was the reasonable norm) and procedural law (as in the codes of civil or criminal procedure that mandated how reasonableness could be attested and proved) was also noteworthy.

Making the French Codes Universal

In the decades following their promulgation, the French codes, most particularly the Civil Code, had enormous resonance throughout Europe and the Americas, and to a lesser degree also in Asia and Africa.[2] Historians attribute this influence to several factors. Napoleon, who perceived himself as undertaking a "civilizing mission," applied French codes in territories under French occupation, such as northern Italy, Belgium, the Netherlands, Luxembourg, Monaco, and several German polities. In other areas, where he lacked political or military hegemony, he used persuasion and urged local leaders to consider the code for adoption. This took place in several German states, in Swiss cantons, and in Poland. But above and beyond what Napoleon himself aspired to achieve, as the nineteenth century advanced, many members of elite groups around the globe came to view the French codes, most particularly the Civil Code, as useful instruments. Some hoped to unify the various laws of their country into a single national system; others considered the code fitting for the demands of modern economic, social, and political conditions. As a symbol for a relatively accessible law that embodied many of the aspirations of the emerging middle classes, such as legal equality and the protection of property, the various French codes (or versions thereof) continued being adopted long after Napoleon was defeated on the military and political battlefields.

Like the French Revolution itself, the universalization of French postrevolutionary codes proposed both the reign of national laws made by the will of the people and a horizon of new commonality based on reason. Codes embodied a legal system particular to a polity and they were used to nationalize a series of divergent local laws, yet they also, paradoxically, were pan-European and universal in orientation. They encouraged "legal transplantation"—the borrowing of laws from one system and country to the next—borrowing that was not restricted to structures, procedures, and terms, but often included substantial solutions that, in the process of being nationalized by their inclusion in a code, were also universalized through their adoption by many different countries.

German Codification: The Second Model

In 1896, almost one hundred years after the promulgation of the French Civil Code, the Germans enacted their own code, the Bürgerliches Gesetzbuch, better known as the BGB. German codifiers had the opportunity to learn from the mistakes of previous codifications, but they also operated under radically distinct circumstances. Unlike the French codes, which were inspired by the Enlightenment and the Revolution and heralded universal reason (even if they were often the product of tradition), the German code was influenced by Romantic and nationalistic visions that sought to codify and modernize the past.

Most historians trace the origin of the BGB to a group of individuals belonging to a "German Historical School" organized around a manifesto published in 1814 by Friedrich Karl von Savigny (1779–1861). In the manifesto, "Vocation of Our Age for Legislation and Jurisprudence," von Savigny responded to a suggestion made by another scholar (A. F. J. Thibaut) that Germany adopt a code similar to the French Civil Code. Law, von Savigny argued, was not a pure construct of reason but instead the product of tradition. It expressed the history, language, culture, and national consciousness *(Volksgeist)* of society, and it grew as a result of silent operating forces, not the arbitrary will of a lawgiver. Customary in orientation, it was the task of jurists, not legislators, to cohere it into a code, and to do so, jurists had to better understand the national legal history.

Most members of the German Historical School opposed the supremacy of reason and the subsequent claim that reasonable laws could be universal, but they disagreed regarding the role of Roman law in German legal history. Was it an alien system whose bad influence limited the growth of local law and therefore had to be purged for the system to be authentic, or was it, like Christianity, a superstructure that, lacking nationality, was a common

European heritage also shared by Germans? Those adhering to the first interpretation were thereafter identified as "Germanists." Those who supported the second vision were classified as "Romanists."

Having positioned themselves against Roman law, Germanists proceeded to discover and reconstruct the so-called authentic, medieval, Germanic traditions that predated the arrival of Roman law and that, according to them, were responsible for the emergence of present-day structures.[3] Many Germanists identified these older traditions with non-erudite, popular law. Among those participating in this quest to recover customary practices were the Brothers Grimm. Best known as collectors and publishers of folk tales, such as *Cinderella, Hansel and Gretel,* and *Snow White,* Wilhelm (1786–1859) and Jacob (1785–1863) Grimm were jurists who studied with Savigny. As part of their interest in rescuing a genuinely German past, they set off to the countryside to record popular traditions. Their efforts resulted in the famous collection known as the *Tales of the Brothers Grimm,* but also in lesser-known yet extremely important compilations of local legal customs.

While Germanists wished to rescue tradition, Romanists, von Savigny among them, sought to understand the interaction between German and Roman law. They studied Roman law in order to understand the concepts and principles that helped fifteenth- and sixteenth-century German jurists organize and systematize local law. This method, known as the Pandect-Science, led Romanist jurists to insist that what Roman law did to German law in the fifteenth century could be done again in the nineteenth century. By using Roman law rather than pure logic, jurists could again systematize and organize German law without being unfaithful to it. For German Romanists, Roman law was not a foreign legal system. Instead it was a repository of methods and instruments that would enable them to describe the existing law with precision and consistency. The study of Roman law was thus a means for constructing a truly German yet rational, modern, and bureaucratic law that was fit for the demands of the nineteenth century.

To understand the meaning of possession, for example, Romanists turned to Roman remedies that protected it, as well as the defenses that litigants could invoke. Examining additional sources such as edicts, formulas, legislation, the opinion of jurists, and the texts of the *Corpus Iuris Civilis,* Romanists came up with the basic rules for possession, which stated that possession depended on one's having control over the thing as well as having the intention to hold it as an owner in good faith.

According to some critics, Pandectists ended up betraying their own agenda. They became obsessed with categories, concepts, and abstract propositions that, according to them, were derived from Roman law but in fact, according to their detractors, were based on their wish to find a few general principles that would rule over absolutely everything. Critics concluded that Romanists ended up proposing a law that, rather than being based on the particular traditions of Germany, was an abstract logical construction profoundly divorced from any social, religious, political, cultural, or economic considerations. Some critics even considered it a system of legal mathematical calculation. Romanists also were accused of anachronism for writing modern notions, such as the centrality of the individual and his will, into Roman law, which lacked them.

Attempts at codifying the law, which had been continuous in the various German states, intensified with the unification of 1871. As part of the state-building processes and accompanied by rising nationalism, between 1874 and 1887 a committee of academics, practitioners, and government officials deliberated on how to prepare a national code for the new, unified German state. Inspired by the Historical School, the committee aimed to use existing compilations, as well as Roman and customary law, to unify the various legal systems of the diverse territories.[4] To undertake this mission, each member of the committee was to write one part of the code. After seven years, the committee met to discuss the results. Six years of debates followed. Eventually the committee published a proposal, sending copies to universities, judges, and scholars. Newspapers were also asked to collaborate with this enterprise by printing parts of the proposal and making space for the debates that might ensue.

The proposal provoked heated contestation. Although some critics objected to codification in general, most criticized the text for failing to accurately represent German law. For some the draft was excessively Roman and insufficiently German. For others its language was far too complex and abstract, indeed so removed from ordinary language that most Germans would fail to understand it. As one of the commentators is said to have remarked, for the proposal of the code to be understood, it had to be translated into ordinary German.

Given these negative comments, a second committee, working between 1890 and 1895, extensively revised the first draft. The text it produced, the BGB, was given statutory force without much debate in 1896. The new code included five parts: an introduction, followed by books dealing with property, obligations, family law, and succession. The introduction included general provisions regarding the law of persons, the classification of things and juridical acts, prescription, and the like. These provisions governed the other parts of the code and complemented their instructions.

The BGB had some 2,385 sections. It introduced many innovations, most importantly in contract law, but it did not cover all areas of private law; for example, commercial law remained mostly outside the code, though it was considered to be influenced by some of the code's basic principles.

Commentators remark that the BGB depended heavily on Roman law. Its arrangement was Roman and some fields, such as obligations, were extremely Romanized. Other fields, such as family law, were anchored in Germanic traditions. The language remained very technical, conceptual, and opaque.

French and German Codification Compared

Despite aspiring to some of the same objectives, the French and the German civil codes were almost complete opposites. Both sought to systematize the law and write it down so to guarantee legal certainty, but they did so in radically distinct ways. The French code was said to break with the past and be based on natural universal reason that nonprofessional legislators could employ. It was meant to be simple and easy to use. The German code, on the contrary, was the product of past traditions, which were compiled by jurists who employed a sophisticated juridical science that made its interpretation a difficult art requiring ample knowledge. The French code was meant to democratize the law and allow citizens to know what their rights and obligations were (even if it failed); the BGB was instead a monument to the constant necessity for the mediation of legal experts. Rather than transferring power to the legislature, it ensured a central role to jurists and universities, where juridical doctrine could be elaborated and debated. Unlike the French code, which eliminated all other normative sources and was meant to usher in a new, revolutionary age, the BGB was not designed to replace the previous law. On the contrary, at least in theory, it codified it. And although both codes sought to unify the legal regime by transforming a series of local regional systems into a single national order, the French code was more successful at achieving this goal, as the BGB left ample room for local arrangements by recognizing the need to conserve them in regulations regarding mines, waters, fish and game, property relations between individuals and the state, public property, religious societies, and insurance.

Despite these differences, the French and German civil codes were also similar in many ways. Both sought to restate the law systematically and concisely by using general, abstract language. Both codes relied heavily on *ius commune,* the previous legal tradition, although the French code did not openly acknowledge this. Ideologically, both obeyed the mandate of a modern society for a sharp separation of powers and consecrated the protection of private property, the liberty of contracts, and legal equality. As happened also in France, in Germany the promulgation of the BGB also ushered in a period of additional codification, with the development, for example, of a fiscal code, a commercial code, a criminal code, a code of criminal procedure, a code of administrative court procedure, and a code of civil procedure.

Eventually historians would point out that, despite its alleged inspiration in Germanic legal traditions, the BGB was understood by many as a universal, rather than national, code. Becoming a second model for what civil codification could look like, the BGB would be imitated around the globe, most particularly in Europe and Asia.[5] In some places it was reproduced almost in its entirety; in other places local legislatures omitted some parts; but nowhere were its solutions understood as being specifically Germanic. The growing international importance and standing of the BGB enhanced the reputation of German jurists—demonstrating that, even in the late nineteenth century, Roman law could still act as a unifying agent. As far as nineteenth-century observers were concerned, it was indeed like Goethe's diving duck.[6]

13

Codifying Common Law

IN A LECTURE AT UNIVERSITY COLLEGE, London, in November 1926, Maurice Amos (1872–1940), a British lawyer, judge, and professor of law, suggested that codification was one of the "great activities and vehicles of civilization."[1] Trying to explain to his compatriots what it meant and what it could achieve, he proposed a hypothetical case. Imagine, he said, that the Duke of Wellington, the foremost British military commander during the Napoleonic wars, had seized power in England in the early nineteenth century. Imagine that, after he did, he asked celebrated legal experts to prepare a civil code based on Blackstone's *Commentaries*. Imagine that this code had absolutely no references to religion or feudalism. Imagine that this Wellington Code would then be applied not only in England but also in Scotland. Imagine that after its enactment, all previous customs and statutes ceased to exist. This scenario, Amos declared, should give the English a fair idea of what Napoleon had accomplished by creating a code that unified, laicized, democratized, and simplified French civil law. It should also explain to them why the French model was so widely imitated around the globe, while the English system was followed only in countries that are or were directly subjected to it.

Amos was one of many admirers of codification in England. Wrong or right, correct in his appreciations or completely mistaken, he spent time and ink explaining to his compatriots why codification was good and what it could do for them. Although in the nineteenth and early twentieth centuries enthusiasts like him were not lacking among common-law experts, it is nevertheless true that most English and American legal professionals turned their back on codification. Suggesting that it was both unnecessary and unwise, or favoring a different type of codification more appropriate to common-law countries, they engaged in heated debates regarding the question whether codification was a suitable tool for reforming the law.

English Response to Codification

At the turn of the nineteenth century, English law was divided into two main parts: statutory law, which included legislation passed by Parliament, and common law, which allegedly encompassed customary law made by judges. Statutory law could be found in a huge variety of acts and statutes that, after being promulgated, were published and conserved in the archives. Common law could be located in the Yearbooks (1263–1535) or their more modern replacement, the Law Reports. From the mid-sixteenth century until 1865, when they became institutionalized, Law Reports were authored by private individuals, some (like Edward Coke's) winning more followers than others. Covering what had transpired in the courts, both the Yearbooks and the Reports were the best source for studying the development of common-law concepts, methods, and doctrines as well as tracing precedents. Published in different editions and by many individuals, not only were these sources of diverse quality, but there was no general index that would help one navigate through them. As a result, many lawyers were reduced to using secondary literature, such as abridgments, to discover which past cases and rulings might be applicable to their case and what they stated.

In short, in order to know what the law dictated, it was necessary to consult both the legislation and case law, which was an extremely arduous task. Because the underlying assumption was that legislation and common law cohered rather than contradicted one another, it was also essential for lawyers to secure an interpretation that upheld them both. Legal practice, including maxims, principles, presumptions, and doctrines, held by legal professionals, both lawyers and judges, also introduced into this mix additional elements that were considered mandatory.

From the sixteenth century onward, many in England lamented this complexity, some demanding the production of an orderly code or the collection of all statutory and case law in a single body. Following such demands, Francis Bacon (1561–1626) and Matthew Hale (1609–1676), two of England's foremost seventeenth-century legal authorities, envisioned a compilation of the laws of England that would include three parts: a first book encompassing legal institutions, legal maxims, and a legal dictionary; a second book reediting the Yearbooks; and a third book reproducing statutory law.

It was not until 1833, however, that a significant move toward codification took place in England, when a committee to reconsider criminal law (a field that, contrary to many others, heavily relied on legislation and thus was more amenable to codification) was appointed by Parliament. The committee was given the task of preparing a code including all statutes, enactments, and common-law principles regarding crimes and their punishment. Yet attempts to pass the committee's proposals for reform and its recommendations for codification in Parliament failed. New proposals for a criminal code in 1878, 1879, and 1880 also did not have sufficient backing.

Attempts at codifying other areas of the law met with similar results. In 1860 the government announced a project to compile and revise English statute law and create a digest of case law with a view to combining both in a single text. The committee appointed in 1866 was dissolved fourteen years later, its main contribution being a series of drafts that became textbooks on the different branches of English law.

Eventually, instead of codifying their laws, what the English did was adopt other means to simplify their system. Most important among these were the consolidation acts (laws) passed by Parliament that collected various pieces of statutory law. Usually covering a particular legal field, consolidation acts sought to reproduce and describe this field exhaustively in a single text that would be promulgated by Parliament. Some parliamentary legislation even sought to go beyond consolidation by combining both statutory and case law; such legislation was sometimes known as "codifying statutes." The Bills of Exchange Act (1882), for example, consolidated seventeen statutes in a single text but also summarized the jurisprudence of some 2,600 law cases scattered in over three hundred volumes of Law Reports.

Although presented as a technical solution intended not to change the law but only to facilitate its knowledge, consolidation acts and codifying statutes were rarely a simple recording of preexisting norms. Instead they allowed selection as well as reordering according to a predefined and selective agenda. According to many observers, they actually changed the law. By making it easier to navigate the legal system, they also propelled new debates. After they were completed, it was no longer clear whether the original decisions or the acts and statutes were more authoritative. Was their power dependent on their common-law origins (the judicial decision that declared their existence), their initial enactment by Parliament, or their reenactment in an act or a codifying statute that now declared them valid?

Eventually lawyers who wanted to understand the law referred most frequently to treatises written by lawyers, judges, and university professors. Beginning with William Blackstone and his *Commentaries on the Laws of England* (1765–1769) and continuing with other notable scholars, such as Frederick Pollock (1945–1937), who authored various treaties on the laws of contract, partnership, and torts as well as *The History of English Law before the Time of Edward I* (1895), English legal experts set out to arrange English law systematically according to general categories. Describing and, to a degree, rationalizing the law, they enumerated and summarized principles, listed precedents, and prepared indexes. Dividing writs according to their subject matter (contract, torts, guardianship, as in the case of Pollock), they often used Roman law principles to describe what the writs instituted. Although these books had no binding force, they became a common, sometimes even authoritative, point of reference that both lawyers and nonlawyers used, and that judges also followed.

The English Position Explained

The traditional explanation for why codification was not adopted in England was that it was both unnecessary and unwise. According to this vision, countries that adopted codification did so because they had no choice. Their legal situation was catastrophic and their system complex, bulky, contradictory, and inaccessible. Divided into a multiplicity of local regimes, many of these countries had no national law nor were their laws adequate to the needs of the nineteenth-century nation-state. Legal development was stalled, requiring the urgent intervention of legislators. All these conditions were absent in England, where legal growth continued and where a national, orderly, and modern legal system already existed.

Even if this description had been correct (it certainly was not), in recent years historians have pointed out that what was most opposed to codification was the very distinct English take on what law was and how it should be created. As described in Chapter 12, Continental codification, most particularly in its French variant, styled codes as the beginning of a new age.

They were to replace tradition with new enactments that, even if they reproduced past solutions (which they often did), would be promulgated by the nation's representatives in Parliament because they were reasonable. Thereafter the norms' validity would depend not on tradition but on their having been promulgated by an assembly that represented the will of the people and that was sovereign and could change the law. Codes were supposed to be comprehensive statements of the law and replace all previous enactments. Using general abstract principles, codes were to be interpreted according to their logical meaning, not past experience, jurisprudence, or doctrine. Under this system, judges theoretically were to exercise absolutely no discretion. All they could do was implement a law that, by definition, had a single reasonable interpretation. No general pronouncements creating new norms were tolerated.

The basic assumption of most English lawyers regarding what law was and where it came from was radically distinct from what is described above. By the nineteenth century, most English lawyers believed that the English legal system was based on common law, which was a customary law that grew organically within the community. Tied to the particular conditions of England, it was anchored in experience, not reason. Because it naturally sprang from societal interactions, it was concrete and casuistic rather than abstract and general, inductive rather than deductive. It consisted of an enumeration of cases that reproduced and explained what judges had decided in the past. Lawyers' task was to compare cases and, highlighting similarities or distinctions, find a fair solution. While judges were central to legal creation, legislators were not. Although legislators represented "the people," their duty was to uphold rather than make the law. They were to ensure that the traditional rights of Englishmen were respected, and they could do so by legislating as long as they did not attempt to innovate. English legal experts also tended to believe that their system was superior to all others because, legislation was formal and inflexible, whereby a customary law made by judges allowed for constant updating and better defended the rights and liberties of individuals. The English system, in short, guaranteed freedom, which the Continental systems, most particularly the French, did not. Many Englishmen also rejected association with ideas that could be identified as French, most particularly those originating in the French Revolution.

These characteristics of common law as understood by nineteenth-century English lawyers made recourse to codification extremely difficult. The common law these actors imagined left relatively little room for legislation and certainly left none for enactments designed to overhaul the existing order. This common law also made it difficult to formulate abstract and general propositions, or to adopt reason rather than experience as a guide. It is therefore not surprising that some English lawyers concluded that it was "naïve to think that the common law could be codified without undergoing a sea change."[2] Common-law lawyers also rejected the claim that codification made the law more coherent and more secure. Identifying judges as the best legal experts, many distrusted Parliament's ability to reproduce or create law effectively. Some also claimed that Continental codes were a failure. Enormous effort was required to elaborate them, but they did not obtain the desired results. They did not create a truly new system, nor were they particularly easy to use.

Despite such claims, codification did find enthusiasts in England. Maurice Amos was one, but the most famous proponent of codification in England was Jeremy Bentham (1748–1832). Founder of a school known as utilitarianism, in his *Introduction to the Principles of Morals and Legislation* (1789) Bentham argued that the purpose of society is to produce the greatest happiness for the greatest number of people. Human beings, he observed, are moved by natural and rational self-interest. A law such as common law, based on oral customs and controlled by judges, cannot guarantee this end. What is required instead is legal security and clarity, and this can be best achieved by combining empiricism with rational analysis.

Bentham advocated the elaboration of codes that would be promulgated by the legislature and that would be comprehensive (with no gaps), exclusive (what was not included would not be part of the law), systematic, and simple. From as early as the 1810s, Bentham was also engaged in developing a constitutional code that, taking into consideration human nature and human reason, would be potentially appropriate to any nation or government.

During the nineteenth century England remained largely immune to codification, but several codes were nevertheless elaborated in British India. Later applied to other English colonies, these included a code of civil procedure (1859), a penal code (1860), and code of penal procedure (1861). Historians have explained that this divergence between metropolitan and colonial developments—England rejecting codification and India embracing it—made perfect sense. Many English lawyers believed codification was an extreme remedy in legal systems that were chaotic. This description, which they wrongly or rightly applied to nineteenth-century Continental Europe, fit colonial situations, in which a multiplicity of indigenous laws that English legal experts found hard to understand, coexisted alongside colonial legislation. Viewing codification as an imperial endeavor, these actors also suggested that it could be a means to "civilize" natives by implementing a new, rational legal system. It enabled the importation of an abbreviated version of English law into the colonies, which were often portrayed as lacking an appropriate legal system of their own or having too many. The undemocratic environment overseas also facilitated codifiers' task because there was no serious public debate regarding the pros and cons of such reform measures.

Codification in the United States

Most historians agree that in the 1820s and 1830s, legislators, governors, and lawyers across the United States asked whether codification was good or bad, necessary or useless. In some territories and states, proposals to adopt codes were entertained, and committees were appointed to study their desirability or even prepare drafts. Yet, most of these initiatives did not prosper, in part because the basic operating assumption of most interlocutors was that common law could not be codified. As a result, debates regarding codification were often understood to include a much larger discussion on whether the United States should keep or abandon its adherence to common law. Those who advocated codification were usually seen as favoring the abandonment of common law. Those who opposed it were understood to support the continuation of the existing legal system. Despite this general stalemate, both Louisiana and New York (and a series of states imitating New York), did proceed to codify their laws.

Louisiana

General surveys of American codification tend to assume that the adoption of codes in Louisiana was self-explanatory. Given its French heritage, they argue, it was only natural that the territory of Orleans (the name Louisiana had before it became a state) chose to codify its civil laws by elaborating a Civil Digest (1808). It was equally natural that, after Louisiana became a state (1812), it enacted a fully fledged Civil Code (1825). These measures expressed local residents' adhesion to their French colonial past and their rejection of federal efforts to introduce common law into their territory. This rejection also found expression in the vote of the Territorial Legislature in 1806 to maintain the existing legal system, and in the 1812 state constitution, which denied the Assembly the power to adopt a different legal system.

If allegiance to tradition was one reason for the adoption of codes in Louisiana, another was the allegedly messy legal situation. According to most scholars, codification was needed in Louisiana because local law was partially French and partially Spanish and most of it was not available in English translation. Chaotic and incomprehensible (at least to outsiders), it required a short restatement in codes that would also translate local norms into English.

Yet to argue that what happened in Louisiana was natural is to undermine the importance of what had transpired. The decisions taken by locals in 1806 (to maintain the previous legal system), 1808 (to adopt a digest), 1812 (to deny the Territorial Legislature the power to adopt a different system), and 1825 (to adopt a civil code) were more than a stubborn insistence on tradition. They involved conscious and strategic moves allowing local actors not so much to conserve the existing system as to engage in its reinvention. These actors intensified rather than gradually abandoned their dependence on French law, while also progressively sidetracking their Spanish heritage.

How and why this happened remains largely a mystery. In 1806, asked what their law was, the local authorities identified as their own the Justinian *Corpus Iuris Civilis,* the writing of *ius commune* jurists, and various Spanish compilations and ordinances. Although they did not mention French law at all, the Civil Digest proposed in 1808 had elements of both Spanish and French law and it was arranged according to the Code Napoléon. This departure from strict adherence to Spanish law was noted by some of the judges who applied the digest. These judges, who tended to interpret it as a mere restatement of Spanish law, refused to take into account the French elements that it included. The judges also rejected the idea that the digest would replace existing law and felt at liberty to use uncodified Spanish law when it was convenient or needed.

Continuing dependence on sources other than the digest, most of which were available only in Spanish, led to the decision to replace the digest by a code. Yet the code adopted in 1825 was not a simple amplification of the digest. Instead, although again including elements of both Spanish and

French law, the French elements were substantially more dominant than the Spanish. The strong affiliation with French law—in part an invented tradition—was clear, for example, in article 3521, which stated that, after its promulgation, all preceding Spanish, Roman, and French law as well as all legislative enactments adopted by local legislators would be repealed. The code further mandated that precodification law could not be invoked in the courts under any circumstances.

Rather than "naturally" following its traditional law, Louisiana therefore underwent a transformation that made it less Spanish and more French over time. From this perspective, the Gallicization of Louisiana's law was as much a result of its incorporation into the United States as it was of its colonial past. As a means that locals adopted to halt the penetration of common law, there was nothing inevitable about these developments, in which the past as well as the present, and visions of the future, played equal roles.

The Louisiana story is further complicated by the fact that adherence to Continental law covered only parts of civil law. In other parts, as well as in criminal, evidentiary, and commercial law, common law reigned without much contestation. Here as elsewhere, attempts to codify these fields mostly failed. Despite the success at passing the civil code, the Louisiana legislature rejected drafts of a penal code and a code of penal procedure. The civil procedure code adopted in 1823 had elements of both Continental and common law and, according to some, was interpreted by judges as reflecting English rather than Continental norms. All these developments suggest that there was more to the Louisiana story than what met the eye.

New York

The New York codification story usually begins in 1846 when state legislators decided to revise, reform, simplify, and abridge the law. The following year David Dudley Field was appointed to head the codifying committee. Field planned five codes for New York: a political code (with rules regarding government), civil and a criminal procedure codes, and penal and civil codes. Field, who was said to be inspired by the French experience, hoped to create codes that would be brief and synthetic and that would eliminate archaic regulation. Considering both common and statutory law, he also sought to identify general principles from which all other legal solutions could be deduced.

Although the codes Field prepared were revolutionary—one observer suggesting that the code of civil procedure was a death sentence for common-law pleading—the code of civil procedure (1848), the code of criminal procedure (1881), and the penal code (1882) were adopted by the New York legislature without much opposition. Yet Field's proposal for a civil code met with strong enough resistance to lead to its abandonment after being subjected to veto by the governor on multiple occasions. Why the other codes were easily accepted and this one rejected is unclear, but there is reason to believe that most lawyers and legislators felt more strongly about private law than about procedural or criminal law and adopted a more conservative attitude with regard to reforming private law. It is also possible that the civil code was rejected because of its strong resemblance to the Napoleonic Code and the instruction that after its promulgation it would replace rather than add to or clarify all previous legal arrangements.

Whatever the reasons for the rejection of the civil code were, what was most surprising about the New York story was not what happened in that state but what transpired elsewhere. The New York code of civil procedure, passed in 1848, was adopted wholesale in Missouri the following year (1849) and, in the next few decades, in twenty-one additional states and territories.[3] The draft of the civil code that the New York legislature rejected met with similar success and was adopted with only minimal changes in the Dakotas (1866), which also adopted the New York penal code. California followed, adopting in 1872 all five New York codes, and so did Idaho, Montana, and Colorado.

Scholars conclude that the adoption of the New York codes elsewhere should be comprehended as implementing a shock treatment or a desperate remedy to chaotic legal situations. Believing that codes were a better fit for frontier territories than for developed regions, these scholars argue that the willingness of states and territories to adopt the New York codes can be explained by the lack of dense legal traditions in those parts of the country. As in colonial India, in these areas codification allowed for the adoption of a superior normative system where none existed or where those that existed were severely flawed. Embodying also a "civilizing mission," the New York codes domesticated the new North American territories by using the purportedly mature deliberations of New York lawyers and legislators. If codification was an option in New York, in the American West it was a necessity.

This account, which reproduced many of the biases English legal experts also expressed, neglected to analyze the legal situation that predated the borrowing of the New York codes, assuming rather than verifying that it required a radical reform. One factor particularly forgotten was that many of the states and territories that enacted the New York codes were in the midst of sometimes heated debates over which legal system they should adopt. California, for example, was a former Spanish and Mexican territory; the Dakotas, Montana, and Idaho as well as most of the midwestern states, were a French possession and large parts of their territories were under the control of indigenous tribes that followed their own legal systems. Were their existing laws so inadequate? Did the bias of common-law lawyers classify them as such or did locals feel the need for reform? Who exactly decided on this adoption and why?

In the 1770s the Continental Congress meeting in Philadelphia declared that the new territories northwest of the Ohio River would be subject to common law. During the nineteenth century, American authorities who assumed control over former French, Spanish, or indigenous territories adopted a similar approach, generally believing that one of their most urgent tasks was to replace the previous legal system(s) with common law. These officials portrayed replacement as necessary and pressing because, according to them, all other legal systems (which they now paradoxically classified as foreign despite being local) were arbitrary to the point that they were not systems at all. Attempts to introduce legal change, however, often met with resistance. Research on upper Louisiana (present-day Missouri) has demonstrated, for example, that residents did not share these pejorative visions of their law and instead believed their system to be orderly and just.

In California, where a sizable and stable community of Spanish and Mexican residents predated the arrival of Anglo immigrants from the East, many demanded the continuation of the Spanish legal system. Others debated the possibility of creating a mixed normative order that would include the English law of evidence, English commercial law, and English penal law, yet civil and procedural codes of Spanish and French inspiration. In 1850, nonetheless, a committee mainly manned by common-law experts recommended the wholesale adoption of common law.

Similar debates took place at the Congress of the Republic of Texas in 1836. Eventually legislators there formally adopted common law for civil disputes as well as criminal offenses, yet local courts continued to use the Spanish civil procedure, which they considered a better fit for local conditions. This practice was formally sanctioned in 1840, when the local legislature declared that the adoption of common law did not include the common-law system of pleading.

There is no convincing explanation as to why common law succeeded in replacing previous systems. Neither do we have sufficient knowledge of how this process took place and how locals reacted. Most historians point to the prejudice of common-law lawyers turned U.S. officials who assumed that common law was civilized and all other systems were not. Historians also mention power relations that favored Anglo immigrants from the East over established residents, and explain that the Anglos preferred common law because it allowed them to dispossess natives, whether indigenous, Spanish, or French.

The growing hegemony of common law perhaps explains why the New York codes found reception elsewhere. Rather than curing chaos or civilizing a defective normative world, the New York codes were mostly welcomed in territories that, having had a different legal tradition (or various traditions), were now transitioning to common law. Rather than being a remedy, the codes were an instrument for imposing a new law, and rather than being contradictory to common law in spirit and design—as most assumed codes were—they were a strategic and useful device by which to impose it.

Without Codes but with Legislation

Louisiana and New York provide two tales about codification in the United States in the nineteenth century. A third story takes a different path that highlights the growing importance of legislation in the United States in the nineteenth and twentieth centuries. According to this story, American law was traditionally more accepting of legislation than the English common law. Much of the colonial legal order was based on written instructions by metropolitan and colonial authorities; and local assemblies in Virginia, Massachusetts, and Georgia, for example, considered themselves authorized to legislate as well as compile and reform the law. This tradition—which made legislation central—was only strengthened after independence as Americans sought to detach their legal system from England's, and as they came under the influence of democratizing impulses that trusted local assemblies more than judges. Americans also appealed to legislation in order to create their states and their federation, which came into being after they adopted constitutions in which legislatures were instituted. All these features aligned to create a legal system in which—despite allegiance to common law—there was a permanent preference for official, written rules explicitly promulgated by appropriate institutions over unwritten customary laws.

As a result, even though during the nineteenth century codification was largely rejected across the United States, most states nevertheless massively turned to legislation to clarify and solidify their existing systems as well as introduce innovations. During this period many legal professionals, acting on their own initiative, took a lead in these developments, preparing drafts that they encouraged the legislatures to enact formally.

Particularly noteworthy in this regard were efforts to unify American law. Motivated by growing interstate immigration, commerce, and collaboration, and propelled by the accelerated mobility allowed by highways and modern transportation, in 1892 a group of eminent lawyers, judges, and law professors founded the National Conference of Commissioners on Uniform State Law. Supported by the American Bar Association, members of the Conference elaborated a series of individual acts, which they proposed to all states for their endorsement. Examples of such acts were the Negotiable Instruments Law (1882) and the Uniform Sales Act and the Law of Warehouse Receipts (both dated 1906).

In 1923 the American Law Institute was founded with the explicit aim of undertaking the simplification of the U.S. legal system. In 1944 the members of the Institute in collaboration with the National Conference of Commissioners on Uniform State Laws (now called the Uniform Law Commission) formally agreed to work toward the elaboration of a Uniform Commercial Code. Published in 1951 and revised in 1962, the Code covered issues such as sales, leases, negotiable instruments, letters of credit, and investment securities. In the years following its elaboration, it was adopted, more or less faithfully, by all fifty states, as well as by the District of Columbia, the U.S. Virgin Islands, and Puerto Rico.

Although the Uniform Commercial Code produced a certain unification across the United States, it was different from Continental codes because it allowed some variations among states, which were allowed to choose between several options, and because it was not intended to replace all previous normative sources. Furthermore, according to some scholars, rather than prescribing solutions, the uniform code mostly indicated issues that needed consideration, suggested questions that judges should ask, and included a catalogue of possible remedies, also listing the possible conditions for receiving them. Contrary to Continental codes, in short, the Uniform Commercial Code allowed, indeed encouraged, wide judicial discretion. It refused to prescribe how each case should be resolved but instead indicated what the judge ought to take into consideration and which methods he or she should follow in order to reach a just decision. In other words, the code supplied a roadmap rather than a destination.

Epilogue

A MARKET, A COMMUNITY, AND A UNION

In 1951, France, West Germany, Italy, the Netherlands, Belgium, and Luxembourg formed the European Coal and Steel Community (ECSC). The aim was to place management of these important natural resources under common control so as to encourage economic growth and interstate collaboration. Five years later in a series of treaties signed in Rome (1957), the six countries proceeded to establish the European Atomic Energy Community (Euratom) and the European Economic Community (EEC; also known as the Common Market). With a much wider scope than the ECSC, the EEC set some basic rules that were to facilitate trade relations, such as abolishing tariffs between the states and setting common trade and agricultural policies.[1]

These developments were focused on economic growth, but the intention of those involved was also to enable greater political union. This was the European response to both the horrors of the Second World War and the intensification of the Cold War. To facilitate this task, the institutional structures created in the 1950s for the three organizations (ECSC, Euratom, and the EEC) were unified in 1967, thereafter forming a single institutional configuration called the European Community (EC).[2] This configuration was given an executive, a legislature, and a judiciary branch that included a commission located in Brussels (executive), a parliament that resided in Strasbourg and collaborated with a legislative council (of ministers of member states), and a court of justice, which sat in Luxembourg. The community also had an assembly (the European Council) that included all heads of member states, who met regularly to discuss European policies.[3]

In the years following these developments, the European Community expanded at a spectacular rate; over the years 1973 to 1986 the United Kingdom, Ireland, Denmark, Greece, Spain, and Portugal joined. This expansion entailed tensions between those who saw the advantages of forming a free trade area and a customs union and those who had more federalist aspirations; and those who were concerned about the concentration of power in a supranational executive, and therefore the loss of national sovereignty, and those who preferred pooling resources and enhancing political integration in order to achieve certain aims. Although these tensions were to become permanent, by the 1980s proponents of integration seemed to have the upper hand. In a gradual and piecemeal process extending from the 1980s to the present, the Community moved from its initial design as an international organization that promoted interstate collaboration to a new structure that, according to many observers, constitutes a state or a quasi-state.

To achieve this gradual transition, in 1986 the member states of the European Community signed yet another treaty (the Single European Act) that, advancing the goals set in 1957, adopted additional steps toward the creation of a true single economic market. Most important among those steps was the transition from unanimity to qualified majority voting in a number of areas, a move that essentially eliminated the veto power of national governments. By signing the Single European Act, member states also committed themselves to a timetable for their economic merger and defined some of the ways in which this merger would take place. The 1986 treaty set a calendar to extend collaboration among member states to fields such as the environment, social policies, education, health, consumer protection, and foreign affairs. The European Parliament, now directly elected by citizens, was given a larger role.

In 1985 five of the ten member states signed the Schengen Agreement. Although set up outside and independently of the structures of the European Community, the agreement advanced the agenda of those who wished for a closer union. It suppressed internal border control among the signing parties and instituted a single external border where immigration checks and visa and asylum policies would be shared.[4] Incorporated in 1997 (in the Treaty of Amsterdam) into European agreements, from 1999 the Schengen principles became part of European law. During that same period, several nonmember countries, such as Norway, Iceland, Liechtenstein, and Switzerland, chose to join Schengen, agreeing to suppress their borders with countries of the

European Community. Meanwhile, three European community members (the United Kingdom, Ireland, and Denmark) decided to implement only parts of Schengen, whereas several others (Bulgaria, Cyprus, Croatia, and Romania) were excluded from some or all of its benefits.

In 1992 the twelve member states signed the Maastricht Treaty, which set in motion the measures necessary to guarantee the free movement of capital, labor, services, and goods between them. Among these measures was common European citizenship, which allowed all citizens of member states to circulate and reside freely anywhere in the community. Another important measure was greater coordination of economic policies and the subjection of member states to financial and budgetary discipline. Maastricht also included provisions regarding common policies in areas such as health, safety at work, social protection, and criminal justice, and it affirmed the identity of the community on the international scene, giving it powers in internal and external security.

Reflecting these changes, in 1993 the European Community was renamed the European Union. By 2013 the Union comprised twenty-eight countries, the biggest expansion having taken place in 2004, when ten new members joined.[5] In 2002 the new European currency, the euro, became official in the twelve countries known as the Eurozone and a central European bank was established in Frankfurt.[6] Efforts to adopt a constitution for Europe, however, were unsuccessful because in 2005 in a public referendum the Dutch and the French refused to ratify the Constitutional Treaty. Although the treaty was rejected, many of its core institutional provisions were incorporated into the legal structure of the Union by yet another treaty (the Treaty of Lisbon, also known as the Reform Treaty) signed in 2007. Among other things, the Treaty of Lisbon reformed the powers of the European Parliament and voting in the Council of Ministers, ratified the European Charter of Fundamental Rights, making it legally binding, consolidated the legal personality of the Union, and provided procedures by which a member state could withdraw from the Union.

Europeans continue to disagree about how wide the Union should be (who should be included) and how deep (what kinds of powers it should have). Some even express disillusionment with what the Union has achieved and have articulated demands, or even voted, to see their country leave it. Motivated by growing concerns regarding the loss of national sovereignty, economic instability, and migration, such reactions give voice to local anxieties but they also echo concerns existing elsewhere. Despite these disagreements and the unknown future that lies ahead, from a legal point of view the formation of the European Union was incredibly important, as it was responsible for the rebirth of a new common European law, indeed a new, modern *ius commune*.

The New European Law: Normative Sources

Economic collaboration, political integration, and the development of central institutions led to the emergence of a new European law created through the various treaties among member states (the *acquis,* literally, "what has been acquired," which must be accepted by new members), the legislation passed by the Council in collaboration with the European Parliament, and the regulations and directives proposed by the European Commission (the executive) and adopted by the Council and the Parliament.

If treaties among states and legislation were important normative sources of this new, emerging European law, no less vital was the jurisprudence of the European Court of Justice in Luxembourg.[7] The European Court of Justice (ECJ) was created in 1958 out of the merger of the separate courts of the European Coal and Steel Community, the European Economic Community, and the European Atomic Energy Community. Its judges are elected for renewable six-year terms by joint agreement of the governments of the member states. In theory, all states need to agree on all nominees; in practice, as the court has one judge per member state, most national governments promote their national candidates and automatically endorse those of other countries.

The European Court of Justice (now called the Court of Justice of the European Union) is charged with authoritatively interpreting European law in cases in which member states and / or European institutions disagree about its meaning, extension, or application. The court is also to rule on questions referred to it by member states' courts regarding the appropriate interpretation and scope of European law. It has the power to check European and member states' institutions, ensuring that they obey the law. In its decisions the Court, whose rulings cannot be appealed (there is no appeal instance), is to take into consideration the treaties signed by members states and legislation passed by European bodies. It is also to consider unwritten, supplementary sources of law such as the general principles said to be shared by all member states, as well as legal customs. These are usually interpreted as including notions such as the rule of law, adherence to public international law, and respect for fundamental rights.

Initially granted fairly limited powers, over the years the European Court of Justice emerged as a principal promoter of European law and European integration. In what was to become one of its most important decisions, in 1963 its judges ruled that European law could be directly applicable in member states' territories without requiring local reception or reenactment *(Van Gend en Loos v. Nederlandse Administratie Belastingen)*. In another key decision dated 1964 *(Costa v. ENEL)* the court held that European law had primacy over national law. Thereafter, and acting as a constitutional court of sorts and exercising a faculty somewhat akin to judicial review, the European Court of Justice determined that national laws that were incompatible with European law could be deemed inapplicable. It instructed all courts of member states to implement this decision, setting aside any provisions of national law that conflicted with European rules. The Court of Justice also guided European institutions and members states on how European law should be interpreted, adopting, among other things, the rule that national laws, even those preceding the formation of European law, should be interpreted as consistent rather than conflicting with European law.

Initially the decisions granting European law immediate applicability in the territory of member states and a superior position vis-à-vis national law were greatly criticized. However, over time member states' national courts acquiesced and adhered to these doctrines. Their acceptance, which was gradual and is still contested on occasions and is conditional on others, truly revolutionized European law. It allowed European law to become operative on the national level, and it empowered private litigants to monitor state compliance with it. Thereafter, European citizens could invoke European law in their national courts while they litigated with one another and with organs and institutions of their own state.

National courts' application of European law eventually became so routinized and so pronounced that many scholars now argue that every national court in the Union is also a European court of justice in the sense that it applies and interprets (and thus also makes) European law. The guardianship of European law by national courts ensures the rule of law within the European Union and guarantees the subjection of national governments to their European legal obligations. Yet national courts' involvement in the

interpretation and enforcement of European law has often generated important tensions. It placed national courts in opposition to what their government or Parliament desired when they passed laws that did not perfectly
cohere with or ignored European normativity. It also placed lower courts in
opposition to higher or constitutional courts, the former challenging the
monopoly of the latter in declaring certain laws or actions unconstitutional.

As a result of these developments, many now argue that de facto, even if
not de jure, the European Union lost its original character as an international body and became a quasi-federal state with a quasi-federal constitution (European law) to which all member states are now subject. Another
important result was the Europeanization of national law. Though scholars
disagree on how to measure Europeanization, according to some estimates
as much as 15 to 45 percent of national legislation across Europe is currently
influenced by European law. This influence was already clear as early as 1992
when, with 22,445 European regulations, 1,675 directives, 1,198 agreements
and protocols, 185 recommendations of the Commission or the Council, 291
Council resolutions, and 678 communications (as counted by the French
Conseil d'État), European law became "the largest source of new law, with
54 percent of all new French law originating in Brussels."[8] It is currently estimated that, to incorporate European law into their national legal order,
new member states are expected to implement approximately 100,000 pages
of legislation. And as the number of cases in the European Court of Justice
rises—it now reviews some 1,500 cases a year—the court not only sets
common standards that are the basis of a new legal order, it also constantly
broadens its activities to fields such as environmental, social, and human
rights law. The court also works to integrate into European law the instructions of the European Union Charter of Fundamental Rights, the European
Convention of Human Rights, and new European and international standards and traditions.[9]

The New European Law: An Idiosyncratic System

What is particularly striking about these developments is the degree to which
they transformed the law. The initial treaties that founded European institutions were intended to institute some measure of economic collaboration,
yet the way they were interpreted greatly transformed them. Discussions
regarding what these treaties meant and what they covered and authorized

confronted actors with diverse agendas and interests. These actors either wished to enhance the institutionalization of Europe and expand its powers, or wished to halt it. Although all of them might have employed a language that was political, the tools they used were legal. These tools allowed the creation of a European legal system that, having originated in international treaties and statutory law (enacted by the European Parliament and the Council) and having been mandated among sovereign powers, came to penetrate into national spaces and depend heavily on judge-made law. This penetration and the judge-made law that enabled it were generated by demands for remedies from European citizens; such demands fuel the work of European and national courts and allow them both to examine compliance with European law and to introduce new norms. A mix and match between Continental and common-law traditions, between international and national law, the new European order is therefore an odd creature that does not subscribe clearly to a single genealogy or trajectory.

Scholars disagree about why these important transformations (from international to domestic, and from legislation to judge-made law) happened. Some suggest that the powers taken on by the European Court of Justice were not foreseen in the original treaties that founded the European Community. These powers were the outcome of a vision shared by a group of lawyers working in European institutions and the judges sitting on the European Court of Justice. Starting in the 1970s these individuals intentionally and energetically supported European integration. Seeking to fill important voids in the 1957 Treaties of Rome, they invented an efficient mechanism to force compliance on national governments by recruiting the help of their citizens.

But even if the European Commission and the European Court of Justice strategically used judicial review to expand their powers and accelerate European integration, it is still unclear why national courts collaborated. After all, by adhering to the interpretation of the European Court of Justice, national courts played an important political and social role in promoting integration.

Many historians suggest that the transformation of European law into a superior, constitutional-like law was not foretold, but others insist that seeds of these developments were already planted in the founding treaties. Rather than being forced into this situation, according to this interpretation, national governments acquiesced to the growing powers of Europe, either because these developments were favorable to them or because politically it was too costly to resist them.

Despite these disagreements, most analysts coincide in concluding that structural issues rather than substantive law drove these processes to fruition. In other words, what made European law authoritative was not a declaration of principles or the signing of yet another treaty but a practical mechanism, proposed by the European court, that pushed European law into primacy by allowing different actors to call upon it to protect their own interests and desires.

The European law that resulted was both domestic and international, both written and oral, both statutory and based on case law. Perceived as a system propelling "integration through law," it gradually transformed what was initially an international organization into a quasi-state with a quasi-constitution. Given these characteristics, some historians imagine European law to be similar to a digital operating system. Like Windows, European law operates in the background. Many users might mistakenly ignore its importance and its effects, but even if they do, this law is nevertheless both constantly present and extremely powerful.

How Could This Happen?

These developments (the creation of the European Community and the European Union, the primacy of European law made of both legislation and judge-made law, and the transformation of an international organization into a quasi-state with a quasi-constitution) took place some 150 years after European law was said to have been nationalized. The legal systems that emerged in Europe after the French Revolution broke away from a *ius commune* that acknowledged wide differences in local practices yet recognized the importance of a shared normative framework that united all Europeans. They proposed to replace commonness with distinctiveness, creating separate national systems. On the Continent, these new systems identified law with legislation and they mandated that legislation would be enacted by a sovereign assembly of elected representatives.

Giving up or moderating these postrevolutionary premises and returning to a common law, which also admitted the power of jurists and judges, was not a simple affair. Neither was the concession of national sovereignty, or the idea that norms emanating from external European institutions could be automatically applicable locally. If each country had its own norms, willed by its people, how could a shared European law emerge? If most Continental countries recognized legislation and codification as exclusive normative sources, how could judge-made law be enforceable? Was the emergence of European law the end of the legacy of the French Revolution? And how should common-law lawyers react to a system that was neither national nor customary nor based on judge-made law?

Some historians have suggested that the wish for greater collaboration among the countries joining the Community / Union reminded at least some Europeans of their common past. It allowed them to point to a period when many Europeans had shared not only a common law *(ius commune)* but also a common religious creed and a belief in the primacy of natural law. If, once upon a time, a shared *ius commune* could bring together thousands of distinct local arrangements by offering overreaching principles, conceptual categories, methods of analysis, and shared norms, why could the same not happen now? If a common metaculture allowed Europeans in the past to perceive themselves as members of a single civilization, why would the case be different in the present? Cannot a contemporary European juridical science provide mechanisms to structure a legal system that admits of both divergence and convergence?

While many scholars have sought to discover, under what some have identified as the bewildering and idiosyncratic mass of casuistry and deeply entrenched legal nationalism, the common legal foundation of Europe, others have concentrated on the present. They argue that despite divergent histories, constitutional arrangements, and legal technologies, most Europeans are now in basic agreement regarding the most essential values and goals. This agreement, which mainly operates on the philosophical level, nevertheless has significant legal consequences because substantial coincidence exists among specific solutions that the diverse European countries have given to similar questions. Driven also by economic considerations, the gradual unification of law across Europe took place long before the formal political and economic project of commonness was proposed. Because differences in needs and desires were becoming smaller across Europe, the laws of the different European countries progressively and naturally converged despite the preeminence of national legislation.

Thus, while the European Court of Justice was busy naming and recognizing the general principles of European law, European scholars sought to identify the basic legal tenets that most European countries shared. Most famous among these attempts was the draft of a Common Frame of Reference (DCFR) by a committee appointed by the European Commission. The committee was charged with identifying as well as sometimes creating a framework of common rules that European and national legislators, courts, and individuals could adopt in legislation, interpretation, or commercial activity. The committee's work gradually covered areas such as marketing relations, service contracts, sales law, lease of goods, unjustified enrichment, and transfer of property. Somewhat similarly, the Common Core of European Private Law project, established in 1993 at the University of Trent (Italy), aimed to identify commonalities in member states' private law, including contracts, torts, and property. Participants in the projects described their quest as "a promising hunt for analogies hidden by formal differences" linked to no political agenda and seeking no particular outcome.[10]

Although many of these efforts at harmonization were encouraged or even supported by the institutions of the European Union and by various member states, attempts to elaborate a common European civil code, which in 1989 the European Parliament declared was desirable, have thus far failed. Those who lament this failure believe the code is necessary because it would enhance collaboration and integration across Europe. For those who criticized the efforts at enacting a code, it was preferable to allow for legal convergence to happen gradually and naturally rather than to impose it through legislation. A few point out that even if legislation were the correct vehicle to introduce changes, it is unclear whether codification is preferable to a restatement. Some suggest that the best way to achieve conversion would be through the creation of a new European common legal science, not additional European legislation. Arguing that the making of rules should be transparent and as apolitical as possible, yet another group seeks to identify procedures that would guarantee that the new European civil code, if enacted, would focus on obtaining a greater social good. Finally, some scholars question the constitutionality of a European civil code altogether, arguing that the European Community lacks competence to move in this direction.

Even though many European jurists believe in the inevitability of either a natural or an imposed convergence, others affirm that even in cases in which specific solutions are deemed comparable, it is vital to remember that multiple legal systems operate in Europe. Particularly important in this regard is the distinction between Continental Europe, which followed *ius commune,* and England, which had its own common law. The distinction between these two systems, it has been argued, is truly insurmountable. Legal epistemologies matter more than the specific solutions that each of these systems adopted. On the epistemological level, Continental and English law are recognizably distinct, with different approaches to what law is, who made it, and how it could change. Whereas Continental systems focus on reason, common law is anchored in experience; whereas Continental systems give primacy to legislation, common law prefers judge-made law.

To such claims, those favoring integration respond by arguing that the stark differences between Continental and common law are mostly fictional. Theoretically, Continental law might restrict judges, forcing them to follow the letter of the law while ignoring all other possible inputs from doctrine or jurisprudence. Yet, in practice, Continental judges have huge discretion in their interpretation of the law; they often incorporate doctrinal assessments and precedents into their thinking and hand down decisions that change rather than interpret the law. Similarly, theoretically common law might allow judges to innovate, yet in practice it now relies heavily on parliamentary legislation as well as precedent. Furthermore, some areas of Continental law, such as administrative law, depend greatly on judge-made law. Meanwhile, some areas of common law, such as criminal law, are based on legislation.

Insisting that theoretical distinctions should not be taken too seriously, that they are stereotypes rather than reflections of reality, and that these distinctions mainly reproduce ideological positions, not empirical analysis, these jurists also point out that there are important ways in which both systems have been gradually converging even conceptually, evolving into a middle ground. This convergence has abolished (or at least minimized) many of the differences between the Continental and the English systems, not only on the level of concrete solutions (which are often identical) but also with regard to how they view legislation and judge-made law, now seen in both systems as complementary rather than opposites. Indeed, the best proof for such a peaceful coexistence is European law itself. Rather than working against one another, in the case of European law, these distinct normative sources (legislation and judge-made law) together have created a new order that is neither Continental nor English, neither traditional nor completely modern, but instead constantly reinventing itself as it adapts to new circumstances, conditions, and constraints.

Europe in a Globalized World

Scholars of European law have also noted that many of the challenges facing the European Union were not particular to Europe. Instead they were embedded in the way modern law developed in a globalized world. Moves to harmonize the law were noticeable, for example, in the United States, where growing interstate commerce led many people to desire the unification of law across the country. To achieve this goal, jurists gathered to draw up and propose model codes, which they hoped would be adopted by most states. Since 1892 the National Conference of Commissioners on Uniform State Laws has proposed a great variety of such codes. Alongside the American Law Institute, beginning in 1944 the members of the commission also elaborated a Uniform Commercial Code. Published in 1951, the code was adopted, more or less faithfully, by all fifty states, as well as by the District of Columbia, the U.S. Virgin Islands, and Puerto Rico.

Moves to unify the law were also pursued by international bodies such as the International Institute for the Unification of Private Law (UNIDROIT), which was established in 1926 as an auxiliary organ of the League of Nations and in 1940 became an independent intergovernmental organization. UNIDROIT aims to modernize, harmonize, and coordinate private and commercial law across the globe. It currently has sixty-three member states, and its experts have prepared dozens of proposals for international conventions, model laws, and legal regulations and guides.

While harmonization, unification, and modernization of the law across the globe are goals that many now pursue, concerns regarding the changing nature of law itself are also evident on a global scale. These concerns focus on several issues. The first centers on the delegation of lawmaking from legislatures to state bureaucracies. This delegation allows the transfer of important regulatory functions to unelected officials who, as employees of state commissions, bureaus, agencies, ministries, and programs, not only execute orders but also adjudicate conflicts and enact new rules. These officials decide cases, build up bodies of precedent, and elaborate internal regulations regarding procedure and substantive law.

Equally new is the demise of state monopolies over regulation because of norm-making by transnational bodies such as commercial companies, sports associations, Internet giants, and intergovernmental organizations, or the growing diversity within national boundaries that challenges the hegemonic

narrative by suggesting alternative jurisdictions that cater to particular mi-
norities, religious denominations, and so forth.

These tendencies lead jurists across the globe to ask how, under these
circumstances, national systems can cope with norm-making and conflict
adjudication. How can they deal with the internationalization of the law?
Alternatively, how can these nonstate systems be controlled, integrated, and
legitimized? Is legal unification at all possible? Can there be agreement on
law among participants who are culturally diverse and whose traditions are
so distinct? Are these agreements necessary at all, or can a progressive globalization be managed in ways other than legal harmonization? Are we, in
short, facing the end of the regulatory power of representatives of the nation
voting in Parliament? Are we facing the beginning of a new age, in which the
will of the people still dominates but in new ways? Could democracy be ensured not by citizens' votes but by open competition among multiple bodies
and interests?

The need to find efficient answers to new challenges is thus matched by
the wish to come up with a new paradigm that would replace the old imagi-
nary of a society made of undifferentiated equal citizens linked by an abstract social contract and expressing their desires by electing representatives
to a Parliament. The new paradigm, instead, would recognize the power of
groups and group solidarity as well as the persistence of inequalities and differences by unmaking the metaphors proposed by the French Revolution.
In this new reality of extreme legal pluralism, where the juridical order of
the nation-state coincides with a multiplicity of other normative orders,
should not jurists center their efforts on proposing methods to imagine a
new legal universe for a new society?

Notes

1. Roman Law

1. Goethe was said to have referred to the "enduring life of Roman law, which, like a diving duck, hides itself from time to time, but is never quite lost, always coming up again alive." Johann Wolfgang von Goethe, *Conversations of Goethe with Eckermann and Soret,* trans. John Oxenford, 389–390 (London: George Bell, 1875), conversation that took place on April 6, 1829.

2. Historians of Roman law have long disagreed whether pontifices only gave authoritative responses regarding the law that other officials implemented or whether they also applied it as judges. Some have suggested a compromise that made the pontifices sometimes legal experts, sometime judges, depending on the case.

3. While this is the standard narrative, some historians have asked whether this portrayal is accurate or whether it was largely invented by later Romans on whose testimonies we depend to reconstruct what transpired during the archaic period.

4. Initially there were only two praetors, but their number grew over time. Rather than being members of an institution, each praetor worked independently. Eventually praetors were also nominated in Roman settlements outside Rome, such as Sicily and Hispania. Praetors were identified as "urban" after the introduction in 242 BCE of a new type of praetor *(praetor peregrinus)* who oversaw cases involving non-Roman citizens.

5. Historians disagree as to when and why the division of the process into two parts took place. They point out that references to *iudex* already existed in

the Twelve Tables, though it is unclear that the work of this individual was necessarily preceded by the work of an official similar to the praetor.

6. On the status of foreigners under Roman law, see below.

7. Papinian was a famous jurist who was also an imperial official. Among his most celebrated works are thirty-seven books of questions *(Quaestiones)* and nineteen books of responsa, as well as several treatises.

8. This was the definition of jurisprudence in the Institute, the second-century CE manual for students authored by Gaius. It was reproduced in the Justinian so-called sixth-century *Corpus Iuris Civilis.*

9. Roman provincial governors, who oversaw conflicts in the provinces between Romans and non-Romans, also participated in the elaboration of *ius gentium.*

10. This name was given in the sixteenth century to the three books described below, and often also to the Novellae, a fourth book including new imperial legislation. Though widely known as such, this title is nevertheless anachronistic.

11. Because the *Digest* included excerpts, historians often warn against trusting it too much. The excerpts did not clarify the context in which the opinion was given, and they were often fragmentary. Scholars of Roman law also suggest that the opinions included dated from different periods and that the *Digest* deliberately underrepresented disagreement among them.

12. As will be explained in Chapter 5, not all of the so-called *Corpus Iuris Civilis* survived, forcing jurists to endeavor to reconstruct it from a multiplicity of fragments. As for the validity of the Corpus in the Eastern empire, historians have asserted that its diffusion there was also somewhat limited and that in many places it did not in practice replace the preexisting local law.

2. The Creation of Latin Christendom

1. Christianity also expanded in the Hellenistic east. Although it is not the main subject of this book, which follows only Latin Christendom, what happened in the East will be briefly mentioned at the end of the chapter.

2. Christianity would eventually be open not only to the Israelites but also to all others willing to enter the covenant. This development is usually attributed to the teaching of Paul, one of the apostles.

3. The Council of Carthage selected the twenty-seven books that would make the New Testament alongside the forty-six books of the Old Testament. This selection was confirmed by the Council of Trent (1545–1563), which redefined Christian dogma in the wake of the Protestant Reformation.

4. This was the original definition of what Catholicism meant before the Protestant Reformation. By calling the Church "Catholic" (that is, universal), it adopted the convention that there was only one belief within the Church.

5. John Van Engen, "Christening the Romans," *Traditio* 52 (1997): 1–45, at 4.
6. Thomas Hobbes. *Leviathan,* chap. 47, discussing the powers of the pope.
7. In recent years, another narrative of the "formation of Europe" has been proposed. Criticizing the above-mentioned analysis for disregarding other ideological frameworks operating in Europe at that time, such as Judaism and Islam, the new narrative also suggests that Christianization and Romanization were not uniquely European phenomena, because efforts at conversion were initially stronger and more persistent in Asia and Africa than in Europe. Undertaken by the Eastern Greek Church, these efforts disseminated a Hellenized Roman law whose presence might have persisted even under Islam.
8. On Byzantine, Eastern law, see Chapter 1.

3. An Age with No Jurists?

1. This period was characterized as "an age with no jurists" by Manlio Bellomo in his *The Common Legal Past of Europe, 1000–1800* (Washington, DC: Catholic University of America Press, 1995), 34.
2. See Chapter 5.
3. See Chapter 4.
4. Although the abandonment of ordeal seemed to have greatly influenced the use of juries in criminal cases, its effect on civil cases is unclear.

4. Lords, Emperors, and Popes around the Year 1000

1. Historians have disagreed whether feudalism reached everywhere in Europe and whether its effects were similar across time and place. The answer to this question was important because scholars assumed that it could account for Europe's distinct patterns of development. In 1929, for example, Ortega y Gasset, the foremost Spanish philosopher of the time, pointed to the lack of feudal experience to explain why Spain was "different."
2. See Chapter 3.
3. Since the late nineteenth century, historians have suggested that although the decree was included in the papal registry that corresponded to the year 1075, it might have been authored at a later date not by Gregory himself but instead by Cardinal Deusdedit, one of his collaborators.

5. The Birth of a European *Ius Commune*

1. *Ius commune* was a term originally used to designate the parts of canon law that were common to all Christians. However, it eventually referred to the

combination of Roman, feudal, and canon law that controlled European law from the twelfth to the nineteenth centuries (if not beyond).

2. See Chapter 1.

3. This task of reconstructing the *Corpus* has usually been associated with one person (Irnerius), one city (Bologna), and one period (the second half of the eleventh century). This image, however, is somewhat misleading, as we know that more than a single person in a single location was involved. Some scholars have even expressed doubts whether Irnerius himself was part of this enterprise, or only his students.

4. I refer here to what would later be known as the *noblesse de robe,* the nobility of those wearing the clothes *(robes)* associated with a law degree, as distinguished from the *noblesse d'épée* (sword), which was based on descent and (theoretically) military achievements.

5. Rogerius, "Questions on the *Institutes,*" in *University of Chicago Readings in Western Civilization,* vol. 4: *Medieval Europe,* ed. Julius Kirshner and Karl F. Morrison (Chicago: University of Chicago Press, 1986), 215–218. According to some, this text was not gloss proper but instead a *questio,* that is, a different form of juristic engagement that sought to answer a particular question.

6. We know very little about Gratian and his work. Historians currently debate whether he authored the entire compilation or only part of it. They all agree, however, that even if he was the author, he did not do this work alone, and that he also heavily relied on compilations proposed by previous scholars.

7. The *Corpus Iuris Canonici* was the body of Church law that, to a large degree, was followed until 1917.

8. See Chapter 3.

9. *Directum* was the antecedent of the Italian *diritto,* the French *droit,* the Spanish *derecho,* and the Portuguese *direito.* It also gave birth to the idea of the right (versus the wrong) direction or simply of being correct.

10. Historians usually count among the present-day European countries that were affected by *ius commune* Italy, France, Spain, Portugal, Germany, Belgium, The Netherlands, Switzerland, Iceland, Slovakia, the Czech Republic, Hungary, Austria, Romania, Poland, Denmark, Norway, and Sweden. Most also include England, at least to some degree: see Chapter 6.

11. This was what the *Ordenamiento de Alcalá* (1348) and the *Leyes de Toro* (1505) attempted to do.

6. The Birth of an English Common Law

1. The laws of king Aethelberth, enacted 602–603 CE.

2. The Laws of Alfred (871–899 CE).

3. Although the Norman invasion is habitually referred to as an "invasion" or a "conquest," William, duke of Normandy, had a legal claim to the English throne and indeed presented himself as the rightful heir.

4. The Laws of Henry I *(Leges Henrici Primi)* and of Edward the Confessor *(Leges Edwardi Confessoris)*, which were drawn up by Norman monarchs, were allegedly aimed at accomplishing this task.

5. Even in the sixteenth century, however, plans to adopt an independent code that would ensure the separation of an English ecclesiastical law from a European canon law never materialized. The result was the continuing validity of at least parts of canon law in England.

6. Frederick Pollock, *Oxford Lectures and Other Discourses* (London: Macmillan, 1890), 75–88, quotation at 88.

7. Historians have debated what this restriction meant and how it was applied. They disagree whether most medieval villagers were free, many suggesting that they were not. Others dismiss this question altogether, pointing out that the status of individuals who requested the king's protection was rarely investigated.

8. Among these courts was the court of Common Pleas, which was eventually located in Westminster, and the King's Bench, which accompanied the king on his travels.

9. Administrative writs were also used by Anglo-Saxon kings, but their extension and meaning were somewhat distinct.

10. In the twelfth and thirteenth centuries royal courts mostly used Latin, and therefore, rather than being identified as "common law," this system initially was designated as the *communi iure* or *commune regni ius*.

11. "Ashby vs. White and Others," in *Thomas and Bellots Leading Cases in Constitutional Law (with Introduction and Notes)*, ed. E. Slade (London: Sweet and Maxwell, 1934), 47.

12. *Ius commune* jurists identified this right to process as *servare ordinem iuris*.

13. The Magna Carta will be discussed in greater detail in Chapter 8.

14. Heneage Finch Nottingham (Earl of), *Lord Nottingham's Manual of Chancery Practice and Prolegomena of Chancery and Equity*, ed. D. E. C. Yale (Homes Beach, FL: Wm. W. Gaunt, 1965), 194, cited in Dennis R. Klinck. "Lord Nottingham and the Conscience of Equity," *Journal of the History of Ideas* 67, no. 1 (2006): 123–147, at 125.

15. There were, of course, important differences between ancient Rome and England. Perhaps the most important structurally was that whereas medieval England allowed for the coexistence of multiple courts (royal, feudal, local) to which subjects could bring their conflicts, each one using its very distinct legal system, Rome did not. Also, in England, lawyers and legal experts never acquired the importance they had in Rome.

16. Charles Donahue, "Ius Commune, Canon law, and Common Law in England," *Tulane Law Review* 66 (1991–1992): 1745–1780, at 1748.

7. Crisis and Reaffirmation of *Ius Commune*

1. Fifth-century St. Vincent of Lérins is credited for having coined this fiction. This was the original meaning of Catholicism before the Protestant Reformation, when this term became associated instead with the part of the Church that remained under papal authority in order to distinguish it from the other part that did not.

2. Paradoxically, the school began in Italy and its first proponent (Andreas Alciatus) was Italian, but many of its adherents (such as Guillaume Budé, Jacques Cujas, and François Hotman) were French and its most important centers of creation (Orleans and Bourges) were in France.

3. The Dutch method of law *(usus modernus Pandectarum)* might have combined *mos gallicus* and *mos italicus*. This method was mostly a product of the seventeenth and eighteenth centuries and was geared toward finding practical solutions to everyday situations. Its practitioners were willing to generalize and draw principles as Italian scholars did, yet they cared about the historical evolution of law and admitted the omnipresence of contradictions between different solutions, as French legal humanists did.

8. Crisis and Reinvention of Common Law

1. See Chapter 6.

2. William Blackstone, *Commentaries on the Laws of England* (Oxford: Clarendon Press, 1765–1769), introduction, third section, 65.

3. Mark Kishlansky, *A Monarchy Transformed: Britain, 1603–1714* (London: Penguin, 1996), 37.

4. Glanvil was said to have authored the *Tractatus de legibus e consuetudinibus regni Angliae* (ca.1187–1189) while Bracton was said to have authored *De legibus et consuetudinibus Angliae* (ca. 1220s–1250s). Both books are considered the most important early essays describing common law (see Chapter 6).

5. Among such authors were John Fortecue, Christopher St. German, Anthony Fitzherbert, and Robert Brooke.

6. John David in his *Iris Reports* (1613), as cited in Alan Cromartie, "The Idea of Common Law as Custom," in *The Nature of Customary Law,* ed. Amanda Perreu-Saussine and James Bernard Murphy (Cambridge: Cambridge University Press, 2007), 203–227 at 214.

7. Only in the twentieth century did judges clearly affirm that the prominence of legislation limited their activities because they could not apply or develop the common law in ways that were inconsistent with the law as laid down in statutes (acts of Parliament).

8. See Chapter 6.

9. From *Ius Gentium* to Natural Law

1. This was an indirect reference to the historical process identified as the "Reconquest" *(reconquista)*. It suggested that from the eleventh to the fifteenth century, the Christian kingdoms of Iberia fought Muslim occupiers in order to reconstitute the political structures that existed before the Muslims invaded the peninsula in 711. This ideological reading of the past, however, has been discredited by most historians, who no longer present the Muslims as invaders nor the Christians as pursuing a religious agenda meant at recuperation.

2. This was not the only possible conclusion. Michel de Montaigne (1533–1592), for example, suggested that what was natural for some, might not be natural for others. He expressed these views in his famous essay *On Cannibals* (ca. 1577), which appeared as chapter 30 in his book of essays, available in multiple editions and also online at https://www.gutenberg.org/files/3600/3600-h/3600-h.htm.

3. Tamar Herzog, *Defining Nations: Immigrants and Citizens in Early Modern Spain and Spanish America* (New Haven: Yale University Press, 2003).

10. North American Developments

1. The states that added a Bill of Rights to their constitutions were Virginia, Pennsylvania, Maryland, Delaware, North Carolina, Vermont, Massachusetts, and New Hampshire. Other states, though not including a separate Bill of Rights, did mention or enumerate rights in their constitutions.

2. The following citations are from the Declaration of Independence.

3. Preamble to the Constitution of the United States.

4. "The enumeration in the Constitution, of certain rights, shall not be construed to deny or disparage others retained by the people."

5. William Blackstone, *Commentaries on the Laws of England* (Oxford: John Hatchard and Son, 1822 [1765–1769]), 105.

6. Historians currently debate whether these clauses in colonial charters gave colonists rights overseas or only bestowed on them the right to be treated as subjects if and when they returned to England.

7. Immanuel Kant, "What Is the Enlightenment?," Lonigsberg, Prussia, September 30, 1784, available, for example, at http://legacy.fordham.edu/halsall/mod/kant-whatis.asp.

11. The French Revolution

1. Preamble of the 1789 French Declaration of the Rights of Man and Citizen.
2. As mentioned in Chapter 10, natural law was uncodified. It was a notion that many philosophers, jurists, theologians, and other intellectuals accepted, but they disagreed on what it included. Rather than an enumeration of norms or a system of specific solutions, natural law was a frame of reference.
3. "It is said that there are 144 customs in France that have the power of law: these laws are almost all different. A man who travels in this country changes law almost as many times as he changes horses." Voltaire, "Courtisans lettrés: Coutoumes," in *Oeuvres complètes de Voltaire,* vol. 7: *Dictionnaire philosophique I* (Paris: Chez Furne, 1835).
4. The French Civil Code, art. 544. On the French civil code, see Chapter 12.
5. Title 3, art. 1.
6. Only in 1958 would the French state introduce a version of judicial review that allowed the magistrates of a special body *(Conseil Constitutionnel)* to review the constitutionality of laws prior to their promulgation. In 2010 these arrangements were extended to allow litigants to invoke unconstitutionality during ordinary proceedings at the court, which would suspend its deliberations and send the constitutional issue to the Conseil for its decision.

12. Codifying the Laws of Europe

1. Though codes would continue to be enacted in France (presently there are some fifty codes), those adopted after the Napoleonic period would be identified as "administrative" rather than "ideological."
2. The list of countries influenced by Napoleonic codification included various Italian city-states (before the Italian unification), Belgium, the Netherlands, Luxembourg, parts of Germany (before its unification in 1871), Austria, Switzerland, Poland, Greece, Romania, Spain, Portugal, Louisiana, Quebec, Dominican Republic, Bolivia, Peru, Chile, Uruguay, Argentina, Mexico, Nicaragua, Guatemala, Honduras, El Salvador, Venezuela, Turkey, Egypt, and Lebanon.
3. Germanists' perception that Roman and German law were opposites rather than complementary was resuscitated in 1920 when the Nazi party called for the replacement of Roman law (identified with a materialistic world order) with a "genuine" (and "good") German law.

4. Before the BGB, as many as thirty diverse legal systems might have operated in Germanic territories, using at least three legal languages (Latin, German, and French). Some regions followed local codes, others were under French control until 1871 and thus followed the French Civil Code, and yet others observed Roman, canon, or customary law.

5. The countries that were said to have been influenced by the BGB included Greece, Austria, Switzerland, Portugal, Italy, the Netherlands, the former Czechoslovakia, the former Yugoslavia, Hungary, Estonia, Latvia, Ukraine, Japan, Brazil, Mexico, Peru, Taiwan, South Korea, Thailand, and, for a while, China.

6. See Chapter 1, note 1.

13. Codifying Common Law

1. Maurice Amos, "The Code Napoleon and the Modern World," *Journal of Comparative Legislation and International Law* 10, no. 4 (1928): 222–236, at 222.

2. H. R. Hahlo, "Codifying the Common Law: Protracted Gestation," *Modern Law Review* 38, no. 1 (1975): 23–30, at 23.

3. These states and territories included California, Iowa, Minnesota, Indiana, Ohio, Washington Territory, Nebraska, Wisconsin, Kansas, Nevada, Dakotas, Idaho, Arizona, Montana, North Carolina, Wyoming, South Carolina, Utah, Colorado, Oklahoma, and New Mexico.

Epilogue

1. The 1950s also featured failed attempts to create a European Defense Community (EDC) and a European Political Community (EPC).

2. The treaty that instituted this single structure, known as the Merger Treaty, was signed in Brussels in 1965 but came into effect in 1967. Because the treaty merged three entities (the ECSC, the EEC, and Euratom), the more appropriate name for the new structure was "European Communities" in plural. Yet most people referred to this complex structure as the European Community (in singular).

3. From its initiation, the European Community had two councils. One, the Council of the European Community (later, of the European Union) is a meeting of the national ministers of member states. In this forum, ministers vote on legislation proposed by the European Commission on matters related to their particular ministry. For example, the Agricultural and Fisheries Council is the meeting of the ministers of agriculture and it votes on legislation on matters of agriculture; the Foreign Affairs Council unites the national

ministers of foreign affairs and votes on legislation on these issues; and so forth. The European Council, on the contrary, is a meeting of the heads of state. It sets the political agenda and discusses the major issues facing the Community / Union, but it does not have legislative functions.

4. The five countries that signed the Schengen Agreement were Belgium, France, Luxembourg, Netherlands, and (West) Germany. Their association constituted an area known as the "Schengen area."

5. As of 2013, the European Union included Austria, Belgium, Bulgaria, Croatia, Cyprus, Czech Republic, Denmark, Estonia, Finland, France, Germany, Greece, Hungary, Ireland, Italy, Latvia, Lithuania, Luxembourg, Malta, Netherlands, Poland, Portugal, Romania, Slovakia, Slovenia, Spain, Sweden, and the UK.

6. Originally, Eurozone countries included Austria, Belgium, Finland, France, Germany, Greece, Ireland, Italy, Luxembourg, the Netherlands, Portugal, and Spain. Currently, however, the Eurozone embraces nineteen member states after the addition of Cyprus, Estonia, Latvia, Lithuania, Malta, Slovakia, and Slovenia.

7. http://www.europarl.europa.eu/atyourservice/en/displayFtu.html?ftuId =FTU_1.3.9.html includes a description of the court, as does http://europa .eu/about-eu/institutions-bodies/court-justice/index_en.htm. The Court itself has a useful website allowing to track its jurisprudence: http://curia.europa .eu/jcms/jcms/j_6/.

8. Karen J. Alter, *Establishing the Supremacy of European Law: The Making of an International Rule of Law in Europe* (Oxford: Oxford University Press, 2003), 15.

9. Proclaimed by the European Council in 2000, initially the charter of fundamental rights was not legally binding. However, in 2009 it was formally integrated into European law. Information on the charter can be found at http://ec.europa.eu/justice/fundamental-rights/charter/index_en.htm.

10. Ugo Mattei and Mauro Bussani, "The Trento Common Core Project," a presentation delivered in the first general meeting, July 6, 1995, available at http://www.common-core.org/node/8.

Further Reading

Introduction

Ecklund, John E. *The Origins of Western Law from Athens to the Code of Napoleon.* Clark, NJ: Talbot, 2014.

Grossi, Paolo. *A History of European Law.* Translated by Laurence Hooper. Chichester, UK: Wiley-Blackwell, 2010.

Hespanha, Antonio Manuel. *A cultura jurídica europeia: Síntese de un milénio.* Coimbra, Portugal: Almedina, 2012.

Kelly, J. M. *A Short History of Western Legal Theory.* New York: Oxford University Press, 1992.

Lesaffer, Randall. *European Legal History: A Cultural and Political Perspective.* Cambridge: Cambridge University Press, 2009.

Merryman, John Henry. *The Civil Law Tradition: An Introduction to the Legal Systems of Europe and Latin America.* 3rd ed. Stanford, CA: Stanford University Press, 2007.

Mousourakis, George. *Roman Law and the Origins of the Civil Law Tradition.* Cham, Switzerland: Springer, 2015.

Robinson, O. F., T. D. Fergus, and V. M. Gordon. *European Legal History: Sources and Institutions.* 2nd ed. London: Butterworths, 1994.

Schioppa, Antonio Padoa. *Storia del diritto in Europa: Dal medioevo all'età contemporanea.* Bologna: Il Mulino, 2007.

Van Caenegem, R. C. *An Historical Introduction to Private Law.* Translated by D. E. L Johnston. Cambridge: Cambridge University Press, 1992.

Chapter 1

Ando, Clifford. *Law, Language, and Empire in the Roman Tradition*. Philadelphia: University of Pennsylvania Press, 2011.

Blume, Fred H., trans. "Annotated Justinian Code." University of Wyoming George W. Hopper Law Library. http://uwyo.edu/lawlib/blume-justinian.

Crawford, M. H., ed. *Roman Statutes*. London: Institute of Classical Studies, 1996.

Crook, John Anthony. *Law and Life of Rome*. London: Thames and Hudson, 1967.

du Plessis, Paul J. *Studying Roman Law*. London: Bristol Classical Press, 2012.

du Plessis, Paul J., Clifford Ando, and G. Tuori, eds. *The Oxford Handbook of Roman Law*. Oxford: Oxford University Press, 2016.

Frier, Bruce W. *The Rise of the Roman Jurists: Studies in Cicero's Pro Caecina*. Princeton, NJ: Princeton University Press, 1985.

Frier, Bruce W., ed., and Fred H. Blume, trans. *The Codex of Justinian: A New Annotated Translation*. Cambridge: Cambridge University Press, 2016.

Gordon, W. M., and O. F. Robinson, trans. *The Institutes of Gaius*. Ithaca, NY: Cornell University Press, 1988.

Honoré, Tony. *Justinian's Digest: Character and Compilation*. Oxford: Oxford University Press, 2010.

Johnston, David. *The Cambridge Companion to Roman Law*. Cambridge: Cambridge University Press, 2015.

———. *Roman Law in Context*. Cambridge: Cambridge University Press, 1999.

Jolowicz, H. F., and Barry Nicholas. *Historical Introduction to the Study of Roman Law*. 3rd ed. Cambridge: Cambridge University Press, 1972.

Krueger, Paul. *Justinian's Institutes*. Translated by Peter Birks and Grant McLeod. Ithaca, NY: Cornell University Press, 1987.

Krueger, Paul, Theodor Mommsen, Rudolf Schoell, and Wilhelm Kroll, eds. *Corpus Iuris Civilis*. 3 vols. Berlin: Weidmann, 1928.

Kunkel, Wolfgang. *An Introduction to Roman Legal and Constitutional History*. Translated by J. M. Kelly. Oxford: Clarendon Press, 1966.

Lambiris, Michael. *The Historical Context of Roman Law*. North Ryde, Australia: LBC Information Services, 1997.

Metzger, Ernest. *Litigation in Roman Law*. Oxford: Oxford University Press, 2005.

———. "An Outline of Roman Civil Procedure." *Roman Legal Tradition* 9 (2013): 1–30.

Mousourakis, George. *Roman Law and the Origins of the Civil Law Tradition*. Cham, Switzerland: Springer, 2015.

Nicholas, Barry. *An Introduction to Roman Law.* Oxford: Clarendon Press, 1962.

Pharr, Clyde, trans. *The Theodosian Code and Novels and the Sirmondian Constitutions.* Princeton, NJ: Princeton University Press, 1952.

Robinson, O. F. *The Sources of Roman Law: Problems and Methods for Ancient Historians.* London: Routledge, 1997.

Schiavone, Aldo. *The Invention of Law in the West.* Translated by Jeremy Carden and Antony Shugaar. Cambridge, MA: Harvard University Press, 2012.

Schiller, A. Arthur. *Roman Law: Mechanisms of Development.* The Hague: Mouton, 1978.

Stein, Peter. *Roman Law in European History.* Cambridge: Cambridge University Press, 1999.

Waelkens, Laurent. *Amne Adverso: Roman Legal Heritage in European Culture.* Leuven, Belgium: Leuven University Press, 2015.

Watson, Alan, ed. *The Digest of Justinian.* Philadelphia: University of Pennsylvania Press, 1985.

———. *Law Making in the Later Roman Republic.* Oxford: Clarendon Press, 1974.

———. *The Spirit of the Roman Law.* Athens, GA: University of Georgia Press, 1995.

Chapter 2

Ando, Clifford. *The Matter of the Gods: Religion and the Roman Empire.* Berkeley: University of California Press, 2009.

Bartlett, Robert. *The Making of Europe: Conquest, Colonization and Cultural Change, 950–1350.* Princeton, NJ: Princeton University Press, 1993.

Biondi, Biondo. *Il diritto romano cristiano.* 3 vols. Milan: Giuffrè, 1952–1954.

Brown, Peter. *The Rise of Western Christendom: Triumph and Diversity, A.D. 200–1000.* Cambridge, MA: Wiley-Blackwell, 1995.

Fletcher, Richard. *The Conversion of Europe: From Paganism to Christianity, 371–1386 AD.* London: HarperCollins, 1997.

Freeman, Charles. *A New History of Early Christianity.* New Haven, CT: Yale University Press, 2009.

Grubbs, Judith Evans. *Law and Family in Late Antiquity: The Emperor Constantine's Marriage Legislation.* Oxford: Oxford University Press, 1995.

Heather, Peter. *Empires and Barbarians: The Fall of Rome and the Birth of Europe.* Oxford: Oxford University Press, 2010.

Humfress, Caroline. *Orthodoxy and the Courts in Late Antiquity.* Oxford: Oxford University Press, 2007.

Lenski, Noel. "Constantine and Slavery: Libertas and the Fusion of Roman and Christian Values." *Atti dell'Accademia Romanistica Costantiniana* 18 (2012): 235–260.

MacCormack, Sabine. "Sin, Citizenship, and Salvation of the Souls: The Impact of Christian Priorities on Late-Roman and Post-Roman Society." *Comparative Studies in Society and History* 39, no. 4 (1997): 644–673.

MacMullen, Ramsay. "What Difference Did Christianity Make?" *Historia: Zeitschrift für Alte Geschichte* 35, no. 3 (1986): 322–343.

Salzman, Michele Renee. "The Evidence for the Conversion of the Roman Empire to Christianity in Book 16 of the 'Theodosian Code.'" *Historia: Zeitschrift für Alte Geschichte* 42, no. 3 (1993): 362–378.

Thompson, John A. F. *The Western Church in the Middle Ages.* London: Arnold, 1998.

Vuolanto, Ville. "Children and the Memory of Parents in the Late Roman World." In *Children, Memory, and Family Identity in Roman Culture*, edited by Véronique Dasen and Thomas Späth, 173–192. Oxford: Oxford University Press, 2010.

Chapter 3

Bartlett, Robert. *Trial by Fire and Water: The Medieval Judicial Ordeal.* Oxford: Clarendon Press, 1986.

Collins, Roger. "Literacy and the Laity in Early Mediaeval Spain." In *The Uses of Literacy in Early Medieval Europe,* edited by Rosamond McKitterick, 109–133. Cambridge: Cambridge University Press, 1990.

Davies, Wendy. "Local Participation and Legal Ritual in Early Medieval Law Courts." In *The Moral World of the Law,* edited by Peter Coss, 48–61. Cambridge: Cambridge University Press, 2000.

Davies, Wendy, and Paul Fouracre, eds. *The Settlement of Disputes in Early Medieval Europe.* Cambridge: Cambridge University Press, 1986.

Davis, Jennifer R. *Charlemagne's Practice of Empire.* Cambridge: Cambridge University Press, 2015.

Grossi, Paolo. *L'Ordine giuridico medievale.* Rome: Laterza, 1995.

Humfress, Caroline. *Orthodoxy and the Courts in Late Antiquity.* Oxford: Oxford University Press, 2007.

Jasper, Detlev, and Horst Fuhrmann. *Papal Letters in the Early Middle Ages.* Washington, DC: Catholic University of America Press, 2001.

Kéry, Lotte. *Canonical Collections of the Early Middle Ages (ca. 400–1140): A Bibliographical Guide to the Manuscripts and Literature.* Washington, DC: Catholic University of America Press, 1999.

Lesaffer, Randall. *European Legal History: A Cultural and Political Perspective.* Cambridge: Cambridge University Press, 2009.

Logan, F. Donald. *A History of the Church in the Middle Ages.* 2nd ed. London: Routledge, 2013.

Lupoi, Maurizio. *The Origins of the European Legal Order.* Translated by Adrian Belton. Cambridge: Cambridge University Press, 2000.

Masschaele, James. *Jury, State, and Society in Medieval England.* New York: Palgrave Macmillan, 2008.

McKitterick, Rosamond, ed. *The Uses of Literacy in Early Medieval Europe.* Cambridge: Cambridge University Press, 1990.

Oliver, Lisi. *The Body Legal in Barbarian Law.* Toronto: University of Toronto Press, 2011.

Radding, Charles M., and Antonio Ciaralli. *The Corpus Iuris Civilis in the Middle Ages: Manuscripts and Transmission from the Sixth Century to the Juristic Revival.* Leiden: Brill, 2007.

Reynolds, Susan. *Kingdoms and Communities in Western Europe, 900–1300.* 2nd ed. Oxford: Clarendon Press, 1997.

Rio, Alice. *Legal Practice and the Written Word in the Early Middle Ages: Frankish Formulae, c. 500–1000.* Cambridge: Cambridge University Press, 2009.

Waelkens, Laurent. *Amne Adverso: Roman Legal Heritage in European Culture.* Leuven, Belgium: Leuven University Press, 2015.

Walters, Dafydd. "From Benedict to Gratian: The Code in Medieval Ecclesiastical Authors." In *The Theodosian Code: Studies in the Imperial Law of Late Antiquity,* 2nd ed., edited by Jill Harries and Ian Wood, 200–216. London: Bristol Classical Press, 2010.

Whitman, James Q. *The Origins of Reasonable Doubt: Theological Roots of the Criminal Trial.* New Haven, CT: Yale University Press, 2008.

Chapter 4

Berman, Harold J. *Law and Revolution: The Formation of the Western Legal Tradition.* Cambridge, MA: Harvard University Press, 1983.

Bisson, Thomas N. *The Crisis of the Twelfth Century: Power, Lordship, and the Origins of European Government.* Princeton, NJ: Princeton University Press, 2009.

Bloch, Marc. *Feudal Society.* Translated by L. A. Manyon. Chicago: University of Chicago Press, 1961.

Blumenthal, Uta-Renate. *The Investiture Controversy: Church and Monarchy from the Ninth to the Twelfth Century.* Philadelphia: University of Pennsylvania Press, 1988.

Brown, Elizabeth A. R. "The Tyranny of a Construct: Feudalism and Histo-
    rians of Medieval Europe." *American Historical Review* 79, no. 4 (1974):
    1063–1088.

Cook, William R., and Ronald B. Herzman. *The Medieval World View: An
    Introduction.* 2nd ed. Oxford: Oxford University Press, 2004.

Davis, Kathleen. "Sovereign Subjects, Feudal Law, and the Writing of History."
    Journal of Medieval and Early Modern Studies 36, no. 2 (2006): 223–261.

"*Dictatus Papae* (Gregory VII), Letter of Gregory VII to Henry IV, Henry IV's
    Position and Renunciation of Gregory VII by the German Bishops (Synod
    of Worms)," and "The Concordat of Worms." In *University of Chicago
    Readings in Western Civilization,* vol. 4: *Medieval Europe,* edited by Julius
    Kirshner and Karl F. Morrison, 142–150, 169–170. Chicago: University of
    Chicago Press, 1986.

Ganshof, François Louis. *Feudalism.* Translated by Philip Grierson. London:
    Longmans, 1952.

Logan, F. Donald. *A History of the Church in the Middle Ages.* London: Rout-
    ledge, 2013.

"Lords, Vassals and Tenants in the Norman Summa de Legibus (1258)." In
    University of Chicago Readings in Western Civilization, vol. 4: *Medieval
    Europe,* edited by Julius Kirshner and Karl F. Morrison, 68–76. Chicago:
    University of Chicago Press, 1986.

Reynolds, Susan. *Fiefs and Vassals: The Medieval Evidence Reinterpreted.*
    Oxford: Oxford University Press, 1994.

Tierney, Brian, ed. *The Crisis of Church and State, 1050–1300.* Englewood Cliffs,
    NJ: Prentice-Hall, 1964.

Chapter 5

Ascheri, Mario. *The Laws of Late Medieval Italy (1000–1500): Foundations for a
    European Legal System.* Leiden: Brill, 2013.

Bartolus de Saxoferrato. *Tractatus Tyberiadis seu de fluminibus,* bks. 1–3: *De
    alluvione, de insula, de alveo; Tractatus de insigniis et armis.* Turin: Bottega
    d'Erasmo, 1964. Available in abbreviated form at http://lafogonera.blogspot
    .com.es/2007/11/de-insula-brtolo-de-sassoferrato-1313.html.

Bellomo, Manlio. *The Common Legal Past of Europe, 1000–1800.* Washington,
    DC: Catholic University of America Press, 1995.

Brundage, James A. *Medieval Canon Law.* London: Longman, 1995.

Cairns, John W., and Paul J. du Plessis, eds. *The Creation of the Ius Commune:
    From Casus to Regula.* Edinburgh: Edinburgh University Press, 2010.

Conte, Emanuele. "Consuetudine, Coutume, gewohnheit and Ius Commune: An Introduction." *Rechtsgeschichte / Legal History* 24 (2016): 234–243.

Coopens, Chris. "The Teaching of Law in the University of Paris in the First Quarter of the 13th Century." *Rivista internazionale di diritto comune* 10 (1999): 139–173.

Gallagher, Clarence. *Canon Law and the Christian Community: The Role of Law in the Church according to the Summa Aurea of Cardinal Hostiensis.* Rome: Università Gregoriana, 1978.

Gratian. *The Treatise on Laws (Decretum DD. 1–20) with the Ordinary Gloss.* Translated by Augustine Thompson and James Gordley. Washington, DC: Catholic University of America Press, 1993.

Grossi, Paolo. *L'Ordine giuridico medievale.* Rome: Laterza, 1995.

Hartmann, Wilfried, and Kenneth Pennington, eds. *The History of Medieval Canon Law in the Classical Period, 1140–1234: From Gratian to the Decretals of Pope Gregory IX.* Washington, DC: Catholic University of America Press, 2008.

Haskins, Charles Homer. *The Renaissance of the Twelfth Century.* Cambridge, MA: Harvard University Press, 1927.

Helmholz, R. H. *The Spirit of Classical Canon Law.* Athens, GA: University of Georgia Press, 1996.

Herzog, Tamar. *Defining Nations: Immigrants and Citizens in Early Modern Spain and Spanish America.* New Haven, CT: Yale University Press, 2003.

———. *Frontiers of Possession: Spain and Portugal in Europe and the Americas.* Cambridge, MA: Harvard University Press, 2015.

Ibbetson, David. "English Law and the European Ius Commune, 1450–1650." *Cambridge Year Book of European Legal Studies* 8 (2006): 115–132.

Larson, Atria A., trans. *Gratian's Tractatus de Penitentia: A New Latin Edition with English Translation.* Washington, DC: Catholic University of America Press, 2016.

Le Goff, Jacques. *Intellectuals in the Middle Ages.* Translated by Teresa Lavender Fagan. Oxford: Blackwell, 1993.

Müller, Wolfgang P., and Mary E. Sommar, eds. *Medieval Church Law and the Origins of the Western Legal Tradition: A Tribute to Kenneth Pennington.* Washington, DC: Catholic University of America Press, 2006.

Peters, Edward. *Inquisition.* New York: Free Press, 1988.

Rogerious, "Questions on the Institutes." In *University of Chicago Readings in Western Civilization,* vol. 4: *Medieval Europe,* edited by Julius Kirshner and Karl F. Morrison, 215–218. Chicago: University of Chicago Press, 1986.

Scott, Samuel Parsons, trans., and Robert I. Burns, ed. *Las Siete Partidas.*
    Philadelphia: University of Pennsylvania Press, 2001.
Vinogradoff, Paul. *Roman Law in Medieval Europe.* Oxford: Clarendon Press, 1929.
Winroth, Anders. *The Making of Gratian's Decretum.* Cambridge: Cambridge
    University Press, 2000.

Chapter 6

Baker, John. *An Introduction to English Legal History.* Oxford: Oxford Univer-
    sity Press, 2003.
————. *The Oxford History of the Laws of England: 1483–1558.* Oxford: Oxford
    University Press, 2003.
Bracton, Henry de. *On the Laws and Customs of England* (*De legibus et
    consuetudinibus Angliae*). Translated by Samuel E Thorne. Buffalo, NY:
    W. S. Hein, 1997.
Brand, Paul. "Chancery, the Justices and the Making of New Writs in
    Thirteenth-Century England." In *Law and Legal Process: Substantive Law
    and Procedure in English Legal History,* edited by Matthew Dyson and
    David Ibbetson, 17–33. Cambridge: Cambridge University Press, 2013.
————. *Kings, Barons and Justices: The Making and Enforcement of Legislation in
    Thirteenth-Century England.* Cambridge: Cambridge University Press, 2003.
Carpenter, David, trans. *Magna Carta.* London: Penguin Books, 2015.
Clanchy, M. T. *From Memory to Written Record: England 1066–1307.* 2nd ed.
    Oxford: Blackwell, 1993.
Dawson, John P. *The Oracles of the Law.* Ann Arbor: University of Michigan
    Law School, 1968.
Doe, Norman. *Fundamental Authority in Late Medieval English Law.* Cam-
    bridge: Cambridge University Press, 1990.
Donahue, Charles. "Ius Commune, Canon law, and Common Law in
    England." *Tulane Law Review* 66, no. 6 (1992): 1745–1780.
Fleming, Robin. *Britain after Rome: The Fall and Rise, 400–1070.* London: Allen
    Lane, 2010.
Glanvill, Ranulf de. *The Treatise on the Laws and Customs of the Realm of
    England Commonly Called Glanvill.* Edited and translated by G. D. G.
    Hall. Oxford: Clarendon Press, 1993.
Goodman, Ellen. *The Origins of the Western Legal Tradition from Thales to the
    Tudors.* Annandale, Australia: Federation Press, 1995.
Harding, Alan. *Medieval Law and the Foundations of the State.* Oxford: Oxford
    University Press, 2002.

Helmholz, R. H. *The Ius Commune in England: Four Studies.* Oxford: Oxford University Press, 2001.

———. *The Oxford History of the Laws of England,* vol. 1: *The Canon Law and Ecclesiastical Jurisdiction from 597 to the 1640s.* Oxford: Oxford University Press, 2004.

Hudson, John. "Magna Carta, the *Ius Commune,* and English Common Law." In *Magna Carta and the England of King John,* edited by Janet S. Loengard, 99–119. Woodbridge, UK: Boydell Press, 2010.

———. *The Oxford History of the Laws of England,* vol. 2: *871–1216.* Oxford: Oxford University Press, 2012.

Hulsebosch, Daniel J. "The Ancient Constitution and the Expanding Empire: Sir Edward Coke's British Jurisprudence." *Law and History Review* 21, no. 3 (2003): 439–482.

Hyams, Paul R. "What Did Edwardian Villagers Understand by 'Law'?" In *Medieval Society and the Manor Court,* edited by Zvi Razi and Richard Smith, 69–102. Oxford: Oxford University Press, 1996.

Ibbetson, David J. "Case Law and Judicial Precedent in Mediaeval and Early-Modern England." In *Auctoritates: Xania R.C. van Caenegem oblata; De auteurs van de rechtsontwikkeling,* edited by S. Dauchy, J. Monballyu, and A. Wijffels, 55–68. Brussels: Wetenschappelijk Comité voor Rechtsgeschiedenis, 1997.

———. "Juge et jury dans le common law." In *Le juge et le jugement dans les traditions juridiques européennes: Études d'histoire comparée,* edited by Robert Jacob, 89–105. Paris: LGDJ, 1996.

Kamali, Elizabeth Papp, and Thomas A. Green. "A Crossroads in Criminal Procedure: The Assumptions Underlying England's Adoption of Trial by Jury for Crime." In *Essays in Honour of Paul Brand,* edited by Travis Baker. Farnham, UK: Ashgate, 2017.

Kelly, Susan. "Anglo Saxon Lay Society and the Written Word." In *The Uses of Literacy in Early Medieval Europe,* edited by Rosamond McKitterick, 36–62. Cambridge: Cambridge University Press, 1990.

Kim, Keechang. *Aliens in Medieval Law: The Origins of Modern Citizenship.* Cambridge: Cambridge University Press, 2000.

Korporowicz, Lukasz Jan. "Roman Law in Roman Britain: An Introductory Survey." *Journal of Legal History* 33, no. 2 (2012): 133–150.

Lewis, Andrew. "'What Marcellus Says Is Against You': Roman Law and Common Law." In *The Roman Law Tradition,* edited by A. D. E. Lewis and D. J. Ibbetson, 199–208. Cambridge: Cambridge University Press, 1994.

Liebermann, Felix, ed. *Die Gesetze der Angelsachsen.* 4 vols. Halle, Germany: Max Niemeyer, 1903–1916.

McSweeney, Thomas. "English Judges and Roman Jurists: The Civilian Learning behind England's First Case Law." *Temple Law Review* 84, no. 4 (2012): 827–862.

Milsom, S. F. C. *Historical Foundations of the Common Law.* 2nd ed. London: Butterworths, 1981.

Musson, Anthony. *Medieval Law in Context: The Growth of Legal Consciousness from Magna Carta to the Peasant's Revolt.* Manchester, UK: Manchester University Press, 2001.

Plucknett, Theodore F. T. *A Concise History of the Common Law.* 5th ed. Boston: Little, Brown and Co., 1956.

———. *Statutes and Their Interpretation in the First Half of the Fourteenth Century.* Cambridge: Cambridge University Press, 1922.

Pollock, Frederick. *Oxford Lectures and Other Discourses.* London: Macmillan, 1890.

Pollock, Frederick, and Frederic William Maitland. *The History of English Law before the Time of Edward I.* 2nd ed. Cambridge: Cambridge University Press, 1899.

Price, Polly J. "Natural Law and Birthright Citizenship in Calvin's Case (1608)." *Yale Journal of Law & the Humanities* 9, no. 1 (1997): 73–145.

Richardson, H. G., and G. O. Sayles. *Law and Legislation from Aethelberht to Magna Carta.* Edinburgh: Edinburgh University Press, 1966.

Seipp, David J. "Jurors, Evidences, and the Tempest of 1499." In *"The Dearest Birthright of the People of England": The Jury in the History of the Common Law,* edited by John W. Cairns and Grant McLeod, 75–92. Oxford: Hart, 2002.

———, comp. "Medieval English Legal History: An Index and Paraphrase of Printed Year Book Reports, 1268–1535." http://www.bu.edu/law/faculty -scholarship/legal-history-the-year-books.

———. "The Reception of Canon Law and Civil Law in the Common Law Courts before 1600." *Oxford Journal of Legal Studies* 13, no. 3 (1993): 388–420.

Stanojevic, Obrad. "Roman Law and Common Law: A Different Point of View." *Loyola Law Review* 36, no. 2 (1990): 269–274.

Van Caenegem, R. C. *The Birth of English Common Law.* Cambridge: Cambridge University Press, 1973.

Watson, Alan. "Roman Law and English Law: Two Patterns of Legal Development." *Loyola Law Review* 36, no. 2 (1990): 247–268.

Wormald, Patrick. *The Making of English Law: King Alfred to the Twelfth Century.* Oxford: Blackwell, 1999.

Chapter 7

Dawson, John P. "The Codification of the French Customs." *Michigan Law Review* 38, no. 6 (1940): 765–800.

Decock, W. *Theologians and Contract Law: The Moral Transformation of Ius Commune (ca.1500–1650).* Leiden: Brill / Nijhoff, 2012.

Grinberg, Martine. "La rédaction des coutumes et les droits seigneuriaux." *Annales: Histoire, Sciences Sociales* 52, no. 5 (1997): 1017–1038.

Hotman, François. *Francogallia.* Edited by Ralph E. Giesey and translated by J. H. M. Salmon. Cambridge: Cambridge University Press, 1972.

Pitkin, Barbara. "Calvin's Mosaic Harmony: Biblical Exegesis and Early Modern Legal History." *Sixteenth Century Journal* 41, no. 2 (2010): 441–466.

Strauss, Gerald. *Law, Resistance, and the State: The Opposition to Roman Law in Reformation Germany.* Princeton, NJ: Princeton University Press, 1986.

Teuscher, Simon. *Lords' Rights and Peasant Stories: Writing and the Formation of Tradition in the Later Middle Ages.* Translated by Philip Grace. Philadelphia: University of Pennsylvania Press, 2012.

Toch, Michael. "Asking the Way and Telling the Law: Speech in Medieval Germany." *Journal of Interdisciplinary History* 16, no. 4 (1986): 667–682.

Witte, John. *Law and Protestantism: The Legal Teachings of the Lutheran Reformation.* Cambridge: Cambridge University Press 2002.

Chapter 8

Aroney, Nicholas. "Law, Revolution and Religion: Harold Berman's Interpretation of the English Revolution." *Journal of Markets and Morality* 8, no. 2 (2005): 355–385.

Berman, Harold J. *Law and Revolution, II: The Impact of the Protestant Reformations on the Western Legal Tradition.* Cambridge, MA: Belknap Press of Harvard University Press, 2003.

"Bill of Rights." Reproduced in *The Roots of the Bill of Rights,* 5 vols., compiled by Bernard Schwartz, 1:41–46. New York: Chelsea House, 1971.

Blackstone, William. *Commentaries on the Laws of England.* Oxford: Clarendon Press, 1765–1769.

Bonfield, Lloyd. "The Nature of Customary Law in the Manor Courts of Medieval England." *Comparative Studies in Society and History* 31, no. 3 (1989): 514–534.

———. "What Did English Villagers Mean by 'Customary Law'?" In *Medieval Society and the Manor Court,* edited by Zvi Razi and Richard Smith, 103–116. Oxford: Oxford University Press, 1996.

Brooks, Christopher, and Kevin Sharpe. "History, English Law and the Renaissance." *Past & Present* 72 (1976): 133–142.

Carpenter, David, trans. *Magna Carta.* London: Penguin Books, 2015.

Clanchy, M. T. *From Memory to Written Record, England 1066–1307.* 2nd ed. Oxford: Blackwell, 1993.

———. "Remembering the Past and the Good Old Law." *History* 55 (1970): 165–176.

Cromartie, Alan. *The Constitutionalist Revolution: An Essay on the History of England, 1450–1642.* Cambridge: Cambridge University Press, 2006.

———. "The Idea of Common Law as Custom." In *The Nature of Customary Law,* edited by Amanda Perreu-Saussine and James Bernard Murphy, 203–227. Cambridge: Cambridge University Press, 2007.

Garnett, George. "'To ould fields': Law and History in the Prefaces to Sir Edward Coke's Reports." *Journal of Legal History* 34, no. 3 (2013): 245–284.

Haskins, George L. *The Growth of English Representative Government.* Philadelphia: University of Pennsylvania Press, 1948.

Helmholz, R. H. *Roman Canon Law in Reformation England.* Cambridge: Cambridge University Press, 1990.

Holt, J. C. *Magna Carta.* 3rd ed. Cambridge: Cambridge University Press, 2015.

Hyams, Paul R. "What Did Edwardian Villagers Understand by 'Law'?" In *Medieval Society and the Manor Court,* edited by Zvi Razi and Richard Smith, 69–102. Oxford: Oxford University Press, 1996.

Ibbetson, D. J. "The Arguments in Calvin's Case (1608)." In *Studies in Canon Law and Common Law in Honor of R. H. Helmholz,* edited by Troy L. Harris, 213–230. Berkeley: Robbins Collection, 2015.

———. "Report and Record in Early-Modern Common Law: Sample Reports." In *Case Law in the Making: The Techniques and Methods of Judicial Records and Law Reports,* 2 vols., edited by Alain Wijffels, 2:27–52. Berlin: Duncker und Humblot, 1997.

Kelley, Donald R. "History, English Law and the Renaissance." *Past & Present* 65, no. 1 (1974): 24–51.

Levak, Brian P. *The Civil Lawyers in England, 1603–1641: A Political Study.* Oxford: Clarendon Press, 1973.

Lewis, Andrew. "'What Marcellus Says Is Against You': Roman Law and Common Law." In *The Roman Law Tradition*, edited by A. D. E. Lewis and D. J. Ibbetson, 199–208. Cambridge: Cambridge University Press, 1994.

"The Magna Carta Project." http://magnacartaresearch.org.

Maitland, Frederic William. *English Law and the Renaissance (The Rede Lecture for 1901)*. Cambridge: Cambridge University Press, 1901.

——. *Select Pleas in the Manorial and Other Seigniorial Courts*. London: B. Quaritch, 1889.

"Petition of Rights." Reproduced in *The Roots of the Bill of Rights*, 5 vols., compiled by Bernard Schwartz, 1:19–21. New York: Chelsea House, 1971.

Pocock, J. G. A. *The Ancient Constitution and the Feudal Law: English Historical Thought in the Seventeenth Century*. Cambridge: Cambridge University Press, 1957.

Rodgers, C. P. "Humanism, History and the Common Law." *Journal of Legal History* 6, no. 2 (1985): 129–156.

Sherman, Charles P. "A Brief History of Medieval Roman Canon Law in England." *University of Pennsylvania Law Review and American Law Register* 68, no. 2 (1920): 233–258.

Smith, David Chan. *Sir Edward Coke and the Reformation of the Laws: Religion, Politics and Jurisprudence, 1578–1616*. Cambridge: Cambridge University Press, 2014.

Tubbs, J. W. *The Common Law Mind: Medieval and Early Modern Conceptions*. Baltimore: Johns Hopkins University Press, 2000.

Williams, Ian. "'He Creditted More the Printed Booke': Common Lawyer's Receptivity to Print, c. 1500–1640." *Law and History Review* 28, no. 1 (2010): 39–70.

——. "The Tudor Genesis of Edward Coke's Immemorial Common Law." *Sixteenth Century Journal* 43, no. 1 (2012): 103–123.

Wood, Andy. *The Memory of the People: Custom and Popular Senses of the Past in Early Modern England*. Cambridge: Cambridge University Press, 2013.

Wormald, Patrick. *The Making of English Law: King Alfred to the Twelfth Century*. Oxford: Blackwell, 1999.

Chapter 9

Arneil, Barbara. *John Locke and America: The Defense of English Colonialism*. Oxford: Clarendon Press, 1996.

Brett, Annabel S. *Changes of State: Nature and the Limits of the City in Early Modern Natural Law*. Princeton, NJ: Princeton University Press, 2011.

The Bull *Inter Caetera*. Reproduced in *Sources Relating to the History of the Law of Nations*, 3 vols., edited by Wilhelm G. Grewe, 2:68–70. Berlin: De Gruyter, 1988.

Cavallar, Georg. "Vitoria, Grotius, Pufendorf, Wolff and Vattel: Accomplices of European Colonialism and Exploitation or True Cosmopolitans," *Journal of the History of International Law* 10, no. 2 (2008): 181–209.

Daston, Lorraine, and Michael Stolleis, eds. *Natural Law and Laws of Nature in Early Modern Europe: Jurisprudence, Theology, Moral and Natural Philosophy*. Farnham, UK: Ashgate, 2008.

d'Entrèves, A. P. *Natural Law: An Introduction to Legal Philosophy*. London: Hutchinson and Co., 1951.

Fitzmaurice, Andrew. *Sovereignty, Property and Empire, 1500–2000*. Cambridge: Cambridge University Press, 2014.

Grotius, Hugo. *The Freedom of the Seas or the Right Which Belongs to the Dutch to Take Part in the East Indian Trade*, 1609. Translated by Ralph van Deman Magoffin and edited by James Scott Brown. New York: Oxford University Press, 1916.

———. *On the Law of War and Peace*, 1625. Translated by A. C. Campbell. London: Boothroyd, 1814.

Herzog, Tamar. *Defining Nations: Immigrants and Citizens in Early Modern Spain and Spanish America*. New Haven, CT: Yale University Press, 2003.

———. "Did European Law Turn American? Territory, Property and Rights in an Atlantic World." In *New Horizons in Spanish Colonial Law: Contributions to Transnational Early Modern Legal History*, edited by Thomas Duve and Heikki Pihlajamäki, 75–95. Frankfurt: Max Planck Institute for European Legal History, 2015.

Kingsbury, Benedict, and Benjamin Straumann, eds. *The Roman Foundations of the Law of Nations: Alberico Gentili and the Justice of Empire*. Oxford: Oxford University Press, 2010.

Locke, John. *Two Treatises of Government*. London: Awnsham Churchill, 1698.

MacMillan, Ken. *Sovereignty and Possession in the English New World: The Legal Foundations of Empire, 1576–1640*. Cambridge: Cambridge University Press, 2006.

Marcoci, Giuseppe. *L'invenzione di un imperio: Politica e cultura nel mondo portoghese (1450–1600)*. Rome: Caroci Editore, 2011.

Pagden, Anthony. *The Burdens of Empire: 1539 to the Present*. New York: Cambridge University Press, 2015.

Parry, J. H. *The Age of Reconnaissance*. Cleveland: World Publishing Co., 1963.

Pufendorf, Samuel von. *Of the Law of Nature and Nations.* 2nd ed. Translated by Basil Kennett and William Percivale. Oxford: Printed by L. Lichfield for A. and J. Churchil, 1710.

The Requirement. Reproduced in *Fontes Historiae Iuris Gentium: Quellen zur Geschichte des Völkerrechts / Sources Relating to the History of the Law of Nations,* 3 vols., edited by Wilhelm G. Grewe, 2:103–109. Berlin: De Gruyter, 1988.

Rommen, Heinrich A. *The Natural Law: A Study in Legal and Social History and Philosophy,* 1936. Translated by Thomas R. Hanley. Indianapolis: Liberty Fund, 1998.

Tuck, Richard. *Natural Rights Theories: Their Origin and Development.* Cambridge: Cambridge University Press, 1979.

Tully, James. *A Discourse on Property: John Locke and His Adversaries.* Cambridge: Cambridge University Press, 1980.

Vattel, Emer de. *The Law of Nations or the Principles of Natural Law Applied to the Conduct and to the Affairs of Nations and of Sovereigns,* 1758. Translated by Charles G. Fenwick. Washington, DC: Carnegie Institute of Washington, 1916.

Vitoria, Francisco de. *Political Writings.* Edited by Anthony Pagden and Jeremy Lawrance. Cambridge: Cambridge University Press, 1991.

Chapter 10

Armitage, David. *The Declaration of Independence: A Global History.* Cambridge, MA: Harvard University Press, 2007.

Bailyn, Bernard. *The Ideological Origins of the American Revolution.* Cambridge, MA: Belknap Press of Harvard University Press, 1967.

———. "Political Experience and Enlightenment Ideas in Eighteenth-Century America." *American Historical Review* 67, no. 2 (1962): 339–351.

Bailyn, Bernard, and Philip D. Morgan, eds. *Strangers within the Realm: Cultural Margins of the First British Empire.* Chapel Hill: University of North Carolina Press, 1991.

Benton, Lauren, and Kathryn Walker. "Law for Empire: The Common Law in Colonial America and the Problem of Legal Diversity." *Chicago-Kent Law Review* 89, no. 3 (2014): 937–956.

Bilder, Mary Sarah. *The Transatlantic Constitution: Colonial Legal Culture and the Empire.* Cambridge, MA: Harvard University Press, 2004.

Billias, George A. *American Constitutionalism Heard around the World, 1776–1989: A Global Perspective.* New York: NYU Press, 2009.

Billings, Warren M. "The Transfer of English Law to Virginia, 1606–50." In *The Westward Enterprise: English Activities in Ireland, the Atlantic, and America, 1480–1650,* edited by K. R. Andrews, N. P. Canny, and P. E. H. Hair, 215–244. Liverpool: Liverpool University Press, 1978.

Brown, Elizabeth G. "The Views of a Michigan Territorial Jurist on the Common Law." *American Journal of Legal History* 15, no. 4 (1971): 307–316.

Clark, David S., "Comparative Law in Colonial British America." *American Journal of Comparative Law* 59, no. 3 (2011): 637–674.

Dinan, John J. *Keeping the People's Liberties: Legislators, Citizens, and Judges as Guardians of Rights.* Lawrence: University of Kansas Press, 1998.

Dunham, William Huse. "A Transatlantic View of the British Constitution 1760–1776." In *Legal History Studies 1972: Papers Presented to the Legal History Conference, Aberystwyth 18–21 July 1972,* edited by Dafydd Jenkins, 50–63. Cardiff: University of Wales Press, 1975.

Golove, David M., and Daniel J. Hulsebosch. "A Civilized Nation: The Early American Constitution, the Law of Nations, and the Pursuit of International Recognition." *NYU Law Review* 85, no. 4 (2010): 932–1066.

Grafton, John, ed. *The Declaration of Independence and Other Great Documents of American History, 1775–1865.* Mineola, NY: Dover, 2000.

Greene, Jack P., ed. *Exclusionary Empire: English Liberty Overseas, 1600–1900.* Cambridge: Cambridge University Press, 2010.

Hart, James S., and Richard J. Ross. "The Ancient Constitution in the Old World and the New." In *The World of John Winthrop: Essays on England and New England, 1588–1649,* edited by Francis J. Bremer and Lynn A. Botelho, 237–289. Boston: Massachusetts Historical Society, 2005.

Hulsebosch, Daniel J. "The Ancient Constitution and the Expanding Empire: Sir Edward Coke's British Jurisprudence." *Law and History Review* 21, no. 3 (2003): 439–482.

———. *Constituting Empire: New York and the Transformation of Constitutionalism in the Atlantic World, 1664–1830.* Chapel Hill: University of North Carolina Press, 2005.

———. "The Revolutionary Portfolio: Constitution-Making and the Wider World in the American Revolution." *Suffolk University Law Review* 47 (2014): 759–822.

Ibbetson, D. J. "Natural Law and Common Law." *Edinburgh Law Review* 5, no. 1 (2001): 4–20.

Konig, David Thomas. "Regionalism in Early American Law." In *The Cambridge History of Law in America,* edited by Michael Grossberg and Christopher Tomlins, 144–177. Cambridge: Cambridge University Press, 2008.

Nelson, William E. *The Common Law in Colonial America*. 3 vols. Oxford: Oxford University Press, 2008–2016.

Rakove, Jack N., ed. *Annotated U.S. Constitution and Declaration of Independence*. Cambridge, MA: Belknap Press of Harvard University Press, 2009.

———. *Declaring Rights: A Brief history with Documents*. Boston: Bedford Books, 1998.

———. *Original Meanings: Politics and Ideas in the Making of the Constitution*. New York: Knopf, 1996.

Reid, John Phillip. *The Ancient Constitution and the Origins of Anglo-American Liberty*. DeKalb: Northern Illinois University Press, 2005.

Roeber, A. G. *Palatines, Liberty, and Property: German Lutherans in Colonial British America*. Baltimore: Johns Hopkins University Press, 1993.

Tomlins, Christopher L. *Freedom Bound: Law, Labor and Civic Identity in Colonizing Early America, 1580–1865*. Cambridge: Cambridge University Press, 2010.

Tomlins, Christopher L., and Bruce H. Mann, eds. *The Many Legalities of Early America*. Chapel Hill: University of North Carolina Press, 2001.

Whitman, James Q. "Why Did the Revolutionary Lawyers Confuse Custom and Reason?" *University of Chicago Law Review* 58, no. 4 (1991): 1321–1368.

Wood, Gordon S. *The Creation of the American Republic, 1776–1787*. Chapel Hill: University of North Carolina Press, 1969.

Chapter 11

Aucoin, Louis M. "Judicial Review in France: Access of the Individual under French and European Community Law in the Aftermath of France's Rejection of Bicentennial Reform." *Boston College International and Comparative Law Review* 15, no. 2: 443–469.

Blaufarb, Rafe. *The Great Demarcation: The French Revolution and the Invention of Modern Property*. New York: Oxford University Press, 2016.

Censer, Jack R., and Lynn Hunt. *Liberty, Equality, Fraternity: Exploring the French Revolution*. University Park: Pennsylvania State University Press, 2001.

Cole, John R. *Between the Queen and the Cabby: Olympe de Gouges's Rights of Women*. Montreal: McGill-Queen's University Press, 2011.

Cox, Marvin R., ed. *The Place of the French Revolution in History*. Boston: Houghton Mifflin, 1998.

Edelstein, Dan. *The Terror of Natural Right: Republicanism, the Cult of Nature, and the French Revolution*. Chicago: University of Chicago Press, 2009.

Hancock, Ralph C., and L. Gary Lambert, eds. *The Legacy of the French Revolution*. Lanham, MD: Rowman and Littlefield, 1996.

Hardman, John, ed. *The French Revolution Sourcebook*. London: Arnold, 1999.

Hulsebosch, Daniel, J. "The Revolutionary Portfolio: Constitution-Making and the Wider World in the American Revolution." *Suffolk University Law Review* 47 (2014): 759–822.

Hunt, Lynn, ed. and trans. *The French Revolution and Human Rights: A Brief Documentary History*. Boston: Bedford Books, 1996.

Jones, Colin. *The Great Nation: France from Louis XV to Napoleon, 1715–1799*. New York: Columbia University Press, 2002.

Polasky, Janet. "The Legacy of the French Revolution." In *The Transformation of Modern France: Essays in Honor of Gordon Wright*, edited by William B. Cohen. Boston: Houghton Mifflin, 1997.

Rousseau, Jean-Jacques. *The Social Contract or Principles of Political Right*, 1762. Translated by H. J. Tozer. Hertfordshire, UK: Wordsworth Editions, 1998.

Royer, Jean-Pierre, et al. *Histoire de la justice en France du XVIIIe siècle à nos jours*. Paris: Presses Universitaires de France, 1995.

Schama, Simon. *Citizens: A Chronicle of the French Revolution*. New York: Alfred A. Knopf, 1989.

Seligmann, Edmond. *La justice en France pendant la Révolution (1789–92)*. Paris: Plon-Nourrit, 1901.

Sewell, William H. *A Rhetoric of Bourgeois Revolution: The Abbé Sieyes and What Is the Third Estate?* Durham, NC: Duke University Press, 1994.

Stewart, John Hall. *A Documentary Survey of the French Revolution*. New York: Macmillan, 1951.

Van Kley, Dale, ed. *The French Idea of Freedom: The Old Regime and the Declaration of Rights of 1789*. Stanford, CA: Stanford University Press, 1994.

Woloch, Isser. *The New Regime: Transformations of the French Civic Order, 1789–1820's*. New York: W. W. Norton, 1994.

Chapter 12

Bellomo, Manlio. *The Common Legal Past of Europe 1000–1800*. Washington, DC: Catholic University of America Press, 1995.

Blaufarb, Rafe. *Napoleon, Symbol for an Age: A Brief History with Documents*. Boston: Bedford Press of St. Martins Press, 2008.

Code Napoléon or the French Civil Code. London: William Benning, 1827.

Dilcher, Gerhard. "The Germanists and the Historical School of Law: German Legal Science between Romanticism, Realism, and Rationalization." *Rechtsgeschichte—Legal History* 24 (2016): 20–72.

Foster, Nigel, and Satish Sule. *German Legal System and Laws.* 4th ed. Oxford: Oxford University Press, 2010.

Freund, Ernst. "The New German Civil Code." *Harvard Law Review* 13, no. 8 (1900): 627–637.

German Civil Code, English-language edition provided by Langenscheidt Translation Service. http://www.gesetze-im-internet.de/englisch_bgb /englisch_bgb.html.

Gordley, James "Myths of the French Civil Code." *American Journal of Comparative Law* 42, no. 3 (1994): 459–505.

Halpérin, Jean-Louis. "Le droit privé de la Révolution: Héritage législatif et héritage idéologique." *Annales historiques de la Révolution française* 328 (2002): 135–151.

John, Michael. *Politics and the Law in Late Nineteenth-Century Germany: The Origins of the Civil Code.* Oxford: Clarendon Press, 1989.

Kozolchyk, Boris. *Comparative Commercial Contracts: Law, Culture and Economic Development.* St. Paul, MN: West Academic, 2014.

Kroppenberg, Inge, and Nicolaus Linder. "Coding the Nation: Codification History from a (Post-)Global Perspective." In *Entanglements in Legal History: Conceptual Approaches,* edited by Thomas Duve, 67–99. Frankfurt: Max Planck Institute for European Legal History.

Levasseur, Alain A. "Code Napoleon or Code Portalis?" *Tulane Law Review* 43, no.4 (1969): 762–774.

Martin, Xavier. *Mythologie du Code Napoléon: Aux soubassements de la France moderne.* Bouère, France: Éditions Dominique Martin Morin, 2003.

Schwartz, Bernard, ed. *The Code Napoleon and the Common-Law World: The Sesquicentennial Lectures Delivered at the Law Center of New York University, December 13–15, 1954.* New York: NYU Press, 1956.

Smithers, William W. "The German Civil Code *(Das Bürgerliche Gesetzbuch):* Sources—Preparation—Adoption." *American Law Register* 50 no. 12 (1902): 685–717.

Vanderlinden, Jacques. *Le Concept de code en Europe occidentale du XIIIe au XIXe siècle: Essais de définition.* Brussels: Université Libre de Bruxelles, 1967.

von Savigny, Friedrich Karl. *Of the Vocation of Our Age for Legislation and Jurisprudence,* 1814. Translated by Abraham Hayward. London: Littlewood, 1831.

Whitman, James Q. *The Legacy of Roman Law in the German Romantic Era: Historical Vision and Legal Change.* Princeton, NJ: Princeton University Press, 1990.

Wieacker, Franz. *A History of Private Law in Europe with Particular Reference to Germany,* 1952. Translated by Tony Weir. Oxford: Clarendon Press, 1995.

Chapter 13

Banner, Stuart. "Written Law and Unwritten Norms in Colonial St. Louis." *Law and History Review* 14, no. 1 (1996): 33–40.

Batiza, Rodolfo. "The Louisiana Civil Code of 1808: Its Actual Sources and Present Relevance." *Tulane Law Review* 46, no. 4 (1971).

Billings, Warren M. "The Transfer of English Law to Virginia, 1606–50." In *The Westward Enterprise: English Activities in Ireland, the Atlantic, and America, 1480–1650,* edited by K. R. Andrews, N. P. Canny, and P. E. H. Hair, 215–244. Liverpool: Liverpool University Press, 1978.

Brown, Elizabeth Gaspar. "Legal Systems in Conflict: Orleans Territory, 1804–1812." *American Journal of Legal History* 1, no. 1 (1957): 35–75.

Cook, Charles M. *The American Codification Movement: A Study of Antebellum Legal Reform.* Westport, CT: Greenwood Press, 1981.

Curtis, Christopher M. "Codification in Virginia: Conway Robinson, John Mercer Patton, and the Politics of Law Reform." *Virginia Magazine of History and Biography* 117, no. 2 (2009): 140–180.

Evans, Beverly D. "The Code Napoleon." *Georgia Historical Quarterly* 6, no. 1 (1922): 28–34.

Farmer, Lindsay. "Reconstructing the English Codification Debate: The Criminal Law Commissioners, 1833–45." *Law and History Review* 18, no. 2 (2000): 397–426.

Fisch, William B. "The Dakota Civil Code: More Notes for an Uncelebrated Centennial." *North Dakota Law Review* 45 (1968): 9–55.

Herman, Shael. "The Fate and the Future of Codification in America." *American Journal of Legal History* 40, no. 4 (1996): 407–437.

Kilbourne, Richard Holcombe. *A History of the Louisiana Civil Code: The Formative Years, 1803–1839.* Baton Rouge: Louisiana State University, 1987.

Kolsky, Elizabeth. "Codification and the Rule of Colonial Difference: Criminal Procedure in British India." *Law and History Review* 23, no. 3 (2005): 631–683.

Langum, David J. *Law and Community on the Mexican California Frontier: Anglo-American Expatriates and the Clash of Legal Traditions, 1821–1846.* Norman: University of Oklahoma Press, 1987.

Masferrer, Aniceto. "Defense of the Common Law against Postbellum American Codification: Reasonable and Fallacious Argumentation." *American Journal of Legal History* 50, no. 4 (2008–2010): 355–430.

McKnight. Joseph W. "The Spanish Legacy to Texas Law." *American Journal of Legal History* 3, no. 3–4 (1959): 222–241, 299–323.

Miller, Perry. "The Common Law and Codification in Jacksonian America." *Proceedings of the American Philosophical Society* 103, no. 3 (1959): 463–468.

Morriss, Andrew. "Codification and Right Answers." *Chicago-Kent Law Review* 74, no. 2 (1999): 355–391.

Morrow, Clarence J. "Louisiana Blueprint: Civilian Codification and Legal Method for State and Nation." *Tulane Law Review* 17, no. 3 (1943): 351–415.

Palmer, Vernon Valentine. "The French Connection and the Spanish Perception: Historical Debates and Contemporary Evaluation of French Influence on Louisiana Civil Law." *Louisiana Law Review* 63, no. 4 (2003): 1067–1126.

Parise, Agustín. "Codification of the Law in Louisiana: Early Nineteenth-Century Oscillation between Continental European and Common Law Systems." *Tulane European and Civil Law Forum* 27 (2012): 133–164.

Reinmann, Mathias. "The Historical School against Codification: Savigny, Carter, and the Defeat of the New York Civil Code." *American Journal of Comparative Law* 37, no. 1 (1989): 95–119.

Ross, William E. "History of Virginia Codification." *Virginia Law Register* 11, no. 2 (1905): 79–101.

Schwartz, Bernard, ed. *The Code Napoleon and the Common Law World: The Sesquicentennial Lectures Delivered at the Law Center of New York University, December 13–15, 1954.* New York: NYU Press, 1956.

Weiss, Gunther A. "The Enchantment of Codification in the Common Law World." *Yale Journal of International Law* 25, no. 2 (2000): 435–532.

Wheeler, Charles B. "The Code Napoleon and Its Framers." *American Bar Association Journal* 10, no. 3 (1924): 202–206.

Witt, John Fabian. "The King and the Dean: Melvin Belli, Roscoe Pound and the Common Law Nation." In *Patriots and Cosmopolitans: Hidden Histories of American Law,* 211–278. Cambridge MA: Harvard University Press, 2007.

Young, Edwin W. "The Adoption of the Common Law in California." *American Journal of Legal History* 4, no. 4 (1960): 355–363.

Epilogue

Alter, Karen J. *Establishing the Supremacy of European Law: The Making of an International Rule of Law in Europe.* Oxford: Oxford University Press, 2003.

Borchardt, Klaus-Dieter. *The ABC of European Union Law.* Luxembourg: Publications Office of the European Union, 2010.

Cappelleti, Mauro. "Is the European Court of Justice 'Running Wild'?" *European Law Review* 12, no. 1 (1987): 3–17.

Claes, Monica. *The National Court's Mandate in the European Constitution.* Oxford: Hart, 2006.

Davies, Bill. *Resisting the European Court of Justice: West Germany's Confrontation with European Law, 1949–1979.* Cambridge: Cambridge University Press, 2012.

Davies, Bill, and Morten Rasmussen. "Towards a New History of European Law." *Contemporary European History* 21, no. 3 (2012): 305–318.

Duve, Thomas. "Global Legal History: A Methodological Approach." *Max Planck Institute for European Legal History: Research Paper Series,* no. 2016-04 (May 20, 2016). http://ssrn.com/abstract=2781104.

European Convention. "Draft Treaty Establishing a Constitution for Europe," July 18, 2003. http://eur-lex.europa.eu/legal-content/EN/TXT/?uri =CELEX:52003XX0718(01).

European Market, Community, Union treaties, legislation, directives and case-law can be consulted online at https://europa.eu/european-union /law_en.

Freda, Dolores. "'Law Reporting' in Europe in the Early-Modern Period: Two Experiences in Comparison." *Journal of Legal History* 30, no. 3 (2009): 263–278.

Grossi, Paolo. "Il messaggio giuridico dell'Europa e la sua vitalità: Ieri, oggi, domani." *Contratto e impresa/Europa* 2 (2013): 681–695.

Hartkamp, Arthur, et al., eds. *Towards a European Civil Code.* 4th ed. Nijmegen, The Netherlands: Kluwer Law International, 2010.

Hyland, Richard. "Codification and the American Discussion about How Judges Decide Cases." In *Codifying Contract Law: International and Consumer Law Perspectives,* edited by Mary Keyes and Therese Wilson, 205–218. Farnham, UK: Ashgate, 2014.

Koch, Henning, et al., eds. *Europe: The New Legal Realism: Essays in Honour of Hjalte Rasmussen.* Copenhagen: Djøf, 2010.

Koopmans, Thijmen. "Towards a New 'Ius Commune.'" In *The Common Law of Europe and the Future of Legal Education,* edited by Bruno de Witte and Caroline Forder, 43–51. Deventer, The Netherlands: Kluwer Law International, 1992.

Legrand, Pierre. "Against a European Civil Code." *Modern Law Review* 60, no. 1 (1997): 44–63.

Lundmark, Thomas. *Charting the Divide between Common and Civil Law.* Oxford: Oxford University Press, 2012.

Mamadouh, Virginie. "Establishing a Constitution for Europe during European Union Enlargement? Visions of 'Europe' in the Referenda Campaigns in France and the Netherlands." *Journal of Cultural Geography* 26, no. 3 (2009): 305–326.

Mashaw, Jerry L. *Creating the Administrative Constitution: The Lost One Hundred Years of American Administrative Law.* New Haven, CT: Yale University Press, 2012.

Mattei, Ugo, and Luca G. Pes. "Civil Law and Common Law: Toward Convergence?" In *The Oxford Handbook of Law and Politics,* edited by Keith E. Whittington, R. Daniel Kelemen, and Gregory A. Caldeira, 267–280. Oxford: Oxford University Press, 2008.

Mattli, Walter, and Anne-Marie Slaughter. "Law and Politics in the European Union: A Reply to Garett." *International Organization* 49, no. 1 (1995): 183–190.

Palmowski, Jan. "The Europeanization of the Nation State." *Journal of Contemporary History* 46, no. 3 (2011): 631–657.

Pescatore, Pierre. *The Law of Integration: Emergence of a New Phenomenon in International Relations Based on the Experience of the European Communities.* Leiden: A. W. Sijthoff, 1974.

Rasmussen, Hjalte. "Between Self-Restraint and Activism: A Judicial Policy for the European Court." *European Law Review* 13, no. 1 (1988): 28–38.

———. *On Law and Policy in the European Court of Justice: A Comparative Study in Judicial Policymaking.* Dordrecht: Martinus Nijhoff, 1986.

Stein, Eric. "Lawyers, Judges, and the Making of a Transnational Constitution." *American Journal of International Law* 75, no. 1 (1981): 1–27.

Sweet, Alec Stone. *Governing with Judges: Constitutional Politics in Europe.* Oxford: Oxford University Press, 2000.

———. *The Judicial Construction of Europe.* Oxford: Oxford University Press, 2004.

Töller, Annette Elisabeth. "Measuring and Comparing the Europeanization of National Legislation: A Research Note." *Journal of Common Market Studies* 48, no. 2 (2010): 417–444.

Ugland, Trygve. "'Designer' Europeanization: Lessons from Jean Monnet." *European Legacy* 14, no. 2 (2009): 149–161.

Vanke, Jeffrey. "The Treaty of Rome and Europeanism." *Journal of the Historical Society* 7, no. 4 (2007): 443–474.

Vauchez, Antoine. *L'union par le droit: L'invention d'un programme institutionnel pour l'Europe.* Paris: Presses de la Fondation nationale des sciences politiques, 2013.

Weiler, J. H. H. "Community, Member States and European Integration: Is the Law Relevant?" *Journal of Common Market Studies* 21, no. 1 (1982): 39–56.

————. "The Community System: the Dual Character of Supranationalism."
   Yearbook of European Law 1, no. 1 (1981): 267–306.
————. "The Reformation of European Constitutionalism." *Journal of
   Common Market Studies* 35, no. 1 (1997): 97–131.
————. "The Transformation of Europe." *Yale Law Journal* 100, no. 8 (1991):
   2403–2483.
Zimmermann, Reinhard. *Roman Law, Contemporary Law, European Law: The
   Civilian Tradition Today.* Oxford: Oxford University Press, 2001.

Acknowledgments

More than with any other of my works in the past, I am conscious that this book was made possible by the generosity, friendship, and collegiality of numerous individuals who agreed to read, patiently and closely, the various chapters and gave me extremely wise, practical, informed, and detailed advice. I would not have dared to publish it without their help. Sincere, heartfelt, and deep kudos are due to Clifford Ando, David Bell, Charles Donahue, Andrew Fitzmaurice, Ruby Gropas, Daniel Hulsebosch, Richard Hyland, Elizabeth Kamali, Dennis P. Kehoe, Amalia Kessler, Bruce Mann, Tom McGinn, Miguel Moura e Silva, Vlad Perju, Jack N. Rakove, Richard J. Ross, and Simon Teuscher. Special thanks to David J. Seipp, who not only read my text but also answered my multiple questions. I am particularly indebted to António Manuel Hespanha, who, since my graduate-student days in Paris and over the last twenty-five years, has been an informal mentor and a true friend. There are endless ways in which Hespanha's scholarship has informed, affected, and intersected with mine. This book is but one. I am also grateful to the Radcliffe Institute for Advanced Study at Harvard University, which has allowed me to have the time and resources to write this book. Last but not least, I would like to thank Yuval Erlich for all these years, which have transformed my life into a wonderful ongoing adventure. Patiently hearing too much about the past and lightly laughing over my obsessions, during the last thirty years, besides being my husband and best friend, Yuval has become my closest and most attentive reader. Each time I write a book I promise to him that it will be my last. Maybe this time I will comply.

Index